D0753164

California Initiatives and Referendums

THE EDMUND G. "PAT" BROWN INSTITUTE OF PUBLIC AFFAIRS

The Edmund G. "Pat" Brown Institute of Public Affairs of the California State University, Los Angeles, is a multidisciplinary center for applied research and analysis of major public issues facing California and the greater Los Angeles metropolitan region. The Institute takes an independent, non partisan approach in addressing these issues and acts as a facilitator of long-range policy discussion and resolution.

The Institute serves the state and its various communities in the following ways:

*By fostering dialogue and interchange among governmental officials, business and labor leaders, community organizations, and academic experts to improve public policies and the governmental process;

*By offering research, forums, consultations, and technical assistance on vital policy issues;

*By publishing important studies and proceedings; and

*By providing internships in public service.

California Initiatives

and Referendums

1912-1990

A Survey and Guide to Research

John M. Allswang

California Direct Democracy Project
Edmund G. "Pat" Brown Institute of Public Affairs
California State University, Los Angeles

10   9   8   7   6   5   4   3   2   1

Library of Congress Cataloging-in-Publication Data

Allswang, John M.
    California initiatives and referendums, 1912-1990
: a survey and guide to research / John M. Allswang.
        p.   cm.
    Includes bibliographical references and index.
    ISBN 1-878644-02-5 : $29.95
    1. Referendum--California--History--20th century.
I. Edmund G. "Pat" Brown Institute of Public Affairs.
II. Title.
    JF495.C24A43 1991
    328.794' 09' 04--dc20   91-36188
                                     CIP

ISBN: 1-878644-02-5

Edmund B. "Pat" Brown Institute of Public Affairs
California State University, Los Angeles
Los Angeles, CA 90032

Manufactured in the United States of America.

Preface

The proper place of direct citizen intervention in the political and governmental process has been controversial since its beginnings at the start of this century. California has been a leading factor in this question, from the start, because of the number and significance of the initiatives and referendums it has considered. And this has become even more the case since the "taxpayer revolt" of Proposition 13 in 1978. Since that time, California's use of the initiative and referendum has expanded considerably, and numerous other states have been following the California Example. Thus, California's past and current experience is of national significance.

Just as the initiative and referendum have become more important in California politics and government, they have also become more controversial, with an increasing number of calls for "reform" of the process. Both critics and defenders have become more outspoken and active, and have tried to use the initiative process to implement their aims. Concerned individuals and citizen groups can easily become confused by all of this, and the purpose of this book is to provide information they can use to understand just what the furor is all about, how the initiative and referendum have been used, and to consider whether and what kind of change, if any, might be beneficial.

The book is divided into several parts, each of which offers specific kinds of information about California direct democracy. Part I, the Introduction, explains the origins of initiative, referendum, and recall early in this century, and provides summary information on the development of the initiative and referendum from 1912 through 1990.

Part II, the largest section of the book, provides information on all statewide initiatives and referendums held in California from 1912 through 1990. The information analyzed and summarized here is derived from a number of sources, including the official voter information pamphlets, and other documents issued or maintained by the office of the California Secretary of State. The propositions are organized chronologically, by election year, and in each case, except where data was not available, the following is provided

- The Proposition's number and official name.
- The type of measure: Initiative Statute, Initiative Constitutional Amendment, Referendum, etc.
- The outcome: whether the measure was approved or rejected by the voters.
- A summary of the proposition.
- A summary of the arguments for the proposition in the official voter information pamphlet and the names of individuals and organizations endorsing the arguments (in both cases combining both the arguments for the measure and the rebuttal to the arguments against the measure). Except in a very few cases where a very large list of endorsers existed, all endorsers are included; occupations and other identifying information for individuals are always included.
- The reverse of the above: arguments and their endorsers against the proposition.

In each case, within the framework of optimizing clarity of analysis and summary, we have tried to maintain the actual language and tone of the original summaries and arguments.

Part III is a bibliography of published, and some unpublished, materials related to the initiative and referendum. It provides interested parties with sources of additional research into the initiative and referendum.

This is followed by a comprehensive subject index.

This project has received funds under three grants from California State University, Los Angeles, for which I am most grateful. Financial support and encouragement were also provided by the Edmund G. "Pat" Brown Institute of Public Affairs at Cal State L.A., under the leadership, formerly, of Dr. Eric Schockman and, currently, of Dr. James Regalado. Dr. Richard Dean Burns of

Regina Books also encouraged the project from the start. I would also like to acknowledge the assistance provided by the California State Archives and the Office of the Secretary of State of California.

Most of the summaries were originally researched and prepared by student research assistants, chiefly Leonard Wynne, Danielle Chupa, and Robert Hooper. Additional student research assistance was provided by Lawrence Guillow. Responsibility for the information and analysis provided is entirely mine.

Los Angeles, CA
September, 1991

Contents

Publications of the
Edmund G. "Pat" Brown Institute
of Public Affairs

Occasional Papers Series

1. Political Battles Over L.A. County Board Seats: A Minority Perspective. Edited by James A. Regalado (1989).

2. *Gang Violence Prevention: Perspectives and Strategies*. Edited by Alfredo Gonzalez, Shirley Better, with Ralph Dawson (1990).

3. *Minority Political Empowerment: The Changing Face of California?* Edited by James A. Regalado (1991).

Monograph Series

1. *The Perfecting of Los Angeles: Ethics Reform on the Municipal Level*. Edited by H. Eric Schockman (1989).

2. *Emergency Disaster Management Patterns of Inter City Mutual Aid (Los Angeles County)*. George C. Littke (1989).

Books

1. *California Initiatives and Referendums, 1912-1990: A Survey and Guide to Research*. John M. Allswang (1991).

Foreword

It is with great pleasure that the Edmund G. "Pat" Brown Institute of Public Affairs publishes this important and timely work by Professor John Allswang on California initiatives and referendums. The Pat Brown Institute is committed to developing forums and publishing works on crucial public policy issues affecting California. This is one such issue area. Increasingly, the voters of this state are asked to perform the demanding and complex task of making public policy decisions largely on the basis of interest group use of the initiative and referendum.

Interest in California's political history and climate extends far and wide. Recently, I was interviewed by a the Japanese newspaper *Asahi Shimbun* concerning forms of direct democracy in California. The publishers were particularly interested in the initiative process, an interest in the "golden state" and its democratic processes that is profound in Japan. In that interview, I maintained that avenues of direct democracy were indeed created to ensure democratic rights on the part of the voters in California above and beyond interests of corrupt public officials linked with private interests. However, I also maintained that the old notions of assuring democracy through the initiative and referendum have become more difficult to argue, especially over the past two decades.

Increasingly, students, scholars, critical observers, and mass media editorial boards have questioned the degree to which moneyed and other special interests have usurped the democratic notions and underpinnings of these historic avenues of direct action. Seemingly, the processes have often gone the way of traditional political campaigns—manipulating voter behavior through lavish spending on media-oriented campaigns.

Some observers contend that this is merely a norm of American politics, including the politics of reform. This largely pluralist contention implies that competitive individuals form competitive (interest) groups that vie in the public policymaking marketplace more or less as equals. More critical observers might contend that whenever large amounts of money are involved in attempting to influence the course of public policy, that the "balanced" marketplace become severely tilted. A severely tilted "playing field" does not equate with the notions of democracy most of us cherish.

Until this publication, no single volume had compiled and summarized all state level initiatives ;and referendums from the beginning days of direct democracy through 1990. For students and scholars of direct democracy and California governance in particular, this work provides a strong tool for understanding historically important policy issues, contending arguments, and individual public policy movers and players.

James A. Regalado, Ph.D.
Executive Director
Edmund G. "Pat" Brown
Institute of Public Affairs

California Initiatives and Referendums, 1912-1990

Part I: Introduction

The process of direct democracy, including the initiative, the referendum, and the recall, has played an important and controversial role in American state and city politics and government since early in the twentieth century. In the initiative, voters by petition are originating statutes or constitutional amendments, to be submitted directly to the electorate for approval or rejection. In the referendum, voters by petition are demanding that a statute passed by the state legislature be submitted directly to the electorate for approval or revocation. Both comprise means of circumventing the legislative process by direct voter action.

At one time, California also had the indirect initiative, wherein a measure by petition is sent to the state legislature, and goes to the voters only if the legislature fails to adopt it. Three such measures ended up on the ballot in the 1940s and 1950s, and are included in Part II.

In the recall, voters by petition are submitting to the electorate a proposal to remove an office-holder. While the recall has been widely used in California cities, it has not played a role at the state level, and will not be included in this book. The terms "direct democracy" and "direct legislation" are used interchangeably, although, literally, the recall doesn't fit into the latter.

Origins of Direct Democracy in California

California was one of the first states to implement direct democracy, first used in South Dakota in 1898, and quickly became a pace-setting state in terms of the frequency of its use. Its origins have to be understood in terms of California progressivism, of which direct democracy was very much a part. California progressivism, however, was often a function of individual group interest and political activity, with cooperation among groups resulting as much from construed need as from construed commonalty of purpose. And the issues that, together, came to be seen as the elements of progressivism, were combined with some reluctance and some happenstance.[1]

It is very unlikely that direct democracy would have been part of California progressivism were it not for one man, John Randolph Haynes. Indeed, neither the origins of the issue, nor its ultimate incorporation in the measures advocated by the progressives as they sought power, nor its implementation under Gov. Hiram Johnson can be understood apart from Haynes, who often seemed the only person in California who really cared about the initiative, referendum, and recall.

John Randolph Haynes was born in rural Pennsylvania in 1853, in a middle class family whose ancestors in England had been involved in both political and religious reform. He established a successful medical practice in Philadelphia, and was very early involved in local politics, opposing the Philadelphia Republican machine, which influenced his lifelong interest in public affairs and his commitment to the political empowerment of the masses.[2] Haynes moved with his family to Los Angeles in the 1880s, where he became extremely wealthy through his medical practice and a variety of investments and other economic interests, at the same time as he became socially prominent and active. Like others of his class, Haynes was active in numerous clubs and organizations, and served on the boards of several corporations. At the same time, however, he was a radical—a Christian socialist, a Fabian, and, even at the height of his medical career, devoted a tremendous amount of time to a wide variety of public issues, including some that were quite unpopular with most middle class Californians.[3]

Haynes shared with other progressives a suspicion of big business, and particularly of its political power, as most significantly seen in the political influence of the Southern Pacific Railroad. The corruption of the state legislature by such power was a central theme in the development of direct democracy.[4] Haynes was deeply involved in other issues, but it was politics and government that became the main focus of his reform interests starting about 1895. Even this area had several aspects, including the short ballot, political corruption, and the direct primary, but, above all, direct democracy. This was an article of faith as well as efficiency:

> Let me confess it gentlemen, democracy is a part of my religion... We find that happiness, enlightenment and prosperity among the people increase in precisely the same ratio as do their power, influence, and participation in government. Responsibility tends to develop the best that is in us.[5]

But if his commitment was moral, his approach was scientific. Haynes studied the practice of direct democracy everywhere it existed, constantly, from the mid-1890s, kept copious clippings and notes, corresponded widely, and became a nationally recognized expert on the initiative, referendum, and recall.[6]

It is interesting to note, in this context, that Haynes, despite the great variety of his reform interests, was never a leading figure in California progressivism. He supported many of the progressive's issues, contributed a good deal of money to them, and wrote to progressives, as to others, in seeking to implement direct democracy. But he remained an outside figure, and appears never to have actually joined the Lincoln-Roosevelt Republican League, the heart of California progressivism, perhaps because it was Republican and he never considered himself one, despite supporting almost all of the Republican progressives.[7] Equally notable is that very few of the other leading California progressives showed much interest in direct democracy. Hiram Johnson, for example, was still unclear on the operation of the initiative, referendum, and recall when he ran for governor in 1910.[8] A major exception was Milton T. U'Ren, who served as Secretary-Treasurer of Haynes's Direct Legislation League.

Like many other progressive causes, direct democracy was first introduced at the city level and later became statewide in focus. The original political impetus came from the Populists, who had raised that issue, among others, locally and nationally. As early efforts at Los Angeles political reform proved unsuccessful, the time became ripe for an effort at structural reform in the mid-1890s.[9] The time of the actual founding of the Direct Legislation League is unclear, but it seems to have begun operation in 1898.[10] It was in 1898 that the local chapter of the Union Reform League, of which Haynes would become president, proposed the initiative, referendum, and recall to the city's Board of Freeholders, which had been created for the purpose of preparing a new city charter. A watered-down proposal without the recall failed to win voter approval. Haynes then became a candidate in the 1900 Board of Freeholders election, vowing to develop a new charter that included real direct democracy. He won the support of both major parties, and received more votes than any other candidate. But the Supreme Court invalidated the Board of Freeholders as an institution, temporarily halting development of the issue.[11] California voters, however, did approve a constitutional amendment in 1902 that permitted home rule cities to amend their charters by initiative local action, and this was a key to implementation of local direct democracy.[12]

When the city council refused to support charter amendments for direct democracy, Haynes invited a group of civic leaders to a dinner in 1902, soliciting support for a new nonpartisan "Committee on Charter Amendments." From this base, Haynes worked for additional endorsements, from the Municipal League, local labor unions, even the mighty Southern Pacific Railroad and the Los Angeles *Times* (which would change its position soon after). Such broad-based support persuaded the city council to act, and the initiative, referendum, and recall were proposed as charter amendments in 1903. In the campaign, the recall was the most controversial, but all three passed, making Los Angeles the first city in the United States to so act.[13] Los Angeles reformers, including Haynes and organized labor, made it also the first city to actually recall a public official—Councilman J. P. Davenport in 1904; they then mounted a recall effort in 1909 against Mayor Arthur C. Harper, who resigned before the election.[14]

Los Angeles also made quick use of the referendum and initiative. The referendum was used twice in 1909 by reform groups, on the sale of street railroad franchises and increased telephone rates. The initiative was first used in 1904 or 1905, for similar measures, and again in 1906 by the Anti-Saloon League. Other California cities rapidly followed Los Angeles's lead; twenty-one of them modified their charters to permit the initiative and referendum by 1910. In almost all cases, direct democracy was part of a package of political reforms, generally including the direct primary and non-partisan local elections.[15] The inclusion of numerous issues expanded the proposals' basis of support, which would be the case, also, at the state level.

Haynes acted immediately to move consideration of direct democracy to the state level, building on the momentum of Los Angeles's success. And until California progressives were well organized in 1907 under the Lincoln-Roosevelt Republican League, it was Haynes and the Direct Legislation League that kept the issue alive. He focused on the new legislature elected in 1902, hoping for constitutional amendments to institute direct democracy. It was, he argued a "great wave" sweeping the United States. There seemed to be general agreement among the neophyte legislators that the process was beneficial at the city and county level, but some feared that it could undercut the powers of the legislature.[16] Once the legislature met, Haynes was personally financing a lobbyist for the direct democracy propositions, and he personally appeared in February, 1903, with his signed petitions and with resolutions from a wide variety of groups, primarily farmers' clubs and labor.[17] The legislative debate was not extensive; the major questioning was over the number of signatures required to put a measure on the ballot. But not a lot of people shared Haynes's deep concern with direct democracy. It passed in the Assembly, but lost by one vote (14-13) in the Senate.[18]

The initiative, referendum, and recall continued to be introduced into subsequent sessions of the legislature, in 1905, 1907, and 1909, but with no effect. It appears that the Southern Pacific clearly turned against it, responding to the fact that the successful implementation of direct democracy in cities across the state was trumpeted by its proponents as a way to overthrow the railroad's influence. This was an important factor in legislator's actions, since the Southern Pacific did have the power to limit their advancement in the legislature.[19]

Haynes and U'Ren were able to maintain the coalition of groups behind direct democracy, and even to broaden it. Like many devotees of a cause, Haynes cared little where the support came from. He even developed a strong, albeit more or less secret association with the Anti-Saloon League, and ministers from the League worked as his assistants for a while.[20] And at the same time, woman suffrage groups, Socialists, the unions, and others continued to be solicited. Money, however, was harder to come by than endorsements, perhaps because to most supporters this was only one of the causes they were interested in. U'Ren constantly complained of the need for funds, and Haynes appears to have personally provided much of the financing.[21]

The key to any possible success was in broadening the basis of support. And that became possible with the inclusion of the initiative, referendum, and recall in the body of proposals advocated by the organized California progressives.

The Lincoln-Roosevelt Republican League *was* the progressive movement in California politics, and as such a key vehicle for making statewide direct democracy happen. It was founded in 1907 by Chester Rowell and Edward A. Dickson, who met in Sacramento when covering the legislature for their respective newspapers, the Fresno *Republican* and the Los Angeles *Express*. Both men were offended by the incapacity and corruption of the legislature, which, they were sure, was due to the power of the "machine," meaning the Southern Pacific.[22]

The early meetings were agreed only on the problem of the Southern Pacific. Little thought had been given by the organizers to the development of a complete program, although some who attended were devoted to various issues. Like any political group, the progressives, if they were to succeed, had to lead in the direction the voters wanted to go, which created an opportunity for advocates of proposals like direct democracy. Haynes worked every meeting, in person when possible, urging the initiative, referendum, and recall; others advocated the statewide primary, workmen's compensation, woman's suffrage, outlawry of race track gambling, and other issues. The result was more or less perfunctory approval of most of these measures; but the real agreement was to focus on the problem of the Southern Pacific machine.[23]

As these issues became increasingly controversial, the breakup of the Republican party progressed, with almost all the reform impetus becoming focused in the Lincoln-Roosevelt Republican League. Debate on the specific issues among progressives was not great, however. The Lincoln-Roosevelt League needed groups like the Direct Legislation League and people like Haynes and U'Ren if it had any hope of succeeding. The followings such organizations and individuals had, and the money they could provide, were key sources of League strength. And the Direct Legislation League was never reluctant about flexing its muscle to achieve its own aims.[24] By the 1909 session of the state legislature, the anti-Southern Pacific forces probably made up a majority of the representatives of both parties. And they had some legislative successes: removing the straight party choice from the ballot and, especially, passing a direct primary bill for all statewide offices. Despite bipartisan support, efforts for more divisive issues like railroad regulation and direct democracy were unsuccessful. The Southern Pacific was still powerful, but its failure to halt the direct primary bill provided the Lincoln-Roosevelt Republican League with one of the tools it needed to take over the Republican party in the 1910 primary.[25]

The Direct Legislation League saw 1910 as the most promising year yet for implementation of its program. Once again it sought to get commitments from candidates of both major parties, in the August primary and again in the November general election. Likewise, it solicited all of its traditional allies, trying, as one supporter put it, "to line up the unions, the improvement clubs, church and temperance folds (*quietly*) and all the progressive forces."[26] The League's greatest success, perhaps, came when both parties adopted planks including the initiative, referendum, and recall.[27]

Hiram Johnson's gubernatorial victory in the 1910 elections was not overwhelming: he won the Republican primary with 47 percent of the vote, and the general election with 46 percent. But it was a historically high plurality, and he did carry 35 of the 58 counties. More important, progressives of both parties did well, while conservatives did badly. Progressivism was in control.[28]

Johnson endorsed the whole progressive agenda in his inaugural address, including the statement that "the first step in our design to preserve and perpetuate popular government shall be the adoption of the initiative, the referendum, and the recall."[29] In the legislature itself, given the number of measures under consideration, quite a few of which proposed significant changes, voting often revolved around one's general attitude toward progressive reform. There was more debate over the recall than the initiative and referendum. To foes of reform, including the Southern Pacific, it seemed particularly threatening. Even some proponents of other reforms, including the initiative and referendum, feared that the recall was not a good idea, and many shared the common view that recall of judges was particularly pernicious. But Haynes and the Direct Legislation League continued working to keep the three measures together, and they did prevail: the initiative and referendum amendment passed the Assembly 71-0 and the Senate 35-1; the recall amendment passed 70-10 and 36-4.[30]

The broad range of proposed constitutional amendments, including direct democracy, woman's suffrage, railroad regulation, and workmen's compensation constituted a fundamental change in California government and politics. Devotees of each issue worked hard to secure its passage in the October 1911 special election, and this was not least the case in terms of advocates of direct democracy.[31]

Their worries, in fact, were excessive: 22 of the proposed 23 amendments passed, and quite easily, except for woman's suffrage which just squeaked through. The direct democracy measures had the highest rate of approval: 76 percent for the initiative and referendum, and 77 percent for the recall (obviously the public did not share the widely voiced fears about the latter). Interestingly, the statistical relationships are quite low between the vote for the various measures, and between the vote for any of the measures and that for Hiram Johnson for governor.[32] That suggests, once again, that each measure had its own constituency, and that the Direct Legislation League had done a very good job of persuasion.

California now had the initiative and referendum, and wasted no time in making extensive use of both.

Development of California Direct Democracy

California has had 266 initiatives and referendums on its ballots since 1912, and an even greater number for which petitions were circulated but not enough signatures obtained. While the frequency of direct legislation measures has varied somewhat, the tool has been used almost constantly since its origin, as Table 1 indicates.

The table suggests some variations over time. Direct legislation was extensively used in its first thirty years or so, and then became increasingly less popular down through the 1960s. The rate of ballot measures then began to increase rapidly, and, if current trends continue, the present decade will see far more initiatives and referendums than at any time in California's history. The success rate of initiatives and referendums has varied somewhat less, but was at its height in the 1970s and 1980s, when the use of the initiative began to increase. Whether the current decline in success rate reflects rising questions about the nature of the direct legislation, and will continue, remains to be seen. Also, as seen in Table 1, the referendum fell quite rapidly into disuse; only five have been on the ballot since 1952 (four of them, of which three dealt with reapportionment, in 1982), and none has been successful.

Table 1: Initiatives and Referendums by Time Period

Date	Initia-tives	Passed	Referen-dums	Passed	Total % Passed
1912-1919	30	6	11	3	21.95
1920-1929	35	10	11	5	32.61
1930-1939	36	10	11	4	29.79
1940-1949	20	6	1	1	33.33
1950-1959	12	2	1	1	23.08
1960-1969	9	3	0	0	33.33
1970-1979	22	9	1	0	39.13
1980-1989	44	21	4	0	43.75
1990	18	6	0	0	33.33
TOTALS	226	73	40	14	32.71

Another way to summarize this large amount of information is by type of proposition. This is an imprecise measure, since an initiative relating to "taxation" might have raised taxes or lowered them. But it does provide some sense of the frequency of certain selected types of measures. This is presented in Table 2 for some of the most frequently recurring topics.

Some topics tended to be quite time-related, such as the regulation of public morality. Fourteen of the thirty-four "Morals" propositions, for example, dealt with prohibition or other control of liquor, all of them between 1914 and the mid-1930s. Likewise, efforts to control boxing, wrestling, horse racing, and various religious practices took place primarily before 1930.

Table 2: Initiatives and Referendums by Subject
Number on Ballot (Number Passed)

Date	Bond Acts	Elections, Voting	Taxation	Economic Regulation	Education	Health	Morals	Environment	Civil Rights & Liberties
1912-1919	2 (1)	6 (0)	6 (1)	5 (2)	1 (1)	2 (0)	10 (2)	0	0
1920-1929	1 (1)	5 (2)	8 (1)	12 (2)	3 (1)	7 (3)	6 (2)	1 (1)	0
1930-1939	1 (0)	2 (1)	7 (0)	11 (4)	3 (0)	3 (0)	8 (3)	7 (1)	0
1940-1949	0	0	3 (1)	3 (0)	3 (2)	1 (0)	3 (0)	1 (0)	1 (0)
1950-1959	0	1 (0)	4 (1)	1 (0)	3 (2)	0	1 (0)	1 (0)	0
1960-1969	0	0	1 (0)	1 (1)	0	0	1 (0)	0	2 (1)
1970-1979	0	1 (1)	5 (3)	1 (0)	3 (1)	1 (0)	4 (0)	4 (2)	4 (2)
1980-1989	1 (1)	4 (3)	11 (5)	8 (3)	2 (2)	10 (5)	0	7 (4)	8 (4)
1990	5 (1)	3 (0)	4 (1)	5 (1)	0	3 (0)	1 (0)	6 (2)	1 (1)
TOTALS	10 (4)	22 (7)	49 (13)	47 (13)	18 (9)	27 (8)	34 (7)	27 (10)	16 (8)

Similarly, questions relating to civil liberties and civil rights appeared only after World War II, reflecting rising national concern with such problems. This is true, also, of measures relating to social welfare, which emerged only after the onset of the Depression and the New Deal in the 1930s.

Measures relating to economic regulation of various kinds, to taxation, to health, and to education, however, tend to be found in all periods. The content of such measures, however, varied widely over time. In the area of health, for example, early concerns were with things like medical professionalism (including control of chiropractors and naturopaths) and vaccination, whereas in recent years there have been four measures focusing on the dangers of AIDS.

There has always been an overlap between economic regulation and environmental propositions. Questions of the economic exploitation of California's oil, water, and gas resources, in relation to conservation and environmental considerations have been raised consistently from the 1920s to the present.

The largest single subject category (not included in Table 2 because it covers such a vast array of specific topics) is government, with fifty-eight measures, 22% of the total. This includes thirteen measures relating to the state legislature, most of them quite recent and four of them in 1990. It also includes twelve measures relating to reapportionment of congressional and state legislative districts, which has been a controversial topic throughout California's modern history.

The voters have approved 32% of the proposed initiatives and 35% of the proposed referendums. But what is perhaps most striking about California direct legislation, as seen in Part II, below, is the immense variety in the measures that Californians have put on their ballots. Equally striking is the lack of any clear correlates of success. Neither partisanship, ideology, nor even type of issue appears to have guaranteed success or failure in initiatives and referendums. The bases of voter discrimination can often be seen in a single brief time period, but overall they are quite unapparent. Critics will argue that this is in part because at least half the voters in any given election don't really understand the measures they are voting on. Alternative explanations are also possible.

What is very clear is that in recent years direct democracy has become increasingly problematic in California. Measures are more complex, cover more points (even though, by law, they should deal with only one thing), and are more draconian in their effects. They are also big business, requiring often enormous sums for signature gathering, publicity, and legal defense. Serious question has been raised about whether California direct legislation is really serving its original purpose, and whether the process requires extensive reform. [33] This book is designed to provide researchers and other interested parties with much of the information they need to evaluate the current state of the direct democracy process, and to derive ideas for productive change.

Notes to Part I

[1]For a fuller exposition of the origins of California's direct democracy and its relationship to progressivism, see, John M. Allswang, "The Origins of Direct Democracy in California: On the Development of an Issue and Its Relationship to Progressivism," Paper presented to Conference in Honor of Samuel P. Hays, Pittsburgh, PA, 4-5 May 1991.

[2]Haynes to Philadelphia *Public Ledger* (letter to editor), 12 June 1905, Haynes mss, UCLA Library; a good overview of Haynes's background and ideas can be found in, Tom Sitton, "California's Practical Idealist: John Randolph Haynes," *California History*, LXVII:1 (March, 1988).

[3]Sitton, "California's Practical Idealist," 3-4, and personal interview with Sitton, who is preparing a book-length study of Haynes; Kevin Starr, *Inventing the Dream: California Through the Progressive Era* (NY: Oxford, 1985), 211-212.

[4]V. O. Key and Winston Crouch, *The Initiative and Referendum in California* (Berkeley: University of California Press, 1939).

[5]"Origins and Future of the Recall, the Initiative, and Referendum," typescript of 1909 lecture to University Club, Haynes mss. Misspellings corrected.

[6]See, e.g., his address to the Joint Constitutional Comm. of the California legislature, 20 Jan. 1905; typescript of address to "Friends and Members of the Economic Club," 8 June 1901; misc. notes and clippings (Box 34); all in Haynes mss.

[7]The progressives, generally, were too moderate in their politics for Haynes to feel really close to them; he was also somewhat older than most progressive leaders, which may have increased a sense of separateness. The result was that he and the progressives mutually used one another, to the advantage of both. See, Starr, *Inventing the Dream*, 211.

Haynes was an important figure in the progressivism of the 1920s, but that was really a different movement, involving different people and issues.

[8]George Mowry, *The California Progressives* (Chicago: Quadrangle, 1951), 135.

[9]Haynes, "The History of the Recall," typescript in Haynes mss; Eric F. Petersen, "Prelude to Progressivism: California Election Reform, 1870-1909" (Unpublished Ph.D. Dissertation, UCLA, 1969), 146-149.

[10]It is probable that there was more than one organization of that name, although with an overlap of personnel. Socialist H. Gaylord Wilshire did have one going in 1898, and Haynes had an organization of that name operational in 1900 for local action, and perhaps a second one in 1902 for statewide action. By the latter date, there seems to be just one organization, definitely under Haynes's leadership. Sitton, "California's Practical Idealist," 5-6, and Sitton to the author, 12 Feb. 1991.

[11]J. W. Park, "The Adoption of the Recall in Los Angeles," typescript, Haynes mss; Haynes, "The History of the Recall," typescript, Haynes mss; Janice Jaques, "The Political Reform Movement in Los Angeles, 1900-1909" (Unpublished Master's Thesis, Claremont Graduate School, 1948), 13-15, copy in Hichborn mss, UCLA Library.

[12]Sitton, "California's Practical Idealist," 5-6; Key and Crouch, *The Initiative and Referendum in California*, 428, 428n. Increased empowerment of the larger cities does not seem to have been very controversial, or partisan, at the time. Los Angeles *Herald*, 23 Jan. 1903.

[13]Park, "The Adoption of the Recall" and Haynes, "The History of the Recall," Haynes mss; Sitton, "California's Practical Idealist," 6-7; Los Angeles *Times*, 8 Nov. 1902. The state supreme court upheld the legality of the Los Angeles measures in 1906 (Los Angeles *Express*, 15 Oct. 1906). This is also a good example of Haynes's practicality as a politician; in pursuit of direct democracy, he was quite willing to work with the Southern Pacific in these years and had important SP officials as officers in the Direct Legislation League. Fred W. Viehe, "The First Recall: Los Angeles Urban Reform or Machine Politics?" *Southern California Quarterly*, 70 (Spring, 1988), 3-4.

[14]Haynes, undated typescript [1910?], "The Recall of Councilman Davenport," and undated, unsigned typescript, Haynes mss. Haynes felt that Harper's narrow election was in part due to the Southern Pacific machine's support. And he believed that the recall effort against Davenport reversed the position of Harrison Gray Otis and the *Times*, in that it made Otis realize that "these measures had shown a capacity for interfering

with his personal designs upon the public treasury." *Ibid.* It is true that the main charge against Davenport was his participation in giving a city printing contract to the *Times* at exorbitant rates. See, Grace H. Stimson, *Rise of the Labor Movement in Los Angeles* (Berkeley: UC Press, 1955), 281-286; Viehe, "The First Recall."

Interestingly, Davenport's recall was later overturned by the courts, on the basis of an insufficient number of valid signatures, anticipating the extremely litigious nature of direct democracy from that time to the present. Viehe, "The First Recall," 23.

[15]Key and Crouch, *The Initiative and Referendum*, 428; San Francisco *Star*, 9 Nov. 1910.

[16]Los Angeles *Herald*, 5 December 1902.

[17]Haynes supported P. B. Preble, of the Alameda County Federated Trades Council, in Sacramento for about eight weeks. Haynes to Preble, n.d.; Preble to Haynes, 17 Mar. 1903 and 29 Mar. 1903; Haynes mss. See also, Los Angeles *Times*, 19 Feb. 1903; Los Angeles *Herald*, 22 Feb. 1903.

[18]N. K. Foster, M.D. to Haynes, 27 Oct. 1902, Haynes mss.; Los Angeles *Herald*, 27 Feb. 1903; Los Angeles *Express*, 14 Mar. 1903.

The question of the political power of the Southern Pacific is central to the history of California progressivism. Certainly, the progressives believed this power was overwhelming, a conclusion shared by leading students like Mowry (*The California Progressives*, 38-39) and Key and Crouch (*The Initiative and Referendum*, 423), but the quantity of hard evidence is not huge. There are demonstrable cases where Walter F. Parker and William F. Herrin of the SP directly forced, bribed, and otherwise promoted or stymied actions by public officials (e.g., affidavit from H. J. Lelande, Los Angeles City Clerk, published in *Pacific Outlook*, 4 Dec. 1909, and Los Angeles *Herald*, 27 and 28 Nov. 1909; E. T. Earl [publisher of Los Angeles *Express*] to Edward A. Dickson, 8 July 1907, Dickson mss, UCLA Library.). And Fred W. Viehe, in "The First Recall," describes the SP's infiltration of the Good Government League in Los Angeles and its corruption of the recall election of 1904. But, overall, it is not an easy phenomenon to pin down.

[19]Alice M. Rose interview with Frank R. Devlin, Rose mss, Stanford University Library; Haynes, "The Birth of Democracy in California," typescript [1912?], Haynes mss. Haynes concluded that "the absolute domination of the Southern Pacific Railroad" was the key factor in this failure, although he probably underestimated the role of lack of interest among many legislators. See also, Franklin A. Hichborn: *Story of the Session of the California Legislature of 1909* (San Francisco: J. H. Barry,

1909); "Sources of Opposition to Direct Legislation in California," *The Commonwealth*, VII:9, Part II (3 Mar. 1931); and "California Politics, 1891-1939," typescript; all in Hichborn mss.

[20]The Revs. Ervin S. Chapman and J. H. Scott of the Anti-Saloon League worked for Haynes. Chapman to Haynes, 22 Aug. 1904, Haynes mss.

[21]U'Ren to Haynes, 12 Jan. 1909, 18 Feb. 1901, 24 Feb. 1901, 6 Mar. 1901, 9 Mar. 1909, Haynes mss.

[22]They shared the common belief that the Southern Pacific machine's influence made the 1907 session of the legislature the most venal ever, and that the railroad had been the real force behind the election of James N. Gillett as governor in 1906. Alice M. Rose interview of Dickson, 27 Dec. 1937, Rose mss; Mowry, *The California Progressives*, 58.

[23]Alice M. Rose interview of Dickson, 27 Dec. 1937, Rose mss; Ida Tarbell interview of Rowell, 24 Mar. 1911, Rose mss; Janice Jaques, "The Political Reform Movement in Los Angeles, 1900-1909" (Unpublished Master's Thesis, Claremont Graduate School, 1948), 71-72; Dickson, "History of the Lincoln-Roosevelt League," Dickson mss.

[24]When the Direct Legislation League was approached by Franklin Hichborn about subscribing to his proposed study of the 1909 session of the legislature, U'Ren asked him how much coverage the League would get in the book. The League wanted 100 copies, but "perhaps this can be enlarged...." Such hardball was not unusual for Haynes and U'Ren. U'Ren to Hichborn, 20 Mar. 1911, Hichborn mss.

[25]Hichborn, *Story of the Session of the California Legislature of 1909*; Hichborn to Sen. Marshall Black, 4 Mar. 1909, Hichborn mss. The U. S. senatorial primary, however, was to be advisory only. The Southern Pacific forces were very well organized, led on the floor by Grove Johnson (Hiram Johnson's father), and were able to defeat a large number of Lincoln-Roosevelt League-supported proposals. Mowry, *The California Progressives*, 82.

[26]A. H. Spencer [Spence?] of the Oakland *Evening Mail* to Haynes, 10 July 1910, 16 Aug. 1910, Haynes mss; emphasis added. The *Evening Mail* was a Scripps paper, all of which supported direct democracy in 1910, as did a large number of other newspapers across the state. Equally important, by 1911 Haynes had managed to get a large part of the progressive leadership officially enrolled as members of the DLL.

[27]Copies of the platforms are in Haynes mss. There was some conflict between the Direct Legislation League and the Lincoln-Roosevelt League (now, actually, the state Republican party), in that the latter found the

former in its way. U'Ren told Haynes that, with the formal adoption of direct democracy, Meyer Lissner, now Republican party chairman, "rather intimated that the League ought to go off and quietly die." U'Ren to Haynes, 22 Nov. 1910, Haynes mss.

[28]Los Angeles Express, 25 Nov. 1910; Hichborn, *Story of the Session of the California Legislature of 1911*, 12-16.

[29]Hichborn, *Story of the Session of the California Legislature of 1911*, i-xvi, and Royce D. Delmatier, *et al.*, *The Rumble of California Politics, 1848-1970* (NY: Wiley, 1970), 165.

[30]"Recall," *Transactions of the Commonwealth Club of California*, VI:3 (1911); Hichborn, "Sources of Opposition to Direct Legislation," 515-16; Key and Crouch, *The Initiative*, 437-438; Hichborn, *Story of ... 1911*, 102-138; Los Angeles *Sunday Tribune*, 9 July 1911; Haynes telegram to Dickson, 1 Jan. 1911, Dickson mss; Johnson to Haynes, 17 Jan. 1911, Haynes mss; Meyer Lissner to Editor, Santa Barbara *Independent*, 17 Feb. 1911, Lissner mss, Stanford University Library.

The recall proposed for California was a rather powerful one, since it combined a yes/no vote on recall with another vote on those nominated to succeed the officeholder if he or she was recalled. Only those who voted on the recall itself would have their votes on the successor candidate tallied. And the successor required only a plurality.

The legislature also passed two statutes in this session permitting non-charter (smaller) cities and counties to implement direct democracy.

[31]U'Ren to Lissner, 5 May 1911, Lissner mss; Hichborn to Johnson, 23 June 1911 and 27 June 1911, Johnson mss, Bancroft Library, UC Berkeley.

[32]See, Allswang, "The Origins of Direct Democracy in California," for a fuller exposition of the significance of these voting patterns.

[33]Good sources of information on this currently controversial topic are: League of Women Voters of California, *Initiative and Referendum in California: A Legacy Lost* (Sacramento: The League, 1987); Philip DuBois and Floyd Feeney, *Improving the Initiative Process: Options for Change* (Davis: University of California, forthcoming); California Commission on Campaign Financing, *To Govern Ourselves: Ballot Initiatives in California* (forthcoming).

Part II: The Propositions

Election of November 5, 1912

PROPOSITION 3: **Appointment of a Registrar of Voters.**
Type: Referendum*
Outcome Rejected
Summary: Rejects the legislature's call for the appointment of a Registrar of Voters to be selected by the County Board of Supervisors, with a fixed term of four years and a salary dependent on the class of the individual county in which the office is held. The legislation removed control of the electoral machine from the office of County Clerk.
Arguments For the existing legislation, Against this referendum: This bill is an attempt by the Alameda County delegation to the legislature to remove the three-time, popular elected, county clerk, John P. Cook. The bill's provision for setting the officer's salary, would violate California's constitutional provision for salary to be determined in direct relation to the duties performed, This is most evident in the suggestion that an annual salary of $3000 be paid to the new officer in Alameda County, while the counterpart in Los Angeles, who has far more duties, would receive a mere $24 per year.
Endorsers: A. L. Frick
Arguments Against the existing legislation, For this referendum: The bill will prevent the supervisors, namely those of Alameda county from consolidating the office of registrar of voters in that of the county clerk's office, which can lead to the domination of the electoral machinery by the special interest of business. **Endorsers:** Edward J. Tyrell, State Sen., Oakland, Ca.
With referendums, there is often confusion between the language in the voter's information pamphlet and that on the actual ballot. The official summary is often of the law under reconsideration, rather than of the referendum itself. And the "Arguments For" in the pamphlet are actually in favor of the existing law and against the change proposed by the referendum. Conversely, the "Arguments Against" in the pamphlet are actually opposed to the existing law and for the

change proposed by the referendum. I have worded the summaries to clarify this. Also, in the Arguments For and Arguments Against sections, when this situation applies, I have followed the organization of the voter's pamphlets, but expanded the section titles to avoid confusion.

PROPOSITION 4: Salaries and Fees of County Offices.
Type: Referendum
Outcome Rejected
Summary: The law amended the Political Code in relation to salaries and fees of officers of counties of the third class; created the office of Registrar of Voters and set the annual salary for the new officer and his deputies.
Arguments For: None recorded.
Arguments Against: None recorded.

PROPOSITION 5: County Officers.
Type: Referendum
Outcome: Rejected
Summary: The law amended the Political Code to provide for the addition of a Registrar of Voters and a Sealer of Weights and Measures to the list of county officers.
Arguments For: None recorded.
Arguments Against: None recorded.

PROPOSITION 6: The Formation of Consolidated City and County Governments.
Type: Initiative Constitutional Amendment
Outcome: Rejected
Summary: Permits the merging and consolidating of contiguous territory of two or more cities, upon majority vote in favor thereof. Any new consolidated city or county will be entitled to the use of any property of such county.
Arguments For: Under the present law, cities like San Francisco and Los Angeles cannot extend their territories or consolidate them. The adoption of this amendment will create possibilities, if desired, for small communities to consolidate with big cities. However, no large city can consolidate with any other large city. This will give every city a fair opportunity to determine for itself if it desires to consolidate with another. By voting, the people will determine how they want their counties to be governed.
Endorsers: Leslie R. Hewitt, State Sen., 38th Dist., Los Angeles County.
Arguments Against: The amendment is not practical for the following reasons: First, San Francisco is the only city that will have the privilege of crossing

county lines and expanding into new areas, while Los Angeles is the only city that could annex or consolidate "contiguous territory" with the new conditions imposed. Second, the amendment will result in the division and dismemberment of local administrative units of the state government. Third, it will be possible for San Francisco and Los Angeles to dominate the political power by controlling nineteen out of forty votes in the Senate, and thirty-eight out of eighty votes in the Assembly. Moreover, cities will be agitated with attempts at annexation that will interfere with investment and enterprise.
Endorsers: W. E. Gibson, Pres., Oakland Chamber of Commerce.

PROPOSITION 7: Racing Commission and Horse Racing.
Type: Initiative Statue
Outcome: Rejected
Summary: Prohibits all horse racing and breeding associations from bookmaking and pool-selling. Advocates a state racing commission to grant horse racing licenses for limited periods. Wagering on horse races will then be permissible only through the parimutuel and auction pool systems.
Arguments For: The change in law will provide a racing commission, appointed by the governor of the state, with authority to grant permits to conduct race meetings. It will bring a great influx of population into California to generate more jobs and prosperity for the state. Ultimately, race meetings will not only improve California's economic situation but also provide a form of recreation for the public.
Endorsers: John C. Kirkpatrick, Chairman.
Arguments Against: The purpose of the initiative is only to revive racetrack gambling in the state of California. It is illogical to say that racing cannot continue without gambling. Gambling not only destroys individual's lives but also the lives of their families. In granting people the right to gamble, the state will not fulfill its moral obligation to the gamblers or their families. There are other methods of raising revenue for the state than gambling.
Endorsers: John M. Eshleman.

PROPOSITION 8: Home Rule Taxation.
Type: Initiative Constitutional Amendment
Outcome: Rejected
Summary: All cities and counties will be allowed to set the rate for property taxes locally. The revenues of counties, cities, towns, and districts are derived from the value of taxation on land; unjust improvements on property may be adjusted for property owners by these local authorities.
Arguments For: Many people believe that the present taxation system is putting them at a disadvantage and injustice. To attain a just taxation system, the

voters of political subdivisions of the state should have the power to raise revenue for local purposes if it does not conflict with the state's revenues. This will allow individual communities to try out new plans of taxation and select that which best fits their needs. Ultimately, this amendment can stimulate business and industry by exempting certain classes of property from taxation.
Endorsers: H. A. Mason, Secy., League of Calif. Municipalities.
Arguments Against: The proposed amendment is neither clear nor concise. Although taxes or exemptions shall be uniform on classes of property, it does not provide how or what property may be exempt from taxes. This would only destroy the uniform system of taxation and exemption. Apparently, this proposed amendment would give any local government the right to enforce such taxes or exemptions as it saw fit without considering the effect of such action upon the broader question of tax uniformity or the rights of other localities. An equitable tax system should advocate agreement between the state and local government. The proposed amendment will only produce more confusion, inequality, and local jealousies, and is likely to result in consequences its proponents have not expected.
Endorsers: N. W. Thompson, State Senator, 35th Dist.

Election of November 13, 1914

PROPOSITION 2: Prohibition.
Type: Initiative Constitutional Amendment
Outcome: Rejected
Summary: Prohibits the manufacture, sale, giving away, or transportation of liquors into the State of California. Violators would be fined not less than two hundred dollars nor more than twenty-five hundred dollars, and imprisoned in the county jail thirty days or more.
Arguments For: The consumption of alcohol often results in sickness, idiocy, insanity, crime, profligacy, and death. The law gives us the choice to "stay dry or die." Liquor costs the taxpayer seven dollars for every dollar received in taxes or license fees. According to the Bureau of Labor Reports, our courts deal with 113,526 misdemeanors, of which 66,930 were "drunks" and 20,000 more were kindred crimes caused indirectly by alcohol. Like laws against opium, cocaine, lotteries, and horse racing, this amendment interferes only with personal license.
Endorsers: None recorded.
Arguments Against: Prohibition is immoral and contrary to the teachings of religion because wine is considered to be part of religious ceremonies. This amendment will destroy property and industries, impoverish thousands of families, and increase unemployment, while not guaranteeing the minimizing of crime or the death rate. Wine and liquor have been in existence for ages

and they are part of many cultures. It is not the wine or liquor that causes people to commit crimes; rather, it is the person who does not know how to control himself or herself when consuming these substances.
Endorsers: None recorded.

PROPOSITION 3: Eight Hour Law.
Type: Initiative Statute
Outcome: Rejected
Summary: Amends the Penal Code to make it a misdemeanor, punishable by fine of up to $50 and/or imprisonment for up to 90 days, for an employer to require or permit an employee to work in excess of eight (8) hours per day, or more than forty-eight (48) hours in one week. The only exception to this shall be under extreme circumstances, as in the case of a natural disaster.
Arguments For: This measure proposes an eight hour day in all occupations, which will serve the interests of laborers and employers. The prohibition of overtime will allow employees and employers to balance their work and social life in order to bring about a better quality of life. People perform better at work when they are well rested and not being exploited.
Endorsers: Thos. W. Williams, State Secy., Socialist Party of Calif.
Arguments Against: The initiative restricts the flexibility of companies and employees. The proposal of an eight hour law is arbitrary to all occupations, whether or not it suits the interests of laborer or employer. Limitation of hours means increased costs of production, and will result in California being at a disadvantage compared to states that do not have such a law. Thus, an eight hour day would lessen employment for people like farmers and compel many farmers to send wives and children into the field.
Endorsers: G.H. Hecke.

PROPOSITION 4: Abatement of Nuisances.
Tpype: Referendum.
Outcome: ADOPTED
Summary: The law being reconsidered declared any building a nuisance that functions to promote acts of lewdness, assignation or prostitution. Established the prevention and abatement of such nuisances by injunction. Any violation of the injunction provided by this act will result in a finding of contempt and a fine not less than two hundred dollars nor more than two thousand dollars, and a term of imprisonment of six months in county jail.
Arguments For the existing law, Against this referendum: This referendum minimizes investments in exploitation of prostitution. Under this act, any citizen can petition to close down a house of prostitution. This will discourage

homeowners from renting out their properties to prostitutes or participating in this business.

Endorsers: Edwin E. Grant, State Sen., 19th Dist.

Arguments Against the existing law, For this referendum: The referendum against nuisances of prostitution was proposed by property owners of this state and reflects their viewpoint. It is not the prostitute's fault that she makes her living in a house of prostitution. If property owners do not approve of this type of business, it is up to them to establish a censor of morals in their buildings. This law makes one act of prostitution, assignation, or lewdness in any building sufficient to cause the building to be abated. If the building is abated, prostitutes will seek other places to run their business while property owners lose money from rental spaces. Essentially, the property owner and his tenant will pay the price of this act of the legislature.

Endorsers: None recorded.

PROPOSITION 5: Investment Companies Act.

Type: Referendum

Outcome: Approved

Summary: The law being reconsidered created a State Corporation Department and Commissioner of Corporations to have control and power of examination over investment companies and investment brokers. Regulated the issuance, sale, advertisement, and subscriptions of securities; created fund from official fees to pay for salaries and expenses; provided for broker's permit and agent's certificate, reports by companies and brokers, appeal to court from commissioner's decision, and penalties for violations.

Arguments For the existing law, Against this referendum: Known as the "Blue Sky Law", this act gives protection to investors in stocks and bonds by requiring corporations to submit plans of operation to a commissioner of corporations. This is a screening process aimed at eliminating fraudulent business and allowing legitimate business to continue.

Endorsers: Lee C. Gates, State Senator.

Arguments Against the existing law, For this referendum: One man is given too much power and responsibility to preside over the vast and complex range of business. The hiring of assistants will not alleviate this burden or reduce impartiality. The act was designed to prevent corruption, however, this only focuses the corruption into the direction of one department.

Endorsers: Francis V. Kessling.

PROPOSITION 6: Water Commission Act.

Type: Referendum.

Outcome: Approved

Summary: The law being reconsidered created a state water commission to control appropriation and usage of waters. The water commission will determine the ascertainment and adjudication of water rights. It would be authorized and empowered to investigate how water is used within cities and counties, and recognize "vested rights" in the use of waters.

Arguments For the existing legislation, Against this referendum: California water rights cannot be settled by lawsuits. The present water laws rest in the hands of rich men and corporations, and they decide who gets to rent their water rights. When there are lawsuits about water rights, it is usually the person with money who wins, even if he is the exploiter. Such conditions interfere with the prosperity of California and only favor the rich. There are no lawsuits over water rights and no riparian rights in states that have water commission laws.

Endorsers: None recorded.

Arguments Against the existing legislation, For this referendum: This plan is not cost effective and involves unlimited expenses. It will cost a great deal of money to ascertain fair riparian rights in a single stream. To obtain this permit, one will need to employ an attorney and engineers to submit a proposal accompanied by maps and other data, which will not prevent rich people and corporations from monopolizing the water rights. Under present law small users have an equal opportunity with large corporations. This amendment also puts a continuous charge, tax, and burden upon every appropriator of water and is equivalent to general taxation. The end result will fall on the shoulders of consumers.

Endorsers: None recorded.

PROPOSITION 9: Regulating Investment Companies.
Type: Initiative Statute
Outcome: Rejected
Summary: Authorizes governor to appoint auditor of investments, to employ deputies and fix their compensation; defines investment companies, and authorizes examination thereof by auditor; defines securities and prohibits company sales to the public before filing a financial statement with the auditor.
Arguments For: This act will completely safeguard the interests of private investors without tampering with the normal workings of corporate enterprises. It requires investment companies, as defined, to file and publish a sworn statement of their financial assets with the auditor. This screening process will enable the investor to make informed decisions, and promote solid business practices.
Endorsers: W. C. Wallace.
Arguments Against: The previous "Blue Sky Law" was enacted to facilitate the screening of illegitimate investment companies while allowing honest business

to operate. This proposed measure obscures and complicates the purposes of the former law. The auditor, formerly commissioner, is empowered to review published statements and decide whether or not to issue certificates, but he cannot confine the activities of said companies. This provision alone will allow loopholes for corrupt business to enter the market.
Endorsers: Lee C. Gates, Senator, 34th. Dist.

PROPOSITION 10: Abolition of Poll Tax.
Type: Initiative Constitutional Amendment
Outcome: Approved
Summary: No poll or head tax for any purpose shall be levied or collected in the state of California.
Arguments For: The poll tax is a denial of democracy. Furthermore, the poll tax is not necessary for the support of public schools or public services. If the poll tax is abolished, public services will still be provided through the taxation of corporate incomes. The poll tax has never been uniformly collected. Wealthy people rarely pay their poll tax, while laborers pay it through deductions from their wages.
Endorsers: Paul Scharrenberg, Secy., Calif. State Fed. of Labor.
Arguments Against: The state poll tax collects about $850,000 annually for public schools, and $260,000 to build roads, hospitals, and improve our transportational systems. This form of tax has been in existence since feudal times, and is very effective. The argument that some escape from the poll tax system ought not be the reason to abolish it; rather we should improve enforcement of the law.
Endorsers: None recorded.

PROPOSITION 11: University of California Building Bond Act.
Type: Initiative Statute/Bond Act
Outcome: Approved
Summary: Allows the State of California to sell state bonds in the sum of $1,800,000 to create a fund for the construction of the University of California in the city of Berkeley.
Arguments For: The $1,800,000 bond issue for the University of California is for the construction of permanent buildings for the university at Berkeley. The objective is to build more buildings in order to meet needs of the student population, which is about 10,000 in California. The benefits which the university gives to the state are greater than what it is asking for.
Endorsers: Allen L. Chickering, Pres., Alumni Assn.
Arguments Against: None recorded.

PROPOSITION 13: Qualification of Voters at Bond Elections.
Type: Initiative Constitutional Amendment
Outcome: Rejected
Summary: States that no elector may vote on a question of incurring bonded indebtedness of the state or its political subdivisions unless he is assessed as an owner of property taxable for payment of such indebtedness.
Arguments For: California has 879,242 taxpayers, and every person is mortgaged $40.00 for an average period of thirty years. Therefore, more people would invest in homes if the tax confined the creating of public debts to the property owners affected; property values will increase. The voting of public bonds is an economic matter and not a political matter.
 Endorsers: Francis Cutting.
Arguments Against: Every citizen, property owner or not, has the right to vote in all government matters. The proposed amendment is based on the false idea that no one is taxed unless he is assessed for taxable property. It is well known that owners of taxable property can shift the tax to those not on the assessment roll. It would be impossible to have public ownership of public utilities if none but property owners were allowed to vote on bond issues.
Endorsers: James H. Barry.

PROPOSITION 14: Voting by Absent Electors.
Type: Initiative Statute
Outcome: Rejected
Summary: Provides for the issuance of certificate of identification and ballot to voters who will be absent or away from home precincts on election day; authorizes said electors to vote at polls in any precinct more than ten miles from polls where registered; provides description of certificate form and canvass of ballot on which the elector will judge and mark in secret and mail to the county clerk where the voter is registered.
Arguments For: Known as the Postal Voting Act, this proposed law is designed in the interest of some thirty thousand commercial travelers, locomotive engineers, trainmen, and railway postal clerks who are generally called away from home on election day. These disfranchised men are prevented from voting and soon lose interest in elections. This measure facilitates the collection of votes from these men through the issuance of certificates of identification. With the certificate, a traveling worker can cast his ballot at polls outside his home precinct.
Endorsers: Fred H. Hall.
Arguments Against None recorded.

PROPOSITION 15: Deposit of Public Moneys.
Type: Initiative Constitutional Amendment
Outcome: Rejected
Summary: Authorizes banks with public money deposits to issue, as security, bonds of districts within municipalities, or of a corporation qualified to act as surety on bonds, to an amount in value, or with a penalty, of at least ten per cent over amount of deposit; provides that at no time may the deposit exceed fifty per cent of paid up capital and surplus of depository bank.
Arguments For: The framers of the California Constitution did not take into consideration the large range of present day bankable securities and collaterals. Hence, there is over twenty-five million dollars idle money in the vaults of various state treasurers. This sum is better suited for circulation to provide security, and the interest can be used to reduce tax burdens on the people.
Endorsers: Leslie E. Burks.
Arguments Against: Moneys in the state vaults are imposed with a special trust that they be available for public use at all times. Since its enactment, the law has given entire satisfaction in every emergency; no semblance of loss has been reported under its function. The proposed amendment seeks to change the standing law for the selfish interests of the surety companies. This amendment allows banks to form surety companies which will lead to collusion and fraudulent acquisition of public moneys.
Endorsers: L. H. Roseberry.

PROPOSITION 18: Non-Sale of Game.
Type: Referendum
Outcome: Rejected
Summary: The law being reconsidered declared that no one is allowed to sell, buy, or trade any wild game except rabbits and geese, with the exception of wild ducks during their hunting season. Anyone who violates this law is guilty of a misdemeanor and upon conviction will be fined no less than twenty dollars nor more than five hundred dollars.
Arguments For the existing legislation, Against this referendum: The excessive killing of wild animals such as buffalo, elk, and antelope, and of wild birds, has brought them to or near extinction. Eliminating the market hunter is the best method to minimize the slaughtering of wildlife.
Endorsers: F.M. Newbert, Pres., Fish and Game Commission.
Arguments Against the existing law, For this referendum: Citizens who hunt or fish, do it for enjoyment. It is part of their recreation. To prohibit them from hunting, they feel, would violate their rights and freedom as individuals. To prohibit hunting does not guarantee that wildlife will be preserved. Hunting is not the issue to be concerned with here, but rather what is the minimal amount of hunting that can safely occur.

Endorsers: None recorded.

PROPOSITION 19: Consolidation of City and County Government and Limited Annexation of Contiguous Territory.
Type: Initiative Constitutional Amendment
Outcome: Approved
Summary: Authorizes chartered cities to establish municipal courts, and to control the appointment of officers and employees. Authorizes the consolidation and annexation of contiguous territory, only upon voter consent thereof, by cities with a population greater than fifty thousand; prescribes procedures for consolidation and annexation.
Arguments For: Known as the 50,000 population amendment, this measure allows the normal, beneficial formation and expansion of combined city and county governments. This eliminates the unnecessary duplication of public offices, and the disintegration of counties is prevented. Double taxation will be eliminated without depriving the communities of benefits.
Endorsers: Charles A. Beardsley.
Arguments Against: Taking San Francisco, Oakland, and Los Angeles as an example of why this amendment will not serve the interest of the state of California, it should be noted that a substitute amendment to Section 8.5 of Article XI of California's Constitution (Proposition 21) was submitted by these three cities. This measure allows these cities to augment their areas, thereby increasing their political powers in the state legislature. Under the disguise of a "mutual alliance," any city with a population above fifty thousand can secede from its original county and create a new county to serve its own interests.
Endorsers: Edward K. Strobridge, State Sen. 30th. Dist.

PROPOSITION 20: Prize Fights.
Type: Initiative Statute
Outcome: Approved
Summary: Any individual within the State of California who engages in or instigates any act to further a fight on Memorial Day or Sunday is open to arrest. Every person who spectates such an event is guilty of a misdemeanor and shall be punished by a fine not exceeding five hundred dollars or by imprisonment in the county jail not exceeding six months. Any sheriff, marshal, policeman, or other peace officer of the city, county, or other political subdivision is obligated to stop such exhibitions whenever it appears to him that the contestants are unevenly matched or for any other reasons.
Arguments For: This act is designed to abolish commercialized prize fighting in California. Amateur boxing is permitted under the restriction that excludes

professional boxing. Amateur boxing and prize fighting are no different from racing and racetrack gambling. The suspension of boxing should decrease professional as well as amateur matches. Prize fighting and amateur boxing have resulted in many deaths. The promotion of these two types of fighting would exploit boxers as well as spectators and encourages barbarous acts.
Endorsers: Nathan Newby.
Arguments Against: Boxing is not brutal; the risk in mortality and injuries are just as high in other sports. The purpose of the sport is to maintain manliness and good health among the participants. Like any other sport, boxing leads to fame, money, and popularity for boxers. It is not right to deny those with the gift of boxing. Therefore, amateur and professional boxing should be permitted.
Endorsers: D. P. Regan, State Sen., 18th. Dist.

PROPOSITION 21: City and County Consolidation and Annexation with Consent of Annexed Territory.
Type: Initiative Constitutional Amendment
Outcome: Rejected
Summary: Amends section 8.5 of Article XI of the Constitution; submitted by San Francisco, Oakland, and Los Angeles. Authorizes chartered cities to control the appointment of municipal officers and employees; authorizes cities with a population over 175,000 to consolidate under charter and to annex any contiguous territory with the consent of such territory and its county; prescribes procedure for consolidation and annexation.
Arguments For: By allowing charter cities to form their own municipal courts, which has proven successful in eastern cities, present inferior courts can be replaced. Through the consolidation and annexation of city and county, complicated problems of government such as water supply, sanitation, and transportation can be readily resolved through the combined resources of the territories.
Endorsers: J. S. Conwell, Pres., Efficiency Comm. of Los Angeles.
Arguments Against: This amendment is designed to fit the needs of the three cities named in the submission. If approved, Los Angeles can form a consolidated city and county government, while San Francisco can lay claim to all the territory it wants. The state of California does not need this kind of "special legislation" to serve its cities.
Endorsers: W. E. Gibson.

PROPOSITION 22: Land Title Law.
Type: Initiative Statute
Outcome: Approved

Summary: Designed to certify title of land and to simplify the process of mortgage or transfer of ownership of the land. In appointing the county recorder as a "registrar of titles" and establishing clear procedures for establishing title, the holder of the title will be protected against fraud.

Arguments For: The measure will lower the cost of searching for the titles to land by consolidating them in one location in each county, virtually eliminating the chances of fraud in the sale or mortgage of property. In addition, the title holder will be protected against unwarned sale to pay taxes. The low fees charged to claim title will pay for the assurance policy given to the title holder, and will not come out of taxes.

Endorsers: Mrs. Wilbur D. Campbell, Pres., Torrens Land League .

Arguments Against: While the need to simplify the process of verifying title to land is needed, the Torrens bill falls far short of what is needed. The liability of the county recorder, which the bill claims must be the result of gross negligence, will prove too great a risk for many mortgage companies to take. In addition, contrary to the opposition's belief, the bill will hurt the poor by greatly opening the market on "tax title speculation." Above all, the system has no provision for removing land title from the books in the event that the individual situation becomes so complicated as to hinder mortgage or sale procedures.

Endorsers: Chas L. Batcheller.

PROPOSITION 38: Los Angeles State Building Bonds.

Type: Initiative Statute/Bond Act

Outcome: Rejected

Summary: Provides for the sale of $1,250,000 in state bonds to construct new buildings in the city of Los Angeles. The bonds will finance the construction of city buildings and accommodate various governmental offices that are located in the southern part of the state.

Arguments For: This money is part of a movement to bring the government closer to the people and will promote governmental efficiency. The expansion of governmental business is inevitable due to the increase in population and the development of agricultural and industrial activities. The erection of a building at Los Angeles in which all the various state offices are located will enable bureaus to serve the people with grater efficiency.

Endorsers: William W. Mines, Pres., Los Angeles Realty Board.

Arguments Against: There are enough offices, departments, and boards of commissions in Los Angeles already. Under this proposed bill, the state will pay $2,537,000 in principal and interest from a sum of $1,250,000 annually. This would only put the state into more debt in the long run. We should be realistic in assessing our needs and not exceed financial capacities with unnecessary buildings.

Endorsers: W.F. Chandles.

PROPOSITION 39: Suspension of Prohibition Amendment.
Type: Initiative Constitutional Amendment.
Outcome: Approved
Summary: Relates to the manufacture, sale, use, and transportation of intoxicating liquors. This amendment suspends Proposition 2 [Nov. 13, 1914].
Arguments For: This amendment's purpose is to correct an oversight in the prohibition amendment that fails to state when it shall go into effect. The amendment will give people who are in the liquor business a period of time to get out of that business. The present law allows only ninety days to close out the business and that is not enough time. The liquor traffic has been recognized by the state as a business and if it were to prohibit this type of business, then liquor businessmen need some time to readjust their financial situation to conform to the law.
Endorsers: F. M. Larkin.
Arguments Against: The idea of extending time prior to implementation of the prohibition act serves to befog the original issue. Alcoholic liquors create crime, hypocrites, falsifiers, lawbreakers, and cowards, and destroy self-respect. If more time is given to these businessmen, the social problems would continue to escalate. If prohibition is not enforced after ninety days, then the lives of individuals are threatened by alcohol; and honesty, temperance, self-respect, and liberty of thought and action of the people are restricted.
Endorsers: C. F . A. Last.

PROPOSITION 45: One Day of Rest in Seven.
Type: Initiative Statue.
Outcome: Rejected
Summary: Prohibits any business to operate more than six days per week. The seventh day is declared to be a day of rest and religious obligation. Violations of this law with exceptions would result in misdemeanors with prescribed penalties.
Arguments For: It is not part of man's nature to work all the time. Yet, many do so against their own will. The six day labor plan is more efficient and effective since he will be able to rest and recuperate before putting in another six days of work. The bill allows industries to rest and employers to appreciate their employees. The more rest employees receive, the more efficient workers they would be.
Endorsers: William Kehoe, State Sen., 1st. Dist.
Arguments Against: The proposed initiative assumes that everyone's religious obligations land on the seventh day. By selecting and establishing Sunday as

the rest day, those who would want another day are not permitted to do so. If they do, there will be a fine for breaking the law. This law violates the Constitution of the State of California, which states that "the free exercise and enjoyment of religious profession and worship, without discrimination or preference, shall forever be guaranteed in the state." The right of individuals to choose their time of labor and rest is a part of basic human rights, which the proposed law violates.

Endorsers: W. Matthew Healey.

PROPOSITION 46: Drugless Practice.
Type: Initiative Statute
Outcome: Rejected
Summary: Creates state board for drugless physicians to regulate examinations and issuance of certificates. Authorizes certificate holders to treat all physical and mental ailments of human beings without drugs or medicine, and to sign birth and death certificates. Exempts from examination any person having practiced the drugless system six months before date of enactment.
Arguments For: Under the present law, ill people are compelled to go to a doctor who uses and practices medicine. This measure seeks to give people the freedom to choose the type of treatment their conscience dictates. Medicine is an inexact science and the strong sentiment against its uses is well advised.
Endorsers: W. H. Jordan, D.C.
Arguments Against: The purpose of medical license laws is to protect the public from incompetent quacks. Drugless practitioners are recognized professionals in the world of healing, but the license must be verifiably and wisely awarded. The proposed law only requires that a man show competency in reading, writing, and arithmetic! To compound this gross underestimation, it will grant a license, without an examination, to anyone who claims to have practiced drugless healing six months prior to the measure's enactment.
Endorsers: George E. Malsbary.

PROPOSITION 47: Prohibition Elections.
Type: Initiative Constitutional Amendment.
Outcome: Rejected
Summary: Proposes prohibiting state elections on the issue of manufacturing, sale, or transportation of liquors for eight years. Does not interfere with the right of any incorporated city, town, or supervisorial district to hold elections to decide on the authorization of selling of liquors within their jurisdiction.
Arguments For: The proposed amendment restores authority to local communities. The holding of liquor elections would accomplish harmony within

communities and alleviate the abuses of the present system. The amendment retains the power of legislative bodies in local governments to establish licenses, fees, and regulations for the sale of liquor, where permitted by law, without the supervision or restriction of the state. As a result, public places such as saloons and hotels can continue to do business and provide to individuals the liberty to consume liquor or not.

Endorsers: Frank G. Roney, Grand Recorder, Grand Lodge, Knights of the Royal Arch.

Arguments Against: The measure is misleading because it disfranchises the people. On one hand, there are voters who favor local prohibition but who do not support state-wide prohibition. To preserve or obtain local prohibition, they may have to vote for state-wide prohibition. On the other hand, there are voters who oppose saloons, and yet are not in favor of absolute prohibition on a local or state-wide level. Under this amendment, they could not vote for anything except absolute prohibition. Thus, people's vote against license would not guarantee the prohibition of traffic in liquors and would leave the entire issue in the hands of local officials.

Endorsers: D. M. Gandier, State Supt., Central and Northern Calif. Anti-Saloon League.

Election of October 26, 1915

PROPOSITION 1: Direct Primary Law.

Type: Referendum

Outcome: Rejected

Summary: Repeals primary law of 1913, which declared the offices of senator, representative, congressional committeeman, delegate, and presidential elector to be partisan, and all others non-partisan. The law defined political parties and regulated the processes of nomination, election, and canvassing, and expenses of elections.

Arguments For the existing legislation, Against this referendum: This "nonpartisan law" prevents the injection of national party lines into state government, thereby increasing the efficiency and productivity of state and national government. Furthermore, it does away with the confusion and expense of voting by six different ballots, as opposed to one, provided under the old law.

Endorsers: C. C. Young, Speaker of the Assembly.

Arguments Against the existing legislation, For this referendum: History has proven that division leads to the downfall of national government. The union has survived well without nonpartisanship, so why must we fix that which isn't broken? Should this measure pass, there would be no way of combatting it,

and the people have the right to remove any undesirable political machinery. Ultimately, nonpartisanship leads to anarchy.
Endorsers: Milton L. Schmitt, Assemblyman, 31st. Dist.

PROPOSITION 2: Form of Ballot Law.
Type: Referendum
Outcome: Rejected
Summary: Prescribes the size, format, and printing of the new ballots to be used for general elections.
Arguments For this referendum: The omission of party designation from the names of candidates is the most important change proposed by this measure. It will induce efficiency by enabling the election of candidates based on merit alone, and will greatly reduce the confusion and length of the present ballot.
Endorsers: C. C. Young, Speaker of the Assembly.
Arguments Against this referendum: The argument levied against the main measure can be applied here. The people have the right to choose their affiliations and know the political platform of the candidates.
Endorsers: Milton L. Schmitt, Assemblyman, 31st. Dist.

Election of November 7, 1916

PROPOSITION 1: Prohibition.
Type: Initiative Constitutional Amendment
Outcome: Rejected
Summary: Prohibits the possession, sale, purchase, and manufacture of alcoholic liquor within the State of California. Under certain conditions, fields such as medicinal, sacramental, scientific, and mechanical can have access to liquor. Any person other than those stated above, caught in possession of alcoholic liquors, shall be punished by a fine not exceeding one thousand dollars or by imprisonment in the county jail not exceeding twelve months.
Arguments For: Alcohol does great damage to individuals. It is a narcotic poison that injures the body, mind, and character. Prohibition is the key to a better and progressive society. Certainly this act will hurt the California wine-grape market, but that market is a small part of California's grape industry. Restricting alcoholic liquor will not only decrease the chances of destroying peoples' lives but will also promote a better place to live.
Endorsers: Albert J. Wallace.
Arguments Against: Prohibition is an unjust law because it denies human beings their natural appetites and makes all conform to a lifestyle approved by a few. Prohibition has neither decreased crime nor helped improve the public health. In France, which has high consumption of wine, there is no intoxication and they are the longest lived people on earth. For sixty years,

state and local government have fostered and protected the California wine industry because it has brought great wealth and publicity to the state. If the prohibition is passed, California as a state will be hurt and California barley growers will have to look elsewhere to continue their business. Ultimately, this law will only bring more conflict between businessman and local government.

Endorsers: James Madison, General Mgr., Calif. Associated Raisin Co.

PROPOSITION 2: Prohibition.
Type: Initiative Constitutional Amendment
Outcome: Rejected
Summary: After January 1, 1918, no alcoholic liquor shall be possessed, given away, or sold in any saloon, dive, store, hotel, restaurant, cafe, club, dance hall, or other place of public resort. Alcoholic liquor transported into the State of California or within the state cannot exceed two gallons unless obtained at a pharmacy. Hence, this prohibition restricts the selling and purchasing of alcoholic liquor at public resorts. Violation will result in a fine of two thousand dollars or more, and an extensive period of imprisonment based on the amount of alcoholic liquor in one's possession.
Arguments For: This prohibition will only close the saloon and end the service of liquor in public places. People will be able to purchase liquor directly from the manufacturer and have it delivered straight to their homes. The amendment will have no appreciable impact upon California's wine industry. Other states have discovered that closing saloons improves business, reduces crime, improves the life of the average person, and is marvelously better for women and children. Thus, California's communities can be improved like other states' communities with this amendment and it will not hurt the wine industry.
Endorsers: Arthur Arlet.
Arguments Against: The amendment eliminates the purchase of liquors in public places. Thousands of tourists would go annually to other parts of the country and world where they could enjoy their holiday without such restriction of their appetites. The sampling and tasting of wine at the place of manufacture will decrease because purchasers cannot go to a winery or brewery and take away with him an unlimited amount that they may wish to buy. This amendment will not only put the winery and brewery industries at a disadvantage, but it will hurt California's economy as well. Prohibition restricts the liberty of individuals to fulfill their appetites, and has never decreased the crime rate or improved the living conditions of man.
Endorsers: James Madison, General Mgr., Calif. Associated Raisin Co.

PROPOSITION 4: Direct Primary Law.

Type: Referendum
Outcome: Rejected
Summary: Amends provisions of the Direct Primary Law of 1913 which governs nominations at primary elections, in order to allow declaration of party affiliation by electors at the polls. It prescribes all names of candidates on official ballots. Electors can only vote for candidates of their affiliation. Thus, this act provides a method for choosing the delegates for political parties to state conventions and for nominating electors for President and Vice-president of the United States.
Arguments For this referendum: The bill permits voters at primary elections to declare in writing the name of their party and be able to vote for its candidates. This will make sure that voters will not venture to claim membership in parties to which they are not affiliated. In addition, it simplifies the process of party nominations and opens the primaries for more participation by the voters. Hence, the passing of this bill will place more responsibility on voters to seriously think about who they vote for, and will encourage more people to vote.
Endorsers: C.C. Young, Speaker of the Assembly.
Arguments Against this Referendum: This law would prohibit party registration and provide only for party declaration at the polls. It would permit of control of a party at the primaries by its opponents. Boss domination in the centers of population would occur. With the provisions of this measure, voters could request a Democratic ballot and vote for a Republican or a Progressive as the Democratic nominee for United States senator.
Endorsers: Alfred L. Bartlett, Assemblyman 63rd. Dist.

PROPOSITION 5: Land Taxation.
Type: Initiative Constitutional Amendment
Outcome: Rejected
Summary: Mandates that all public revenues shall be raised by taxation of land values with the exception of improvements. The taxation of labor product is prohibited. Land ownership shall be equally assessed, according to value for use or occupance without considering improvements on the land. Essentially, this initiative aims to take for public use the rental and site values of land, and to reduce landholding to those only who live on or make productive use of it.
Arguments For: According to the Constitution of California, "The holding of large tracts of land, uncultivated and unimproved, by individuals or corporations, is against the public interest." Corporations have millions of acres in the state that are uncultivated and unimproved. Yet, they pay no taxes. Meanwhile, farmers pay indirect taxes on what they consume and produce because agriculture is an industry. Is this just? If there were a flat tax fee on land values, the farmer would pay half of what he is paying now, and the city

landowner would pay more than enough to make up the difference. This measure will lower all taxes on land and meet the interests of all the people.
Endorsers: Charles James and Lona Ingham Robinson.
Arguments Against: The theory of single tax is not a realistic one. No state in the Union has put this theory into practice and no economists advocate it. If other forms of property are exempt from taxation, people must pay more for their land. In the event that people cannot continue to pay tax for their land, it would be confiscated. The value of the land would disappear under any form of the single tax. For farmers, the new amendment would be ruinous. For private landowners, including thousands who own small homes, the amendment would impose a heavy sacrifice in value. Thus, a single tax will hurt everyone and not just farmers.
Endorsers: John S. Drum.

PROPOSITION 6: Ineligibility to Office.
Type: Initiative Constitutional Amendment
Outcome: Approved
Summary: Declares that no Senator or Member of the Assembly shall hold or accept any other positions aside from the one that they were elected to during their years in office. However, this provision does not apply to any office filled by election of the people.
Arguments For: The American theory believes that those who execute the law should not be the ones who make the law. Yet the present law allows individuals to be both elected legislators and members of the executive department. Wearing two hats will create greater likelihood of conflicts of interest, and result in decisions upon political pressures instead of an independent frame of mind. Individuals who hold both offices may be prone to the abuse of power.
Endorsers: Richmond P. Benton, Assemblyman, 66th. Dist.; Dr. John R. Haynes.
Arguments Against: The passing of this amendment implies that every governor and member of the state legislature is dishonest and has no integrity or character. Under this amendment, senators or assemblymen could not take a civil service examination for a state position. The prevention of wearing two hats does not guarantee that corruption won't exist among political officials. It is not the office that makes a person corrupt; rather, it is the individual's own character.
Endorsers: Thos. P. White, Presiding Judge, Police Court, Los Angeles.

Election of November 5, 1918

PROPOSITION 1: Liquor Regulation.
Type: Initiative Statute
Outcome: Rejected
Summary: Effective July 1, 1919, prohibits the keeping of saloons and sale of liquor; regulates the transport, licensing and consumption of liquor; prescribes penalties for violations.
Arguments For: The welfare of the state's citizenship has deteriorated because of disreputable saloons and roadhouses. This measure seeks to eliminate the abuse of alcoholic beverages while retaining the legitimate uses of beers and light wines.
Endorsers: J. A. Rominger, State Sen., 33rd. Dist.; Frank T. Swett, Member, State Board of Viticultural Commissioners.
Arguments Against: Intemperance should not be the sole cause for restrictive laws which are designed to strip away civil liberties. Mandating a meal be purchased with an alcoholic beverage will only lead to a waste of food because this law implies that a person is hungry when he is thirsty. Temperance and character can only be developed by the individual through construction and not restrictions.
Endorsers: Harry Ryan, State Organizer, Calif. Trades Union Liberty League.

PROPOSITION 3: Usury Law.
Type: Initiative Statute
Outcome: Approved
Summary: Restricts and regulates the interest rates on the loan of money or property; limits fees and commissions on such loans and provides penalties for violations.
Arguments For: California has never had a usury law, and the result is personal bankruptcy and illegitimate competition among bankers. By fixing the interest rate, widows and orphans in adversity can be protected from loan sharks. The assertion that a fixed interest rate will drive capital out of the state is absurd because lenders will take what they can to do business.
Endorsers: William E. Brown, State Sen., 37th. Dist. ·
Arguments Against: This measure would drive millions of dollars out of California by providing a monopoly for loan sharks. Legitimate businesses can't compete with the loan sharks because they will be restricted to a fixed rate. This deceptive measure would drive out legal business and the victims will be those for whom this law was conceived.
Endorsers: A. W. Sorenson.

PROPOSITION 17: Tax Levy Limitations.
Type: Referendum

Outcome: Rejected

Summary: The law being reconsidered mandated county officers to file financial statements with governing body of county for tax levy. Regulated amounts produced by tax levies by counties, limited to a yearly increase of five percent of production.

Arguments For the existing legislation, Against this referendum: This measure is designed to effectively curb and regulate the rising cost of government through tax limitation. Public officials need to budget expenditures in order to relieve tax burden on the public.

Endorsers: Clyde L. Seavy

Arguments Against the existing legislation, For this referendum: The budget cutting effect of this measure endangers the public education system. It limits income to a constant growth rate of five percent. How is this determined when growth is not a uniform quantity? School districts under similar "scientific legislation" have reported dramatic declines in attendance. Clearly, this law demonstrates that strict budgeting and limitations do not always serve the interests of the public.

Endorsers: Mark Keppel, Supt. of Schools, Los Angeles County.

PROPOSITION 18: County and School Tax Limitations.

Type: Initiative Statute

Outcome: Rejected

Summary: Creates State Board of Authorization. Mandates county officers and respective governing bodies to file budget statements to the state board before making tax levies; limits annual increase in amounts raised to five percent of previous production year. School increases are determined by average daily attendance. The legislature can amend or repeal this act.

Arguments For: Intelligent tax limitations will not impair the necessary costs of government operation. Proper budgeting of proposed expenditures will eliminate wastefulness and facilitate the improvement of education. Estimation of school income based on attendance is a reasonable method that will ensure the preservation of schools.

Endorsers : Mark Keppel, Supt. of Schools, Los Angeles County.

Arguments Against: This cumbersome measure may benefit the schools, but it is harmful to the other branches of government. It removes the matter of local taxation further away from the people through the Board of Authorization, which is not acquainted with the conditions and needs of each locale.

Endorsers : Rob E. Callahan, Chairman, Sacramento County Bd. of Supervisors.

PROPOSITION 19: Land Values Taxation.

Type: Initiative Constitutional Amendment
Outcome: Rejected
Summary: Effective January 1, 1919, taxation will be based on the value of land, regardless of improvements thereon, for all public revenues, state, county, municipal, and district. War veterans, churches, and colleges are exempt. Prevents speculative holding of land, and applies to the community any land value it creates.
Arguments For: The conscription of California's twenty million idle acres of land will lead to immediate food production and jobs for people. Farmers and builders will cultivate the land, and, thereby, increase the worth and growth of California. No longer will labor and industry be denied access to natural opportunities. The Single Tax should fall upon the three percent of the population who own ninety percent of the land in California.
Endorsers: Lona Ingham Washington; Luke North.
Arguments Against: America is great because it originally enabled every citizen to become a land owner. The Single Tax would devalue real estate, bonds, and stocks based on land value. The envisioned growth and prosperity from the usage of "idle millions of acres" is absurd because, in order to develop the land, the common man must borrow a large amount of capital. And who will lend him money if his land is single taxed?
Endorsers: E. P. Clark; Carl C. Plehn.

PROPOSITION 21: Dentistry.
Type: Initiative Statute
Outcome: Rejected
Summary: Requires members appointed to the Board of Dental Examiners to have the degree of Doctor of Dental Surgery or Dental Medicine. Permits applicants with good moral character and five years of practice to be given license without examination upon paying twenty-five dollars. Forbids the administering of anesthetic except in the presence of a third adult. Charging low fees is not to be considered unprofessional.
Arguments For: Dental combines have purposely kept legislators and the public in the dark about the issue of dental care. As a result, these combines have manipulated the laws for their own purposes. This measure will end the current practices of unqualified "professionals" and raise the active role of the people in regard to their dental care. The requirement of a third person when administering anesthetic is not an added hardship or expense; its wisdom does not require an explanation.
Endorsers: Painless Parker.
Arguments Against: This is a shameful example of abuse of initiative power. It attempts to degrade the dental profession by allowing nonprofessionals from other states to be licensed and practice in California without the benefit of

an examination. These derelicts are willing to charge low fees in order to compete with honest, board certified dentists.

Endorsers: Guy S. Milberry, D.D.S., Dean, College of Dentistry, Univ. of Calif.

PROPOSITION 22: Prohibition.

Type: Initiative Statute

Outcome: Rejected

Summary: After December 31, 1918, any party that sells intoxicating liquors, except denatured alcohol, is guilty of a misdemeanor punishable by twenty-five dollars fine and twenty-five days imprisonment for first offense; each subsequent offense will double the penalties.

Arguments For: Patriotic Americans should stand up and fight this liquor battle on the home front in order to support victory in the big war. Breweries and distillers waste resources and manpower that is much needed for the war effort overseas. Going Bone Dry is the only salvation our nation can hope for.

Endorsers: G. F. Rinehart, Manager, Bone Dry Fed. of Calif.

Arguments Against: There are no absolutes in life, and yet this measure seeks to completely forbid the use of alcohol for purposes other than medical. While it is true that alcohol can be destructive if abused, its moderate use should be allowed. Religious freedom, not to mention civil rights, cannot be sacrificed for the sake of winning the war.

Endorsers: Hilliard E. Welch, Pres., Lodi National Bank.

Election of November 2, 1920

PROPOSITION 1: Alien Land Law.

Type: Initiative Statute

Outcome: Approved

Summary: Allows aliens eligible for citizenship to acquire and transfer real estate to same extent as citizens. Permits companies and corporations to acquire and transfer real property as prescribed, but prohibits the appointment of minors as guardians of estates thereof. Provides escheats in certain cases. Provides for penalties and repeals conflicting acts.

Arguments For: California has the right to preserve her lands for Americans. Aliens ineligible for citizenship, largely Japanese, are buying up land, thereby denying American citizens this opportunity. These people use dummy corporations and native minors as fronts to acquire land that belongs to Americans. This measure enables ineligible aliens to acquire land only as prescribed by the Japan treaty. Thus, the equities of innocent holders are fully protected without violating treaty rights and citizenship of the native born.

Endorsers: V. S. McClatchy.

Arguments Against: This measure proposes a discriminatory classification of aliens, giving rights to one class while withholding rights from another. Under the treaty, Japanese here may own and operate property for residential or commercial purposes. Targeting the Japanese is a destructive blow at American liberty.
Endorsers: John P. Irish.

PROPOSITION 2: Prohibition Enforcement Act.
Type: Referendum
Outcome: Rejected
Summary: The law being reconsidered defined intoxicating liquor as that with more than one half of one percent alcohol. It prohibits the possession, production, transport, sale, and serving of alcohol except for medical or religious usage, and regulates the dealing of alcohol for non-beverage purposes.
Arguments For the existing legislation, Against this referendum: The Constitution is not self-executing because it doesn't provide for penalties or means of enforcing the laws. Regulation of intoxicating beverages is aimed at maintaining proper citizen conduct as prescribed by the constitution, while permitting legitimate usage. The real issue is not prohibition, instead it is law and order.
Endorsers: M. B. Harris, State Senator, 26th District.
7. **Arguments Against the existing law, For this referendum:** California will be under double prohibition, federal and state, if this law passes. To say that this type of legislation is productive and reflects the political sentiments of the people is at best speculative. This will eventually lead to an oppressive government that strips away civil rights, rights which are synonymous to our glorious hospitable California.
Endorsers: E. M. Sheehan, Pres., California Grape Growers' Exchange.

PROPOSITION 3: Salaries of Justices.
Type: Initiative Constitutional Amendment
Outcome: Rejected
Summary: Increases salaries of Justices of the Supreme Court from $8,000 to $10,000 per year, and of judges of the District Courts of Appeal from $7,000 to $9,000 per year.
Arguments For: The present salaries were set in 1906 when these amounts were considered reasonable compensation. Since that time, the purchasing power of these salaries has greatly diminished. This measure is designed to offset inflation instead of increasing the amount of compensation.
Endorsers: Bradner W. Lee.
7. **Arguments Against:** None recorded.

PROPOSITION 4: Initiative: 25% Instead of 8% Signatures.
Type: Initiative Constitutional Amendment
Outcome: Rejected
Summary: Increases the number of signatures of electors required on initiative petitions for assessment or collection of taxes. Such number to be 25%, instead of the present 8%, of the number of votes for all gubernatorial candidates at the preceding election.
Arguments For: This measure requires a 25% petition on matters affecting the assessment and collection of taxes only. It is designed to protect the people and will curb the activities of single tax advocates. The ease with which the supporters of the single tax secure an 8% petition encourages them to continue their activities, thereby incurring great expense for the public.
Endorsers: E. P. Clark.
Arguments Against: This dangerous act asks people to surrender control over taxation—the most important function of government. The 25% requirement would mean the signature of one in every four voters; this impossibility can only be met by the richest and most powerful interests. Once enacted, it would be a herculean task to modify or repeal this act because of the same 25% requirement. The claim to curb single tax is misleading because California has defeated the single tax on four occasions. It isn't necessary to destroy the current initiative in order to defeat single tax.
Endorsers: Dr. John R. Haynes, Los Angeles.

PROPOSITION 5: Chiropractic.
Type: Initiative Statute
Outcome: Rejected
Summary: Authorizes the governor to appoint a Board of Chiropractic Examiners. Prohibits the practice of chiropractic without license; requires licensees to observe regulations regarding disease control; authorizes licensees to sign birth and death certificates; and prescribes healing methods.
Arguments For: The need for a Board of Chiropractic Examiners arises because the State Board of Medical Examiners does not know, teach, or believe in chiropractic; therefore, it isn't competent to examine chiropractors. If established, the chiropractic board will ensure the competency of its practitioners through careful examination and licensing. Furthermore, such board would not be an added cost to the public because of the fees imposed on its members, thereby making it self-supporting.
Endorsers: Josh A. Sanford.
Arguments Against: The current State Board is empowered and qualified to examine all applicant's knowledge of the human body and its diseases. California insists that those who desire to treat patients for physical ills shall

possess qualifications determined by the board. The demand of a small number of chiropractors for a special Board of Chiropractic Examiners, based on the asserted incompetence of the Medical Board, is unreasonable. If chiropractors were granted a special board then all other cults would demand and be equally entitled to special boards. The result would be multiple boards, divided authority and loss of proper control.

Endorsers: Dudley A. Smith, M.D., Pres., League for Conservation of Public Health.

PROPOSITION 6: Prohibiting Compulsory Vaccination.

Type: Initiative Constitutional Amendment

Outcome: Rejected

Summary: Declares that no form of vaccination shall hereafter be a requirement for admission to any educational institution, or for employment in any public office.

Arguments For: The efficacy of vaccination is a debatable issue on which medical opinion is not agreed. This measure does not seek to interfere with lawful quarantine and medical treatment. Instead, it prescribes that vaccination shall not be made compulsory. If vaccination is as beneficial as claimed, then no compulsion should be made on its behalf; however, if vaccination does not protect from smallpox, then mandating it would violate the people's right to make decisions regarding their welfare.

Endorsers: Lewis P. Crutcher, M.D.

Arguments Against: The State Board of Health is responsible for warning the public of any present or approaching dangers that threaten the health of the people. Should this measure pass, the people of California will be in constant danger of a smallpox epidemic and the board will be powerless to monitor and control it. Many diseases are not the fault of the individual and are not within his power to avoid or control. The life and health of the public is a fundamental principle which depends on scientific health work aided by community cooperation.

Endorsers: George E. Ebright, M.D., Pres.,Calif. State Board of Health.

PROPOSITION 7: Prohibiting Vivisection.

Type: Initiative Statute

Outcome: Rejected

Summary: Declares it unlawful for anyone to dissect, vivisect, or torture living persons or living animals for experimental purposes at any institution in California. Vivisection of a living person is allowed with that person's consent and only in case of physical injury, deformity, and sickness.

Arguments For: The foundation of vivisection is the unnecessary torture of humans and animals. It is experimenting on living animals by means of cutting, injecting, starving, burning, etc. The results of such experiments have accomplished nothing for the benefit of science and life. It violates the laws of God and nature, and feeds the vaccine and serum factories built on the tortured bodies of God's sentient creatures.

Endorsers: Rosemonde Rae Wright.

Arguments Against: This special legislation is based on prejudice and misinformation. There is no cruelty in the laboratories of the state; no one will tolerate cruelty to animals. Those involved are people of the highest character, working selflessly for the benefit of mankind. Because of these necessary and humane efforts, we no longer need to fear scourges of smallpox, cholera, typhoid, yellow fever, and a host of other diseases. It is unfortunate that any life must be sacrificed in order to save life or gain life-saving information, but the quality and safety of mankind depends on it.

Endorsers: Ray Lyman Wilbur.

PROPOSITION 8: Poison Act.

Type: Referendum

Outcome: Approved

Summary: The act being reconsidered limited the preparation and use of poisons except for established remedies. Regulated the amount of opium, morphine, cocaine, and heroin which licensed physicians can prescribe to habitual users except in cases of incurable disease, ailment, or injury. Regulated the distribution and possession of hypodermic syringes and needles.

Arguments For the existing legislation, Against this referendum: This act amends portions of the "Poison Law" and facilitates better administration of that law. It is intended to prevent unlicensed practitioners from prescribing narcotics and to prohibit the purchase of drugs without a prescription. The goal is to curtail the illicit drug traffic by strengthening the law, thereby increasing its efficiency.

Endorsers: J.S. O'Callaghan.

Arguments Against the existing legislation, For this referendum: In 1901, no one would contend that minor surgery could be done without the use of local anesthetics. Osteopathic surgeons have been licensed to practice major and minor surgery since 1913. This bill provides that osteopaths may possess a hypodermic syringe and needles, but denies them the right to purchase local anesthetics. This type of discrimination deprives citizens from employing the physician of their choice because he could not lawfully care for minor surgical conditions.

Endorsers: W. W. Vanderburgh.

PROPOSITION 9: Highway bonds.
Type: Initiative Statute/Bond Act
Outcome: Approved
Summary: Creates State Highway Finance Board to serve without compensation. Directs cancellation of unsold bonds; authorizes other bonds to be issued at times and interest rate, not exceeding six percent, to be determined by the board; governs said bonds and proceeds thereof. Relieves counties from payments to state on account of highway construction.
Arguments For: State Highway bonds are now unsalable because they are not competitive. State bonds bearing 4.5% interest can't hope to compete with United States or commercial bonds which are yielding more than 7%. Therefore, the proposed law creates a Finance Board, composed of various state officials, to raise or lower the interest rate on previously unsold state highway bonds. This allows future adjustment to meet the market fluctuations at times when the money is required for state highway works. Furthermore, counties should be relieved of all interest payments owed the state on account of highway construction because the highways are for everyone.
Endorsers: M. B. Johnson, Senator, 11th. Dist.
Arguments Against: The proposal to shift the payment of highway bond interest from the counties to the state is dangerous and deceptive because the expected gain cannot justify the cost involved. This reckless financing and unjustified extravagance will destroy the state's economic well being for at least 40 years.
Endorsers: Will H. Fischer, Director, Taxpayers' Assn. of Calif.

PROPOSITION 12: State University Tax.
Type: Initiative Constitutional Amendment
Outcome: Rejected
Summary: Creates an ad valorem tax of 1.2 mills per dollar on property, based upon its assessed value. The revenue, which the university could utilize for operational expenses or payment of deficits, would be placed in a "State University Fund," separating the university system's source of funds from that of the public school system.
Arguments For: The University, which is suffering from financial hardships, faces the crisis of an expanding student population for which it cannot provide adequate facilities or teachers. The tax, which would cost the average taxpayer just dollars a year, would allow the university to plan for the future, and to keep the system tuition free.
Endorsers: Warren Gregory, Pres., Alumni Assn. of the University of California.
Arguments Against: This measure is fundamentally wrong! Unlike the previous tax, this one will remain out of control of the legislature and the people, who may some day need to draw upon the annually increasing fund.

The fund, which unjustly gives the burden to the people and not business, would be at the complete disposal of the University Regents.

Endorsers: Clyde L. Seavey.

PROPOSITION 13: Community Property.

Type: Referendum

Outcome: Rejected

Summary: The law being reconsidered would amend the Civil Code to declare one-half of community property exempt from inheritance tax and legal assessments on the death of one spouse. In addition it would add a provision that a spouse may not will his/her half of the community property without the signed consent of the other, except when the property is willed to the other spouse or a decedent.

Arguments For the existing legislation, Against this referendum: The law would restore the right of a woman to leave her share of community property to her husband or children. The law does not take away the husband's control of the property while he is alive, nor does it affect property obtained before or after marriage.

Endorsers: Chester H. Rowell.

Arguments Against the existing legislation, For this referendum: The law is unfair to men, who are the "bread winners" and the ones who bear sole liability for their wife and children. For many men this will mean a loss of at least one-half of their good credit. If women want the same equal rights, they should have equal liability. This law will lead only to more court battles and provide the right of women to leave their share of property to children from previous marriages, yet prevent them from leaving their share to worthy charities without the consent of their spouse.

Endorsers: L. H. Poseberry.

PROPOSITION 14: Insurance Act.

Type: Referendum

Outcome: Rejected

Summary: The law being reconsidered prohibits state banks and their subsidiaries, officers, and employees from operating or managing insurance companies within the state, except within cities with a population of 5,000 or less.

Arguments For the existing legislation, Against this referendum: Banks must stay out of the insurance business! In order to prevent abuses, which could result from bank officers suggesting a customer use their insurance company as a condition for loan approval, bank officers should not have influence in the insurance business. Cities of less than 5,000 have been excluded from this, as the state feels abuses in these areas would be minimal, if any.

Endorsers: Burt L. Davis.

Arguments Against the existing legislation, For this referendum: This bill is unfair and illogical. It will only hurt the people by eliminating competition in favor of insurance company monopolies, yet it will not lessen or regulate the cost of insurance. The measure also discriminates against bank shareholders who, because they have an interest in a bank, cannot hold an interest in an insurance agency. If there is a threat to the people by having insurance agencies affiliated with banks, the state should offer equal protection to the small communities which it excludes from this measure.

Endorsers: James A. Bacigaluipi.

PROPOSITION 15: Irrigation District Act.

Type: Referendum

Outcome: Approved

Summary: The law being reconsidered seeks to amend the 1897 act to allow for the organization of irrigation districts by a simple majority vote, rather than a 2/3 majority. Sets procedures for petition to the Board of Supervisors, and establishes the State Engineer's duty to review the feasibility of the project, and determine whether it should be allowed to proceed.

Arguments For the existing legislation, Against this referendum: Water is a scarce resource, and should be utilized for good arable land, not kept in the hands of a selfish minority. The provision for the State Engineer to review the proposed projects will protect the people from abusive schemes.

Endorsers: L. L. Dennett, State Senator, 12th Dist.

Arguments Against the existing legislation, For this referendum: The existing act was designed to prevent the large number of irrigation district failures which were once abundant. This law would put the control in the hands of a small majority, which, if the district takes in part of a city, could leave the land owners with virtually no say. It would lead to many more irrigation district failures.

Endorsers: J. B. Ociese.

PROPOSITION 16: School System.

Type: Initiative Constitutional Amendment

Outcome: Approved

Summary: Amends the Constitution to add kindergartens to the public schools and to create a state high school fund. Requires the state to pay, from revenues, a minimum of $30 per pupil in the day and evening public elementary, secondary, and technical schools. Requires, as well, that individual counties levy taxes to provide at least $30 per pupil in the elementary grades and a minimum of $60 per pupil in the secondary and technical schools. The primary intent of the measure would be to provide for an increase in teacher salaries. **Arguments For:** This measure will bring teachers' salaries up $270 per year to $1270 annually, which only slightly compensates for the tremendous increase in the cost of living. Teachers hold the future of America in their hands, and are not compensated adequately for the services. Many shall leave the profession, and this will especially impact the farming areas, from which families will move seeking adequate schools. This measure will adequately supply all schools with the means to provide good education by upholding the principle that school money should "be raised where income is, and distributed where children are."

Endorsers: Will C. Wood, Supt. of Public Instruction.

Arguments Against: While all good Americans favor adequate pay for efficient teaching, we must consider the means by which this money is to be raised. This measure is set up in such a manner that it cannot, without an expensive campaign and a popular vote, be reversed or amended. As a result, the sum of money required for each pupil calculated with the ever increasing attendance will soon lead to astronomical proportions, and will become an extreme burden on the taxpayers.

Endorsers: W. A. Doran, Assemblyman, 18th Dist.

PROPOSITION 20: Land Value Taxation.
Type: Initiative Constitutional Amendment
Outcome: Rejected
Summary: Amends the Constitution as of 1 Janaury 1921 to exempt from personal property taxation items such as plants, trees, and vines, and to limit taxation on improvements to the land. Effective 1 Jaunary 1924, requires that all public revenues be raised by taxation of land, exclusive of improvements. Will not affect war veteran, church, and college exemptions, nor would it effect public utilities using public highways.
(There is no additional information on this measure in the voter's information pamphlet.)

Election of November 7, 1922

PROPOSITION 1: Veterans' Validating Act.
Type: Initiative Constitutional Amendment
Outcome: Approved
Summary: Seeks to validate the measure, passed unanimously by the legislature, for the state to aid veterans of wartime service in the purchase or development of homes or farms. This measure would be carried out regardless of whether or not the accompanying bond issue is approved by the voters.

Arguments For: This measure would provide veterans the ability to settle in homes or on farms, as the state overcomes any constitutional difficulties which would deny the veterans what the people of California, through their legislators, unanimously support.

Endorsers: Hunter Liggett, Major General U. S. Army, ret.

Arguments Against: No Argument Recorded

PROPOSITION 2: Prohibition Enforcement Act.

Type: Referendum

Outcome: Approved

Summary: The law under reconsideration makes the 18th Amendment to the U.S. Constitution and the "Volstead Act" the law of the State of California, and vests in local law enforcement agencies and judicial officers the responsibility for enforcement. These laws will change in accordance with those of the federal government.

Arguments For the existing legislation, Against this referendum: This act will stop bootlegging, without threatening our constitutional rights, and show that California respects the Constitution of the United States. It will create no new offices, nor will it cost the state any more, yet it will provide the counties with revenue now going to the federal government. It would be a "pledge of Allegiance to the ideals of American citizenship."

Endorsers: T. M. Wright, Assemblyman, 44th Dist.

Arguments Against the existing legislation, For this referendum: This "Wright Act" would force the state to the expense of eventually enforcing all federal laws, and would change the priorities of law enforcement, leaving innocent citizens at the mercy of burglars while the police chase bootleggers. Its careless reverence to the federal Constitution will lead to the weakening of the state's power to make and change its own laws, and would lead to ultimate chaos in the confusion and intermingling of state and federal duties.

Endorsers: C. E. McLaughlin.

PROPOSITION 5: State Housing Act.

Type: Referendum

Outcome: Rejected

Summary: The law being reconsidered repeals the "State Tenement House Act," "State Hotel and Lodging House Act," and the "State Dwelling House Act," and combines their provisions. In addition, it includes the definition and requirements for fire resistant building materials in incorporated areas.

Arguments For the existing legislation, Against this referendum: This act would provide for restrictions against the use of dangerous wood shingles, and the require the use of fire resistant building materials. It will, however, apply only to hotels and lodging houses, and not to family residences.

Endorsers: Lester G. Burnett, State Senator, 19th Dist.

Arguments Against the existing legislation, For this referendum: This measure would give unchecked authority to municipal inspectors to approve or disapprove of products, even though they may be nationally known for their fire resistance. It would also eliminate the use of shingles on most structures in California, despite years of proven safe and dependable usage. The measure would also lead to a gross decline in sanitary regulation by allowing for cheap walls, which allow odor and vermin to pass, as long as they are painted, and for its lack of provisions for employees' toilets at hotels.

Endorsers: Paul Scharrenberg, Member, Calif. Comm. of Immigration and Housing.

PROPOSITION 10: Taxation of Publicly Owned Utilities.

Type: Initiative Constitutional Amendment

Outcome: Rejected

Summary: Amends the constitution to provide for the taxation of any land owned or operated by a county or municipality for the purpose of providing a public utility service, in the same manner as property owned by private corporations.

Arguments For: Under the current system, consumers who are served by private utilities pay the taxes imposed as a part of their service fee. Customers of publicly owned utilities pay no such fee, as the public utilities are exempt from this taxation. The continued acquisition of utilities by county or municipal agencies will further, and unfairly, shift the tax burden to those served by private utilities, and will lead to decreased state revenues which will require new taxes to compensate for their loss.

Endorsers: W. A. Sutherland, V.P., Los Angeles Trust and Savings Bank, Managing Director, Fidelity of Fresno Branch.

Arguments Against: This tax would discourage the public ownership of utilities and further tighten the grip of private monopolies on the people of this state. It is a fact of economics that any tax which increases the cost of services essential to human existence or happiness is unjust. The measure also ignores the fact that many public systems purchase services from private corporations, and in paying the factored-in tax, would thus be stuck with double taxation. This tax is illogical and unfair.

Endorsers: H. A. Mason, W. J. Locke, Secretaries of the League of Calif. Municipalities.

PROPOSITION 11: Regulation of Publicly Owned Public Utilities.

Type: Initiative Constitutional Amendment
Outcome: Rejected
Summary: Amends the constitution to bring publicly owned utility services under the regulation of the Railroad Commission, to, with the exception of issuance of securities, regulate service and fees in the same manner as those of privately owned utilities.
Arguments For: This measure would establish reasonable and honest rates, and eliminate preferential treatment or rates. In addition, it would provide the consumer with the same rights and guarantees to reasonable and fair service as enjoyed by consumers supplied by private corporations.
Endorsers: W. A. Sutherland, V.P., Los Angeles Trust and Savings Bank, Managing Director, Fidelity of Fresno Branch.
Arguments Against: The purpose of this bill is to deprive the cities and municipalities of the control of their own public utilities. Municipalities, which provide the services only for themselves, do not need the regulation that a private corporation with multiple interests requires. The public utilities often provide the services at much cheaper rates and thus drive the private competition rates down. Public utilities which charge the same as private corporations can often channel the excess profits into additional public services, while this profit would be lost revenue in private hands.
Endorsers: Mayor Louis Bartlett, Berkeley, Pres., League of California Municipalities.

PROPOSITION 12: State Budget.
Type: Initiative Constitutional Amendment
Outcome: Approved
Summary: Requires the governor to submit a budget, containing all estimated expenditures and revenues for the next fiscal year, to the legislature within thirty days of each regular session. Prescribes the procedure for passage of the budget bill, and for referendum against items contained within that bill, except those of current annual expenditure. In addition, authorizes the governor to reduce or eliminate any item of appropriation, and prohibits the governor from making additional appropriations.
Arguments For: Government is a business, and should be run like a business. A state budget is vital to the state at this time, as it will assure that the financial condition of the treasury is not jeopardized, and will eliminate wasteful use of state funds. In the long run this will save the taxpayers money and assure that, before the state appropriates funds, it will also have the revenue to secure these appropriations.
Endorsers: Albert E. Boynton, San Francisco, CA.
Arguments Against: None recorded

PROPOSITION 16: Chiropractic.
Type: Initiative Statute
Outcome: Approved
Summary: Provides for a five member Board of Chiropractic Examiners to be appointed by the Governor, in order to prescribe and regulate the practice of chiropractors in accordance with all state and local public health regulations. The Board would set the minimal standards of education and would issue a license to all qualified applicants. A fee of $25 will be charged to each applicant, out of which and salaries of the members of the board shall be paid, with the remaining revenue to be placed under the State Controller in a "State Board of Chiropractic Examiners Fund."
Arguments For: This measure would assure that chiropractors, in order to be licensed and practice legally, would be required to have proper education and training as determined by the standards set by the board of review. this measure would not interfere with the current Medical Act, nor would it allow the chiropractors to practice surgery or administer drugs. It would, however, prevent this remarkable technique from being destroyed by the political doctors of the Medical Board who, not wishing to have any competition, have attempted to kill its practice in California.
Endorsers: G. A. Lynch.
Arguments Against: To create two additional boards (see Proposition 20) would be unwise both in terms of economics and public heath standards. The current board of examiners is sufficient to govern the practice of chiropractics, and has issued certificates to those who have qualified. A major result of the new board would be the lowering of educational standards to practice chiropractics, and would result in many "fly by night" schools for training inferior chiropractors, who will receive licenses with practically no training at all. Another consideration is that with nearly twenty-seven "drugless cults" in the state, granting a new board for chiropractors would lead to a new board for each of these fields.
Endorsers: Bomer R. Spence, Assemblyman 35th. Dist.

PROPOSITION 19: Water and Power.
Type: Initiative Constitutional Amendment
Outcome: Rejected
Summary: Amends the constitution to provide for the appointment of a Water and Power Board by the Governor, and subject to recall. The board will have the authority to issue 50 year bonds, not exceeding $500,000,000, to develop and provide water and electric energy.
Arguments For: This measure's greatest benefit is that it will prevent the remaining areas of water and power potential from falling into the hands of monopolistic private interests. State owned and operated utilities can provide

water and power to cities at reasonable rates, and as control will be maintained by a public board open to review, it will prevent the domination of selfish corporate interests.

Endorsers: Rudolph Spreckles; Clyde Seavey, City Manager of the City of Sacramento.

Arguments Against: This plan will only cost the taxpayers more in the long run. Currently, all the cheapest sources of water and power have been appropriated, and the cost of developing the state projects would greatly surpass current estimates which are based on those of 1914. In order to pay for these additional costs the bill permits the board to draw on the state treasury without limit. It will then be necessary to levy additional taxes to repay this money to the treasury. The ultimate result of this measure will be to pass on the added costs the public. This bill is socialist, autocratic, bureaucratic, undemocratic, and should be defeated."

Endorsers: Mark L. Requa, former president, Tax Association of Alameda County.

PROPOSITION 20: Osteopathic Act.
Type: Initiative Statute
Outcome: Approved
Summary: Creates a Board of Osteopathic Examiners to be appointed by the Governor. The board would have the responsibility of regulating schools of osteopathy and the graduates of these schools as provided by the Medical Act of 1913, which powers are currently exercised by the State Board of Medical Examiners. The Board of Osteopathic Examiners will conduct all reviews and examinations of osteopathic students, and the issuance of any form of certificate currently issued by the State Board of Medical Examiners. The salaries of the board will be paid from the collection of licensing fees.

Arguments For: Osteopathy is a complete system of healing which includes general medicine and surgery, and the schools of osteopathy teach all general medical and surgical subjects in addition to osteopathy. Medical doctors, who are the competitors of osteopaths, would like to kill the practice and have used their control of the Board of Medical Examiners to discriminate against practitioners of osteopathy. The current physician and surgeon law is right. Its administration is wrong.

Endorsers: Dr. Charles H. Spencer.

Arguments Against: The measure which would create an additional board of review would only serve to confuse the process of licensing and regulation of physicians and surgeons. Under this measure, any graduate of a college of osteopathy may be licensed as a physician or a surgeon, the results of which would be detrimental to public health. Over the last eight years, 48% of osteopathic graduates have failed the physician and surgeon examinations

Endorsers: Dr. W. T. McArthur, Secy., League for the Conservation of Public Health.

PROPOSITION 24: Regulating Practice of Law.
Type: Referendum
Outcome: Rejected
Summary: The law under reconsideration makes it a crime for any unlicensed person to act as an attorney, or to offer the services of legal advice or representation in a court of law. It would not prohibit any person from preparing ordinary business agreements, nor apply to charitable or non-profit organizations in their dealings with the affairs of their members, or embarrassed debtors. It does not apply to proceedings in justices' or police courts.
Arguments For the existing legislation, Against this referendum: The measure will protect the public against two major threats: 1) It will protect them from lawyers who have been disbarred for lack of integrity and lawyer-client confidence. 2) It will protect individuals from major trust companies engaged in the practice of law to meet for the sake of their corporation's own benefit. The act will not prevent business from conducting its own business transactions as some have implied.
Endorsers: Maurice E. Harrison, Dean, Hastings College of Law.
Arguments Against the existing legislation, For this referendum: This act has not been proposed for the good of the public. It is in fact a bill sponsored by lawyers, for lawyers, to create a monopoly in the field of law practice. It would make it illegal for men and women such as bankers and real estate brokers to share the vast wealth of legal knowledge many have in regards to their field of occupation. It would only serve to give a monopoly to a "special class" and impose unneeded additional fees on the public.
Endorsers: Sylvester L. Weaver, Los Angeles, CA.

PROPOSITION 27: Signatures for Initiative Petitions.
Type: Initiative Constitutional Amendment.
Outcome: Rejected
Summary: Amends the procedures for initiatives on matters related to taxation, or the amendment of this provision, to require that the number of signatures required be raised from 8% to 15% of the total votes cast for all candidates in the last gubernatorial election in which a governor was elected.
Arguments For: This measure will prevent abuse of the initiative system by small groups, by requiring an increase in the number of signatures required to place a initiative on the ballot. Its main benefit will be to prevent the need to battle the "single tax" supporters every two years. The 15% figure is the same percentage that city and county governments require to prevent abusive

changes to their charters, and the state should have equal protection. This measure will not, as claimed by its foes, affect any measures other than those related to taxation and the amendment of these provisions.

Endorsers: Epi Clarke, Office of the Attorney General.

Arguments Against: This measure is a "deadly attack upon democracy." Since most legislation involves taxation, it might be ruled that this measure would thus apply to all future legislation. It would thus have the ultimate effect of robbing the people of California of one of their greatest rights. The supporters fail to mention that raising the percentage of required signatures to 15% would require a very large number of signatures, owing to the fact that petitions usually require 40% more signatures than required in order to offset the error margin. This would leave all the real power of taxation with the legislature and with wealthy special interests.

Endorsers: John R. Haynes, Los Angeles.

PROPOSITION 28: Prohibiting Vivisection.

Type: Initiative Statute

Outcome: Rejected

Summary: Would prohibit vivisection, or any act which might be considered tortuous, upon human beings or animals for scientific or medical research. It would authorize a justice of the peace to issue warrants to prevent such operation, and to levy fines and/or imprisonment upon those who conduct such experiments. This act would not prohibit the branding of animals, nor would it prohibit surgical operations on humans or animals to prevent or correct medical disorders.

Arguments For: The current system in seeking progress tortures animals as well as prisoners, orphans, and patients of insane asylums. From a moral standpoint we have no right to do evil so that good may come. The use of animals to test medications for human use is illogical, as the medical effects of these medications on animals cannot mirror the effects they will have on humans.

Endorsers: Rosemonde Rae Wright.

Arguments Against: People who put the rights of animals above the welfare of mankind cannot intelligently vote for this act. The ultimate effect of this act would hurt animals as well, as much of the experimentation provides cures for many animal diseases. There is no truth to the slander that inhumane experimentation is being conducted upon orphans and the mentally ill. Much of the work is done by refined young women, and the work is devoted to advancing human welfare. Finally, this act is illogical as it continues to allow acts such as branding, which are done without anesthetic.

Endorsers: Walter V. Brem, M.D., Los Angeles.

PROPOSITION 29: Land Franchise Taxation.
Type: Initiative Constitutional Amendment
Outcome: Rejected
Summary: Abolishes the present taxation system; declares that private property rights pertain only to products of labor and not to land. The holding of land in monopoly by virtue of a franchise or title is a privilege, and the rent for this privilege belongs to the people collectively. The franchises shall be assessed annually for their full rental value, and the money, which is rightfully the people's, is to be divided among state and local treasuries. Failure to pay this rental can result in forfeiture and foreclosure of the franchise.
Arguments For: Under the current system the government must tax homes and goods to compensate for the revenues lost by the land profiteers who keep valuable land out of use. To tax this land at its full rental value would make land speculation worthless, and bring more land into use, thus relieving the burden which high taxation places upon the people. It will abolish poverty and lay the foundations for a better world.
Endorsers: Lona Ingham Robinson.
Arguments Against: This "single tax' act is absurd. It suggests that the state own all land and that the people become mere "vassals of the commonwealth." This is the system of Russia, and we all know the results of "Sovietism." This act would destroy the value of land, rob those who have worked hard for it of their ownership. It would free large companies of much taxation, while placing the burden on the people, and it will bankrupt many financial institutions which have large sums invested in real estate.
Endorsers: Albert E. Kern, Pres., Anti Single Tax Assn. of California.

PROPOSITION 30: Franchises.
Type: Initiative Constitutional Amendment
Outcome: Rejected
Summary: Gives the Railroad Commission the exclusive power to grant franchises for street rail, interurban rail, or motor vehicle transportation by the right of eminent domain. The commission would also provide regulation of service and rates. The franchises granted will terminate upon the acquisition of the property by state or local government. Utilities now owned by state or local government will not be subject to the provisions of this amendment.
Arguments For: The value of land, and thus the state, is suffering from inadequacies in public transportation. This has been brought about by too many local restrictions and taxes which prevent transportation companies from improving and extending service to meet the needs of our growing state. We must act now before we fall too far behind in transportation.
Endorsers: C. C. C. Tatum, Pres., Calif. Real Estate Assn.

Arguments Against: This amendment would only give a commission, which already has too much power, more control over our state. It would rob our communities of the right to control over their own streets, and allow the Commission to grant a right of way on streets and property against the communities' wishes. It is unwise to grant to five men the right to decide the fate of a community, when they likely know nothing of that community.
Endorsers: Jess E. Stephens, City Atty. of Los Angeles; George Lull, City Atty. of San Francisco.

Election of November 4, 1924

PROPOSITION 1: State Taxation of Highway Transportation Companies.
Type: Initiative Constitutional Amendment
Outcome: Rejected
Summary: Would require all companies which own and operate common carriers to pay a tax of 4% tax on total gross receipts. This will be in lieu of all other taxes, with the exception of payment of bonded indebtedness outstanding at the time of this election.
Arguments For: This measure, which will not affect carriers that operate solely within an incorporated city, will be to the benefit of the state. The revenues collected will go to the state, where the funds are most needed; it will provide for construction and maintenance of highways. It taxes common carriers in the same manner as public utilities, will prevent double taxation, and allow these companies to expand service, and it will protect the future interests of the people.
Endorsers: H. W. Kidd.
Arguments Against: This measure is supported by the only people who will benefit from it, the common carrier companies. The provision which makes it "in lieu of other taxes" will make it exempt from registration and franchise taxes. The revenue collected will go directly to the state, and the cities and counties will suffer from a loss of revenue.
Endorsers: Walter H. Duval, Assemblyman 60th Dist.

PROPOSITION 7: Boxing and Wrestling Contests.
Type: Initiative Statute
Outcome: Approved
Summary: Creates a commission to authorize and regulate wrestling and boxing in which a purse or door fee is paid. Matches would be allowed a maximum of twelve rounds, four rounds for amateur contests, and would be under full authority of the commission if an admission fee is paid.

Arguments For: California is one of the few states that still prohibits boxing and wrestling matches. Many more men are hurt in baseball and football than in boxing and wrestling, but the opposition has been misinformed. The heads of the army and the navy encourage these sports as it builds better men. Since much of the money earned will go to old soldiers homes, voting yes will be an act of patriotism, helping veterans whom the state now inadequately supports.
Endorsers: Harry F. Morrison, Assemblyman 29th Dist.
Arguments Against: The brutality which led to the prohibition of such matches in the first place is known by all, and thus not necessary to mention. What this act will do is create a commission that will be at the mercy, financially, of the contest promoters. This, combined with the unlimited expense accounts of the commission, will lead to a total drain of the revenues, and only if there is money left over will that go to the retired soldiers home.
Endorsers: Chester H. Rowell.

PROPOSITION 11: Klamath River Fish and Game District.
Type: Initiative Statute
Outcome: Approved
Summary: Creates the Klamath River Fish and Game District from the confluence of the Shasta and Klamath rivers in Siskiyou County to the mouth of the Klamath River in Del Norte County. Prohibits construction or maintenance of any dam in the district, and provides for fines and penalties for violations.
Arguments For: This measure will save the beautiful Klamath River which, by virtue of its importance to salmon and trout breeding, is irreplaceable. There are enough opportunities in the other rivers to provide power and water without sacrificing the Klamath.
Endorsers: J. A. Ager, Chairman, Bd. of Supervisors, Siskiyou County; Frank M. Newbert, Pres., Fish and Game Comm. of Calif.
Arguments Against This measure will not increase the fish potentials in the state, as laws already prohibit obstruction of their passage upstream. What this will do is forever prevent us from harnessing the water and electric potentials which could be provided by the 170 mile stretch of river. Development of the river will mean thousands of jobs and millions of dollars in state revenues.
Endorsers: R. J. Wade, Secy., Eureka Chamber of Commerce; Fred M. Kay, County Clerk, Humbolt County.

PROPOSITION 16: Water and Power.
Type: Initiative Constitutional Amendment
Outcome: Rejected

Summary: Would create a board, appointed by the governor and subject to recall, which would be given authority to acquire land, by any legal means, for the development and distribution of water and electric power. The board would be authorized to issue bonds to finance the measures, and would thus relieve private corporations of the responsibility of expanding water and power facilities.

Arguments For: This measure will, under the cheapest possible means of financing, provide the state with insurance against flood or drought, while providing a plentiful supply of inexpensive hydroelectric power. This new power will, without preventing private companies from making a legitimate profit, make California first among industrial states. The board answers to the people, and it is far safer to trust our remaining resources to such a board than to a private corporation. Finally, the state's financing of the measures, which can be done at the lowest possible rate, will save the consumers money, whereas if private corporations undertook the development the consumers would pay much higher rates to meet the costs.

Endorsers: Col R. B. Marshall, author of the Marshall Plan.

Arguments Against: It would be a mistake to appoint a board which will go almost unchecked in its authority. Further abuse can come from the lack of civil service requirements for employees appointed by the board, which will lead only to a system of corrupt patronage. The real problem in California right now is drought. With half of our dams empty there is no need for the state to enter the water and power business. The answer is not in public ownership, but in effective regulation, as is the case with utility corporations. This measure is just another reissue of the bill defeated two years ago and it is time these agitators stop abusing the initiative system by continual resubmission of bills.

Endorsers: A. H. Breed, Pres. Pro Tempore, Calif. Senate.

Election of November 2, 1926

PROPOSITION 3: Oleomargarine.
Type: Referendum
Outcome: Rejected
Summary: The law under reconsideration regulates the manufacture and sale of oleomargarine. Dairy terms and symbols cannot be used in connection with oleomargarine. There is an annual license plus a payment of 2 cents per each pound of oleomargarine sold during each quarter (except when sold outside of the state).

Arguments For the existing legislation, Against this referendum: This act clarifies the meaning of the original law. It assures that oleomargarine cannot be misrepresented as a dairy product. It also provides its own funds for enforcement. No money has to come from the taxpayer.

2. **Endorsers:** Sam H. Greene.

Arguments Against the existing legislation, For this referendum: It places oppressive restrictions on margarine sales. This is the first direct tax on any food product and it will affect everyone.

Endorsers: Fred J. Blakeley.

PROPOSITION 4: Gas Tax.

Type: Initiative Statute

Outcome: Rejected

Summary: All distributors of gas must pay a license tax of 1 cent per gallon plus the already existing 2 cents license tax required. The additional tax will pay 1/3 of refunds with the balance going to the State Highway Construction Fund. Effective January 1, 1927, subject to amendment or repeal by legislature after January 1, 1939.

Arguments For: The additional tax will help complete our state highway system. This is the fairest, most equitable way of raising money for highway purposes.

Endorsers: A.H. Breed, Pres., Pro Tempore, Calif. Senate; Ed P. Sample, State Senator, 40th Dist.

Arguments Against: There are no plans on how the revenue will be spent. Now auto owners must pay for the cost of constructing state highways as well as maintaining them. It does not finance the improvement of streets in cities or towns. It will increase the cost of transportation as well as the cost of living. Plus it cannot be repealed by the Legislature for 12 years.

Endorsers: Harry A. Chamberlain, State Senator, 31st District; and J.J. Deul, Manager Law and Utilities Dept., Calif. Farm Bureau Federation.

PROPOSITION 6: Racing.

Type: Initiative Statute

Outcome: Rejected

Summary: A board is created (appointed by the Governor) to regulate and license horse racing. Pari-mutuel wagering is allowed. The board limits the racing period at each track. No licenses will be issued at tracks constructed without the board's approval after November 1, 1926. The licensee's return is limited to 9% on capital invested. The license fees are $500 at each race day. Fees will go to the Board's salaries and expenses, the Veterans' Welfare Board, and the state Agricultural Board.

Arguments For: It will restore horse racing under strict control by a racing commission.

Endorsers: H.J. Macomber, Chairman, No. Calif. Exec. Comm.; and Joseph M. Schenck, Chairman, So. Calif. Exec. Comm.

Arguments Against: This will legalize gambling. Demoralization will occur again. It will corrupt the people.

Endorsers: George I. Cochran and F.M. Larkin.

PROPOSITION 8: State Highways.

Type: Initiative Constitutional Amendment

Outcome: Rejected

Summary: Classifies highways as primary and secondary. Appropriates $5 million annually for 12 years for highway construction, allocating three-fourths of the funds to primary highways and one-fourth to secondary.

Arguments For: It guarantees that funds won't be diverted to unimportant roads. It adopts a "cash payment" plan for new construction and therefore avoids bond interest and selling charges.

Endorsers: H.W. Keller, Pres., Automobile Club of Southern Calif.

Arguments Against: It destroys state unity by creating two districts. It does not provide enough money to finish the state highway system. The money taken for this will have to be replaced, which will mean increased taxes.

Endorsers: Chas. W. Heyer, Pres., County Supervisors Assn.

PROPOSITION 9: Repeal of Wright Act.

Type: Initiative Statute

Outcome: Rejected

Summary: The Wright Act provided for the enforcement by California of the 18th Amendment, which prohibited all acts or omissions prohibited by the Volstead Act. It adopted penal provisions of that Act, imposed duties on courts, prosecuting attorneys, sheriffs, grand juries, magistrates, and peace officers, as well as extending their jurisdiction.

Arguments For: Prohibition is unsound in principle. The Volstead Act is prohibition against liquor. Since its adoption, drinking and drunkenness have increased. Prohibition has failed to achieve its objectives. We still have a liquor trade but now it is unregulated and operated by criminals. We need to repeal the Wright Act which allowed for the enforcement of the Volstead Act.

Endorsers: Matt I. Sullivan, Pres., Wright Act Repeal Assn.

Arguments Against: We need this act to enforce the 18th Amendment. If it is repealed we couldn't beat the bootleg menace.

Endorsers: David Starr Jordan.

PROPOSITION 17: Requiring Bible in Schools.
Type: Initiative Constitutional Amendment
Outcome: Rejected
Summary: Amends Section 8 of Article IX. No public money can be appropriated to support sectarian or denominational schools. Teaching sectarian or denominational doctrines is prohibited in public schools. Public funds can be used to purchase Bibles and they can be placed in the library and classroom. Daily study and reading by the teacher is permitted, but no pupil can be required to read or hear it read, contrary to the wishes of the parent or guardian.
Arguments For: We believe in separation of Church and State but not separating religion from civil government. The kids need the principles of morality taught to them.
Endorsers: Wiley J. Philips.
Arguments Against: Religion is a private matter. Religion is not the business of the State. We should not impose religious duties on the government.
Endorsers: C. Fickenscher, Pastor, Trinity Lutheran Church, Sacramento.

PROPOSITION 18: Water and Power.
Type: Initiative Constitutional Amendment
Outcome: Rejected
Summary: A board is created (subject to recall) that will develop and distribute water and electric energy, and acquire any lands (including state lands) for this purpose. State and political subdivisions are given preferential rights against privately owned public utilities selling water and energy to the public. Bonds of up to $500,000,000 will be used for this purpose.
Arguments For: California's waters must be developed by California. Development will not deprive existing corporations.
Endorsers: Rudolph Spreckels.
Arguments Against: This act has been twice rejected by the people already. The Board would be unrestricted and unrestrained. There is no public need for the state to embark in the power business. The utilities are already regulated. We do not need public ownership.
Endorsers: Arthur H. Breed, Pres. Pro Tempore, Calif. Senate.

PROPOSITION 20: Reapportionment Commission.
Type: Initiative Constitutional Amendment
Outcome: Rejected
Summary: Creates a Reapportionment Commission composed of the Secretary of State, Attorney General, and Surveyor General. If the legislature fails to adjust districts after each census, the commission will do so within 3 months.

Arguments For: Without adjustment, as in 1920, many have suffered taxation without representation. If the commission also fails to adjust, the Supreme Court shall have the power. This act will protect your equal representation rights.
Endorsers: Ralph Arnold, Exec. Chairman, All Parties Reapportionment Comm.
Arguments Against: Reforming of districts would be placed in the city's control at the expense of the rural area. Keep the control with the balanced (city and rural) legislature.
Endorsers: C. C. Teague.

PROPOSITION 28: Legislative Reapportionment.*
Type: Initiative Constitutional Amendment
Outcome: Approved
Summary: The Legislature must divide the State into 40 Senatorial and 80 Assembly Districts using the 1920 census. The Reapportionment Commission shall be created and will do the reapportionment if the Legislature fails to do so.
Arguments For: If districts are reapportioned according to the present law, many will be disadvantaged. No county or city can have more than one Senator.
Endorsers: David P. Barrows
Arguments Against: It is unfair and impractical as it relates to Senatorial Districts. One Senatorial District in cities like Los Angeles would lead to underrepresentation. We need representation based on population.
Endorsers: Dana R. Weller.
Revoked by Proposition 1, Nov. 6, 1928.

Election of November 6, 1928

PROPOSITION 1: Reapportionment of Legislative Districts.
Type: Referendum
Outcome: Approved
Summary: The law under reconsideration establishes that districts are reapportioned according to Section 6 of Article IV of the Constitution of November 2, 1926 [Proposition 28].
Arguments For the existing legislation, Against this referendum: The law was already enacted by the mandate of the voters. This is a good law because it is based on population and territory.
Endorsers: J.M. Inman, State Senator, 7th District; Frank S. Boggs, State Senator, 10th District; David P. Barrows.

Arguments Against the existing legislation, For this referendum: According to the Constitution, the legislature should have done the reapportionment after the 1920 census but it failed to do so. A constitutional amendment was adopted in 1926, but it restricted counties to one senatorial district. This disadvantaged areas like Los Angeles that were paying a large part of the taxes. Cities are being deprived of representation.

Endorsers: Ralph Arnold, Exec. Chairman, All Parties Reapportionment Comm.; Henry E. Carter, Assemblyman, 71st Dist.

PROPOSITION 5: Boxing and Wrestling Contests.

Type: Initiative Statute
Outcome: Rejected
Summary: Repeals the act of November 4, 1924 [Proposition 7], which allowed twelve-round matches and prize fights regulated by the State Athletic Commission. Would revert to the laws in effect prior to 1924, which limited boxing and wrestling matches to four rounds and which prohibited prize fights.
Arguments For: Boxing as a sport would be lawful but prize fighting would be unlawful. All the degrading elements of the sport would be removed. Money has become the most important issue to all involved, while the skill of the athlete, in addition to his health ad safety, have been replaced by the desire to win the purse even at the risk of life itself.
Endorsers: F.M. Larkin, Executive Secy., Calif. State Church Fed.
Arguments Against: Today's boxing is on the highest level it has ever occupied in California. To revert to the laws of 1924 would only result in "bootleg" boxing matches. This would deny the state a profitable source of revenue, collected through the Athletic Commission. The supporters of this measure, who would also like to see an end to Sunday baseball and entertainment, hope to undo what the voters approved in 1924.
Endorsers: Harry F. Morrison, Assemblyman, 29th Dist.

PROPOSITION 8: Motor Vehicle Registration Fees.

Type: Referendum
Outcome: Approved
Summary: The law under reconsideration increased registration fees for vehicles transporting passengers or property. Fees increase on a weight basis.
Arguments For the existing legislation, Against this referendum: Trucks wear out the highways quicker and should pay increasing fees. Rates are graduated on an equitable basis. Compared to fees elsewhere, these are moderate.
Endorsers: Dixwell L. Pierce, Secy., State Bd. of Equalization; Ralph W. Bull, Chairman, State Highway Comm.; J.I. Wagy, State Senator, 32nd Dist.

Arguments Against the existing legislation, For this referendum: If you increase the cost of transportation, it will increase the cost of food.
Endorsers: J.F. Vizzard.

PROPOSITION 21: Prohibiting Certain Acts with Animals and Use of Certain Instruments to Control Them.
Type: Initiative Statute
Outcome: Rejected
Summary: Defines prohibited acts including wild animal racing and bull riding. Prohibits use of spurs to make an animal buck, or terrifying it by any means for sport, exhibition, or amusement. This does not apply to farming, dairying, branding, or breaking animals in raising cattle, horses, or mules. Biting, chewing, or twisting a part of an animal is prohibited, as well as trying to control it by an instrument.
Arguments For: We want to get rid of the cruel features of rodeos. The acts condemned are not typical of authentic frontier life.
Endorsers: Herbert W. Erskine.
Arguments Against: Rodeo shows draw a great number of visitors. California statutes already provide ample protection for all animals. This is a symbol of manliness and Americanism.
Endorsers: Marco H. Hellman, Fred H. Bixby, Orie O. Robertson.

Election of November 4, 1930

PROPOSITION 7: Daylight Saving Act.
Type: Initiative Statute
Outcome: Rejected
Summary: At 2:00 a.m. on the last Sunday in April, Standard Time will be advanced one hour, and at 2:00 a.m. on the last Sunday in September, it will be retarded one hour.
Arguments For: This will give Californians more hours of sunlit leisure. This change in hours has also helped decrease juvenile delinquency. Businesses will also benefit. Employees will be healthier and rested. We will have an added hour of communication with the east.
Endorsers: Frank B. Beecher, Pres., Calif. Daylight Saving League.
Arguments Against: We tried this once in 1918 and it failed. Many oppose it. It will confuse hotel and railroad schedules. The churches and the post office will not adopt the change.
Endorsers: Herbert C. Jones, Senator, Santa Clara County; Edward J. Hanna, Archbishop of San Francisco; Harold B. Franklin, Pres., Fox West Coast

Theaters; Paul Scharrenberg, Secy., State Fed. of Labor; Robert A. Condee, Pres., State Board of Agriculture; E.D. DeGroot, Boys' Welfare Official.

PROPOSITION 10: Usury Law.

Type: Initiative Statute
Outcome: Rejected
Summary: A written agreement for interest rate is unnecessary. Corporations cannot recover treble amounts of interest paid. Excepts agreements giving borrower option to pay before maturity. If maturity is accelerated by default, interest paid in advance is not usurious.
Arguments For: Construction loans are encouraged. Corporations cannot plead the act to defeat their contractual obligations. Industrial loan companies and pawnbrokers are not subject to regulation by the Legislature.
Endorsers: Lawrence W. Beilenson, Los Angeles, drafter of the Act; Ransom Henshaw, Financial Editor, Los Angeles Evening Express; George S. Walker, San Francisco, formerly State Building and Loan Commissioner.
Arguments Against: This law is wholly in the interest of the money lender and against the borrower. It eliminates stating the rate of interest in writing. Corporations can be charged any rate of interest, and there is an arbitrary date that the interest on a loan for construction on a building should begin.
Endorsers: William A. Alderson, Los Angeles; William R. Geary, Oakland.

PROPOSITION 11: Fish and Game.

Type: Initiative Constitutional Amendment
Outcome: Rejected
Summary: A five-person Fish and Game Commission is created, to be appointed by the Governor. It will establish districts and issue licenses.
Arguments For: This is a necessary conservation measure. It has been successful in other states.
Endorsers: Sanborn Young, Chairman, Senate Fish and Game Comm.
Arguments Against: The Commission would be unregulated by the legislature. There is no process for review by the Supreme Court.
Endorsers: C.C. Baker, State Senator, 17th Dist.

PROPOSITION 14: Registration of Voters.

Type: Initiative Statute
Outcome: Approved
Summary: Requires new state-wide registration of voters beginning January 1, 1932. The registration will continue until canceled upon request, death, judgment for cancellation, or failure to vote. Registration will continue on

odd-numbered years, and voters must re-register if they failed to vote in past elections.

Arguments For: The present registration requires re-registering every 2 years. It is a waste of money. Permanent registration is quite practical.

Endorsers: W. M. Kerr, Registrar of Voters, Los Angeles; J.H. Zemansky, Election Commissioner, San Francisco.

Arguments Against: Permanent registration will not furnish the necessary clean list of registered electors. This will cost more than re-registering every 2 years. Fraud can occur by using dead persons' names. California tried this from 1873 to 1898 and it failed.

Endorsers: Henry A. Pfister, Pres., County Clerks Assn.

PROPOSITION 26: Sunday Closing Law.
Type: Initiative Statute
Outcome: Rejected
Summary: All businesses must close on Sunday, with the exception of necessary, recreational, or charitable works.

Arguments For: This is an institutionalized weekly day of rest. The family does not have a "real" Sunday if the father must work.

Endorsers: Henry S. Guio, Pres., Calif. Master Barbers Assn.; Daniel F. Tattenham, Secy., State Assn. Journeymen Barbers.

Arguments Against: It impinges on personal liberty to impose religious ideas upon the people. Too many businesses need to stay open on Sunday (such as groceries). People should have the chance to decide whether to work or not.

Endorsers: Edwin Higgins, Managing Dir., Calif. Oil and Gas Assn.

Election of May 3, 1932

PROPOSITION 1: Oil Control.
Type: Referendum
Outcome: Rejected
Summary: The law under reconsideration prohibits the waste of crude petroleum oil. A conservation commission is created, which can investigate oil production and determine if waste is committed.

Arguments For the existing legislation, Against this referendum: This is a conservation measure to deal with overproduction and waste. The act is practical, simple and sound.

Endorsers: Will R. Sharkey, State Senator, 9th Dist.; Ralph H. Cook, State Senator, 33rd District.

Arguments Against the existing legislation, For this referendum: There is doubt as to whether it is truly a conservation measure. Many believe it will

ultimately increase the price of gas. The landowners or lessors have no voice in choosing the commissioners. It is not sound to permit producers alone to determine the quantity of oil and gas.
Endorsers: Ray W. Hays, State Senator, 30th Dist.

PROPOSITION 2: Preventing Leasing of State-Owned Beach Lands for Mineral and Oil Production.
Type: Referendum
Outcome: Approved
Summary: Amends Political Code Section 675, Chapter 325, to eliminate the recent provision authorizing the Director of Finance to lease state owned tide and beach lands for the purpose of mineral and oil production.
Arguments For the Referendum: The new law was supposed to merely enumerate the powers of various state officials, but secretly included a provision permitting the Director of Finance to lease state-owned tidelands. Approval of this referendum will revert to the statutes of 1929, which forbade the leasing of state tide and beach lands for mineral production. Beaches should be preserved.
Endorsers: Bert B. Snyder, Assemblyman, 42nd Dist.; William G. Bonelli, Assemblyman, 54th Dist.
Arguments Against the Referendum: By developing oil, your taxes will be decreased. Private corporations are already drilling right next to state-owned lands, draining the oil under state lands; they are the backers of this referendum.
Endorsers: Elson G. Conrad, Mayor, City of Huntington Beach; L.W. Blodget, City Atty., City of Huntington Beach.

Election of November 8, 1932

PROPOSITION 1: Wright Act Repeal.
Type: Initiative Statute
Outcome: Approved
Summary: Repeals the Wright Act, which enforced the 18th Amendment of the Constitution and prohibited all acts prohibited by the Volstead Act. The Wright Act imposed duties on courts, prosecuting attorneys, sheriffs, grand juries, magistrates, and peace officers.
Arguments For: Prohibition is a failure. The 18th Amendment and Volstead Act have not prevented the illegal production of liquor. There is an overwhelming popular sentiment against prohibition.
Endorsers: Matt I. Sullivan; Eleanor B. MacFarland.

Arguments Against: National prohibition can only be repealed by national action. Until then, peace officers are still needed.
Endorsers: Chester H. Rowell; Mrs. Susan M. Dorsey.

PROPOSITION 2: State Liquor Regulation.
Type: Initiative Constitutional Amendment
Outcome: Approved
Summary: If the Wright Act is repealed, California shall have the exclusive right to license and regulate the manufacture of liquors. Saloons can be prohibited. Wine and beer are permitted to be served with meals. The legislature is permitted to authorize the sale of liquor in stores.
Arguments For: Every state should have the right to control and regulate liquor traffic within its borders. Because the federal government failed to enforce prohibition, the state should be able to gain control. The state is more capable of this task than the federal government.
Endorsers: Matt I. Sullivan; Eleanor B. MacFarland.
Arguments Against: This is an amendment to prevent the possible passage of certain laws in a hypothetical future contingency. If national power was removed the state constitution is not required to confer on the state the right to regulate. This proposition has no present reason and effect.
Endorsers: Chester H. Rowell; Mrs. Susan M. Dorsey.

PROPOSITION 3: Foreclosure of Mortgages and Trust Deeds.
Type: Initiative Statute
Outcome: Rejected
Summary: Mortgage is defined as a contract, trust deed, or instrument. Makes specific real property security for performance without changing possession, and forbids power of sale therein. Requires action dismissed and mortgage reinstated, upon mortgagor paying, before judgment, amount delinquent.
Arguments For: This amendment will make a few changes: a) gives the owner 12 months equity of redemption; b) gives the owner the right to defend his title in court; c) gives the owner the right to reinstate the mortgage. It will help eliminate deficiency judgments. There will be no unjust foreclosure without the right of redemption.
Endorsers: Harry A. Goldman, Los Angeles; Philip O. Solon, Oakland; Hugh E. MacBeth, Los Angeles; Coleman E. Stewart, Santa Barbara; Charles H. Vance, Stockton.
Arguments Against: It will give no relief to borrowers who have given trust deeds or mortgages to secure their loans. It will delay a revival of building construction. By requiring all to go to court to foreclose a mortgage, it will

increase foreclosure costs. It does not prevent the taking of deficiency payments.

Endorsers: H.L. Carnahan, Former Lt.-Gov. of Calif.; William May Garland, realtor; William H. McCarthy, Pres., Home Value Protective League; Henry W. O'Melveny, member, O'Melveny, Tuller and Meyers, Attorneys; George A. Schneider, lecturer on real estate finance, USC; Charles D. Roeth, Pres., No. Calif. Building Congress.

PROPOSITION 5: Racing.

Type: Initiative Statute

Outcome: Rejected

Summary: Creates state Racing Board, empowered to regulate race track licensing and wagering. Racing periods are limited. Fees are used for salaries and expenses, with the balance to the Veterans' Welfare Board and State Board of Agriculture.

Arguments For: California is missing revenue by excluding license fees or taxes to be paid by the racing association. Racing already exists so we should regulate it.

Endorsers: A.J. Uniack, Chairman, So. Calif. Campaign Comm.; William A. O'Neill, Chairman, No. Calif. Campaign Comm.

Arguments Against: It would affect intercollegiate tracks as well. Amateur events would be required to pay fees. Immoralities will also increase with race track gambling.

Endorsers: George I. Cochran, Pres., Pacific Mutual Life Insurance Co.; F.M. Larkin, Secy., Calif. State Church Fed.

PROPOSITION 9: School Funds. Income, Sales Tax.

Type: Initiative Constitutional Amendment

Outcome: Rejected

Summary: An income tax on individuals will provide money for the state public school equalization fund. There will be county and district school taxes which are required to meet district budgets.

Arguments For: This will relieve the burden from individual taxpayers. It will transfer to the state the present burden of county taxes for schools. The state will levy a net income tax and a selective sales tax. This will not affect the local control of schools. It provides equal educational opportunities for all children. Also, it will not increase teachers' salaries.

Endorsers: R.V. Blackburn, Pres., Calif. Farm Bureau Fed.; W. I. Hollingworth, Director, Calif. Real Estate Assn., Los Angeles; John F. Forward, Jr., Pres., Union Title Insurance Co., San Diego; Samuel Leak, member, Governor C.C. Young's Commission on Educational Problems, Calif.

merchant; Ralph E. Swing, State Senator, 36th Dist., Chairman, Senate Finance Comm.; J. Bradley Clayton, Vice Pres. Jas. A. Clayton and Co.; First National Bank, San Jose; V. Kersey, Supt. of Public Instruction.

Arguments Against: It is an impractical attempt at tax relief. It places no limit on taxes, budgets or expenditures.

Endorsers: Arthur H. Breed, State Senator, Alameda County; Harry H. Baskerville, Pres., City Board of Education, Los Angeles; Donzel Stoney, Chairman, Property Owners Div., San Francisco Real Estate Board; Reynold E. Blight, Former State Franchise Tax Commissioner, Los Angeles.

PROPOSITION 11: Tideland Grant to City of Huntington Beach.
Type: Initiative Constitutional Amendment
Outcome: Rejected
Summary: Huntington Beach is granted the tidal and submerged lands situated within the borders of said city. The city can use it for accommodation of recreation, harbor, commerce, fisheries and production of minerals. The city can lease lands for such purposes. Fifty percent of income from lease will go to the general fund.
Arguments For: It will decrease taxes and create jobs. The Standard Oil Company is developing and taking all the oil adjacent to the Huntington Beach lands. The oil belongs to the taxpayers.
Endorsers: E.G. Conrad, Mayor of the City of Huntington Beach; Ray H. Overacker, City Atty. of the City of Huntington Beach.
Arguments Against: The true purpose of this is to develop oil. The city has no title to the land and the Huntington Beach Chamber of Commerce completely opposes this measure. Our beaches must be saved.
Endorsers: C.G. Ward, Chairman Civic Betterment Comm., Huntington Beach Chamber of Commerce; Willis H. Warner, Secy. and Treas., Beach Protective Assn., Huntington Beach.

Election of December 19, 1933

PROPOSITION 1: Water and Power.
Type: Referendum
Outcome: Approved
Summary: This measure will revoke the statute that created a Water Project Authority empowered to construct and operate a system of works called the Central Valley Project. The Project would develop water and electric energy in Sacramento and San Joaquin Valleys, and issue revenue bonds to finance their construction.
(No voter's information pamphlet is available for this measure.)

Election of November 6, 1934

PROPOSITION 2: Intoxicating Liquors.
Type: Initiative Constitutional Amendment
Outcome: Approved
Summary: The consumption and sale of liquors except beer is prohibited. The possession, sale, consumption and disposition of all liquors is permitted in hotels, restaurants, eateries, and clubs after one year of operation. The Board of Equalization is given the power to issue licenses, collect license fees and occupation taxes. The State Liquor Control Act continues.
Arguments For: Proposition 2 allows for liquor to be served with or without meals in eating places but prohibits the return of hard liquor saloons. It keeps the control of liquor in the hands of the state. With this passed, the people will show their support for temperance, business stability, and increased employment.
Endorsers: S.F.B. Morse, Pres.; No. Calif. Business Council; Byron C. Hanna, Pres., So. Calif. Business Men's Assn.
Arguments Against: The act really intended was for the removal of all restrictions on the manufacture, sale and consumption of intoxicating liquors.
Endorsers: Nathan Newby, Los Angeles.

PROPOSITION 3: Selection of Judges.
Type: Initiative Constitutional Amendment
Outcome: Approved
Summary: A Supreme or Appellate Court Justice can declare as a candidate to succeed himself. Otherwise, the governor can nominate one candidate on the ballot to be voted for or against. The governor will appoint a justice until the next election if the nominee is defeated. The nominee or appointee must be approved by a commission of the Chief Justice, Appellate Court Justice, and Attorney General. The retirement system is required and it makes constitutional removal and recall provisions applicable.
Arguments For: To avoid having judicial offices being prizes fought in the political arena, this initiative will make the tenure of judges subject to the will of the people or to retirement or to removal by law. This amendment requires that candidates appearing on a ballot be recommended by the Governor and commission based on qualifications.
Endorsers: Mrs. Duncan S. Robinson, Vice Pres.-at-Large, Calif. Fed. of Women's Clubs, Rio Vista; Rufus B. von Kleinsmid, Pres., University of Southern Calif.
Arguments Against: None recorded.

PROPOSITION 4: Attorney General.
Type: Initiative Constitutional Amendment
Outcome: Approved
Summary: Gives the Attorney General the power to enforce state laws, supervise the district attorneys, sheriffs, and enforcement officers, and prosecute violations within the superior court's jurisdiction. It prohibits the Attorney General from private practice, and provides a salary equivalent to that of a Supreme Court Associate Justice.
Arguments For: In order to catch criminals, we need better organization of our law enforcement agencies. This amendment allows for the coordination of county law enforcement agencies. The Attorney General would have his duties expanded to include that supervision.
Endorsers: Earl Warren, Dist. Atty. of Alameda County and Secy. of the District Attorneys' Assn. of Calif., Oakland; W.C. Rhodes, Sheriff of Madera County, Madera.
Arguments Against: None recorded.

PROPOSITION 5: Permitting Comment on Evidence and Failure of Defendant to Testify in Criminal Cases.
Type: Initiative Constitutional Amendment
Outcome: Approved
Summary: In any criminal case, whether defendant testifies or not, the court or counsel may comment on his failure to explain or deny any evidence against him. Allows the court to instruct the jury regarding the law applicable to the case. Informs the jurors that they are the exclusive judges of all questions of fact submitted.
Arguments For: Without this initiative, the judge and district attorney do not have the right to comment to the jury on the failure of the accused to testify, denying the offense charged. With this initiative, the judge is allowed to give his analysis of the evidence and express an opinion on the merits of the case, but only in an advisory role.
Endorsers: American Legion of Calif.; Executive Board of Calif. Fed. of Women's Clubs; League of Women Voters of Calif.; Comm. on Administration of Justice of the State Bar of Calif.; Arthur S. Bent, Pres., Bent Bros., Inc., Los Angeles; S.G. Tompkins, Attorney-at-Law, San Jose.
Arguments Against: None recorded.

PROPOSITION 6: Pleading Guilty Before Committing Magistrate.
Type: Initiative Constitutional Amendment
Outcome: Approved

Summary: Requires a defendant charged with a felony to be brought before a magistrate; if the felony is not punishable by death, the defendant may plead guilty. The magistrate shall then commit the defendant to the sheriff and certify the case to the superior court.

Arguments For: This amendment will save on expenses of preliminary examinations, shorten time to complete cases, and reduce pressures put on defendants to plead guilty.

Endorsers: William A. Beasley, Chairman, Subcommittee on the Administration of Criminal Justice, State Bar of Calif., San Francisco; Agnes L. McEuen, State Chairman of Legislation, Calif. Fed. of Women's Clubs, Riverside.

Arguments Against: None recorded.

PROPOSITION 7: State Civil Service.

Type: Initiative Constitutional Amendment

Outcome: Approved

Summary: Permanent appointments and promotions in state civil service are to be made on merit, efficiency, and fitness as ascertained by competitive examination. The Personnel Board shall administer state civil service laws. Temporary appointments are prohibited unless eligible list is unavailable.

Arguments For: The amendment's goal is to prevent political interference with the efficient administration of state business. A nonpartisan Personnel Board will help eliminate the "spoils system" of employment.

Endorsers: Will C. Wood, Former Supt. of Public Instruction; Earl Warren, Dist. Atty., Alameda County; Manchester Boddy, Publisher, Los Angeles Illustrated Daily News.

Arguments Against: None recorded.

PROPOSITION 9: State Chiropractic Act.

Type: Initiative Statute

Outcome: Rejected

Summary: Amends the Chiropractic Act. Creates the State Chiropractic Association to regulate this practice, establish qualifications for licensees, fix license fees, and prescribe penalties for violations.

Arguments For: The statute will give injured workers the privilege of being treated by a licensed chiropractor. It gives people the right to have licensed chiropractors in public institutions, partially or wholly supported by public funds. It raises examination requirements and educational standards for licensing, and allows for the investigation of chiropractic schools and the revocation of licenses. All actions of the board will be subject to court review.

Endorsers: Dr. C. Russell Willett, Pres., State Board of Chiropractic Examiners; Dr. C.O. Hunt, Secy., State Board of Chiropractic Examiners; Dr. A.F. Blair, Chairman, Affiliated Chiropractors of Calif.

Arguments Against: This is a useless and dangerous proposal. It opens the door to fraud and racketeering. It will grant too much power to the State Board of Chiropractic Examiners.

Endorsers: Calif. Chiropractic Assn. Officers: James C. Tobin, D.C., State Pres.; Selma M. Geese, D.C., State Secy.; H.A. Rockwell, D.C., Chairman, State Legislative Comm.

PROPOSITION 11: Making State Board of Education Elective. Abolishing Superintendent of Public Instruction. Providing for Director of Education.

Type: Initiative Statute

Outcome: Rejected

Summary: Repeals Section 2 and amends Section 7 of Article IX of the Constitution. Abolishes the Office of Superintendent of Public Instruction. Establishes elected State Board of Education of 10 members. The Board appoints the Director of Education.

Arguments For: This measure gives every district in the state equal representation on the State Board of Education. It also separates the state school system from politics. The board members serve for ten years without salary so they will have the welfare of children in mind.

Endorsers: Willard E. Givens, City Supt. of Schools, Oakland, and Pres., Calif. Teachers' Assn.; Susan M. Dorsey, Former Supt. of Schools, City of Los Angeles.

Arguments Against: It will be more costly to taxpayers to import eastern printed books. Also, some would do all possible to elect friendly members to the board.

Endorsers: Harry Hammond, State Printer.

PROPOSITION 13: Local Option.

Type: Initiative Constitutional Amendment

Outcome: Rejected

Summary: Adds Section 23 to Article XX of the Constitution. Within 30 days of an affirmative vote, holds it unlawful to manufacture, sell, offer for sale, transport, or possess beverages with more than one half of one percent of alcohol. The question posed to the electors is, shall the traffic in and possession of beverages with more than one-half of one percent of alcohol be prohibited?

Arguments For: Presently, four men of the Board of Equalization have the exclusive right and power to license and regulate intoxicating liquor in

California. Local option restores to communities the power of self-determination in the matter of beverage alcohol.

Endorsers: Alonzo L. Baker, Mountain View; J. Frank Burke, Santa Ana; A.M. Wilkinson, Hollywood.

Arguments Against: This will return prohibition to California. The transportation and sale restriction does not even make exceptions for sacramental or medicinal purposes. It will threaten the vineyards and their lure to tourist travel.

Endorsers: Byron C. Hanna, Pres. So. Calif. Business Men's Assn.; S.F.B. Morse, Pres., No. Calif. Business Council.

PROPOSITION 17: Naturopathic Act.

Type: Initiative Statute
Outcome: Rejected
Summary: Regulates practice and licensing, investigation of naturopathic colleges. Fixes education requirements, fixes license fees, and provides penalties for violations.

Arguments For: The naturopaths limit their practice to drugless therapy. Presently, judges have ruled that they can do nothing more than adjust the spinal column. It is a self-sustaining and self-regulating act.

Endorsers: Dr. N.F. Jensen, Dr. P.M. Lovell, and Dr. M.O. Richardson.

Arguments Against: The act places no restriction on the practices of those who may be licensed under it.

Endorsers: Calif. Chiropractic Assn., officers: James C. Tobin, D.C., State Pres.; Selma M. Geese, D.C., State Secy.; H.A. Rockwell, D.C., Chairman. State Legislative Comm.

Election of November 3, 1936

PROPOSITION 2: Personal Income Taxes.

Type: Initiative Constitutional Amendment
Outcome: Rejected
Summary: Amends Section 11, Article XIII of the Constitution. No income tax on an individual or his estate or trust is valid unless it is approved by the majority with this initiative, following its passage by two-thirds of all members of each house of legislature. This would repeal the 1935 Personal Income Tax Act.

Arguments For: The amendment will prevent the state legislature from directly taxing the people's income. It will allow the people to approve any future personal income tax sponsored by the Legislature.

Endorsers: Dr. LeRoy H. Briggs; David R. Faries.

Arguments in Against: Retain the 1935 Tax Act because net income tax is fair, it is productive and practical, it can be economically administered, and it supplies the state with revenue. Double taxation is not peculiar to net income tax and would not be eliminated by California's repeal. The tax law can be changed by legislative action if needs arise.

Endorsers: Von T. Ellsworth, Head of Research Department, Calif. Farm Bureau Fed., and Executive Secy. Calif. Taxation Equalization League which represents Alta Calif., Inc.; Calif. County Tax Equalization Assn.; Calif. Farm Bureau Fed.; Calif. Teachers' Assn.; Economic Council of Southern Calif.; State Assn. of County Auditors; State Department of Education; State Supervisors' Assn.; Calif. Retailers' Assn.; Calif. School Trustees' Assn.

PROPOSITION 3: Liquor Control.
Type: Initiative Constitutional Amendment
Outcome: Rejected
Summary: Amends Section 22 of Article XX of the Constitution, relating to liquor. Creates an Alcoholic Beverage Commission of three appointed members with 6-year terms, to take over the role of the State Board of Equalization to regulate and license liquor. The Commission will have 25 non-civil service employees. Seventy-five percent of license fees will be returned to respective areas for local enforcement of state liquor laws.

Arguments For: This provides an improved method of state control of the sale of liquor. The duty of enforcing compliance with the liquor control laws lies with local authorities, and monies for that purpose are provided by the license fees. The amendment would abolish abuses and provide efficient administration of the law.

Endorsers: Byron Hanna; Hugh K. McKevitt.

Arguments Against: Presently, the Board is elected by the people. With this amendment, the Commission would be appointed by the governor and would be difficult to remove. The Commission could grant a license for liquor in any eating place and the people could not protest.

Endorsers: J.E. White; Nathan Newby.

PROPOSITION 4: Prohibiting Tideland Surface Oil Drilling. Authorizing Slant Drilling from Uplands.
Type: Initiative Statute
Outcome: Rejected
Summary: Prohibits drilling from the surface of the tide (submerged lands not leased). Allows the Director of Finance to execute 30 year leases at fourteen and two-sevenths percent royalty to the state for extracting oil, gas, and other

hydrocarbons from submerged lands slanted from uplands. Half of this revenue must go to maintaining beaches and parks.

Arguments For: This measure prohibits tideland oil drilling. It protects beaches and prohibits pollution, such as illegal drainage. It allows for money to purchase more beaches and parks as well as maintaining them. The state can regulate drilling. It reduces general taxes and safeguards natural resources. Counties and cities can regulate drilling.

Endorsers: Wm. E. Colby, Chairman, Calif. State Park Commission; Mrs. W. D. James, Pres., Calif. Fed. of Womens Clubs; Hartley Russell, Grand Pres., Native Sons of the Golden West.

Arguments Against: This would grant Standard Oil exclusive right to extract oil and gas. The measure provides that leases of state-owned tidelands shall only be granted to the owners of land bordering the tidelands, which are owned by Standard Oil.

Endorsers: Culbert L. Olson, Senator, 38th Dist., Chairman of Special Comm. of State Senate Investigating Extraction of Oil and Gas from State Tidelands.

PROPOSITION 7: County and Municipal Civil Service.
Type: Initiative Constitutional Amendment
Outcome: Rejected
Summary: Adds Section 21 to Article XI of the Constitution. It would require that appointments to county, district, and municipal offices be based on integrity, character, merit, fitness, and industry. Dismissals can only occur with hearings. Appointees are prohibited from political activity.

Arguments For: This would abolish the spoils system in California and replace it with the merit system.

Endorsers: Lynn Ballard, Long Beach Civil Service Commissioner and former Chamber of Commerce Managing Dir.; Clarence E. Dowd, Secy., Fresno Labor Council; Edgar Williams, Palo Alto, former Pres., Calif. Civil Service Comm.

Arguments Against: It does not express the real principles of the merit system but deals primarily with permanent life-time jobs. Also, this will meddle with the establishment and operation of civil service. It will introduce employee political domination, and substantially increase governmental expense. Public personnel administrators denounce it as unsound and unworkable. Executive control is weakened, which lowers efficiency. It will hamper the orderly conduct of public business.

Endorsers: Mrs. Paul Eliel, Pres., Calif. League of Women Voters; Francis V. Keesling, Attorney at Law, San Francisco; James L. Beebe, Attorney at Law, Los Angeles.

PROPOSITION 9: Intoxicating Liquors. Local Option.

Type: Initiative Constitutional Amendment
Outcome: Rejected
Summary: Adds Section 26 to Article XX of the Constitution. This would repeal Section 22 of Article XX, relating to intoxicating liquors. Allows every city and county to regulate the sale of alcoholic beverages within its limits.
Arguments For: The State Board of Equalization has admitted the failure of the present system. Without local control, residential districts have been invaded by liquor stores.
Endorsers: J.E. White; Nathan Newby.
Arguments Against: This will only help to restore national prohibition. It will open the door to bootleggers and liquor tax evasions. With a state appointed commission we have removed the issue from politics.
Endorsers: Byron Hanna; Hugh K. McKevitt.

PROPOSITION 10: Motor Vehicle Fuel Taxes and License Fees.
Type: Initiative Constitutional Amendment
Outcome: Rejected
Summary: Adds Article XXVI to the Constitution. Requires fees to be used for highway purposes and vehicle regulation. A portion will be used for aiding assessment districts and paying local bonds issued. Fees and taxes must be equal. Continues the 1935 statute of vehicle license fees based on value.
Arguments For: The amendment will prevent diversion of money for non-highway purposes. It will continue aid to street or highway special assessment districts, continue the retirement of general county highway bonds, continue repayment by counties to the state of money borrowed for unemployment relief, and continue the 1935 motor vehicle tax.
Endorsers: Standish L. Mitchell, Secy. and General Manager, Automobile Club of Southern Calif.; Stanley Abel, Supervisor, Kern County; Leland W. Cutler, Calif. Highway Council, Inc.; Calif. Highway Commission.
Arguments Against: It will serve the interests of those who manufacture or use diesel powered equipment.
Endorsers: Arthur H. Breed, Former State Senator for Alameda County and Former Pres. Pro Tem., Calif. Senate.

PROPOSITION 11: Instructors' Tenure.
Type: Initiative Constitutional Amendment
Outcome: Rejected
Summary: Adds Section 16 to Article IX of the Constitution. Creates the State Tenure Board of three members. Specifies instructors affected by the amendment. There is a two-year probationary period before permitting permanent tenure. Specifies causes of dismissal of instructors. The Board hears charges

against the instructor, hears defenses by instructors, and can sustain or overrule decisions of the local school board.

Arguments For: Presently, the legislature can repeal all tenure laws; this measure prevents the legislature from dealing with the civil service status of teachers. The tenure question will be taken out of politics. It will provide a fair way to remove teachers. The Boards of Education will no longer be on trial for teachers' dismissals. The law will give teachers permanent tenure until 65 years; they can then retire on a pension. It protects against arbitrary dismissal of probationary teachers. Civil service rules will be applied to tenure. Schools will not be subject to the spoils system. It will eliminate the incompetent political teacher. There will be no cost to the taxpayer.

Endorsers: George W. McDill, Member, Los Angeles Board of Education; Holland D. Roberts, Secy., State Fed. of Labor.

Arguments Against: California already has a tenure law. A tenure board is discriminatory and undemocratic. It discriminates against teachers because they must be certified at all levels: elementary, high school, and junior college. It invades local self-government rights by denying local school boards the right to determine which teachers shall be permanently employed.

Endorsers: John F. Brady, Vice Pres., Calif. Teachers Assn.; E.B. Couch, Chairman, State Tenure Comm., Calif. Teachers Assn.; Ray C. Eberhard, attorney for Affiliated Teacher Organizations of Los Angeles.

PROPOSITION 18: Oleomargarine Tax.

Type: Referendum

Outcome: Rejected

Summary: This is a referendum against the act (Chapter 51, Statutes 1935) providing an excise tax on all oleomargarine containing any fat or oil ingredients, with some exceptions. The tax is 10 cents per pound on oleomargarine sold in California.

Arguments For the existing legislation, Against this referendum: If manufacturers use American-grown products there will be no tax imposed. Exclusion laws protect American labor from the competition of Oriental "Coolie." This law will only tax oleomargarine grown by "Coolie" labor.

Endorsers: F.T. Robson; Stanford Vina Rand, Vina, Calif.

Arguments Against the existing legislation, For this referendum: Many Californians who can't afford to buy butter and use oleomargarine are now faced with a 10 cent tax increase per pound. Oleomargarine does not compete with butter and it nourishes the poor.

Endorsers: Carolyn Weber.

PROPOSITION 22: Retail Store License.

Type: Referendum
Outcome: Rejected
Summary: Repeals the legislation (Chapter 849, Statutes 1935) requiring all businesses engaged in retail sales to pay an annual licensing fee of from $1 to $500, depending upon the number of stores owned. Exceptions are made for filling stations, ice distributors, restaurant facilities, newspaper offices, stores offering personal services, and theaters.
Arguments For the existing legislation, Against this referendum: This is the first serious attempt by the state to regulate the "Economic Royalists," who, through the spread of chain stores, have established monopolies at the expense of the public. This procedure currently works in 26 states and has been upheld by the U. S. Supreme Court. The legislation does not increase taxes, does help independent shop owners, and will promote competitive pricing.
Endorsers: Chris N. Jespersen, Senator, 29th District; Melvyn I. Cronin, Member of the Assembly, 25th District.
Arguments Against the existing legislation, For this referendum: The current law is unfair and discriminatory in singling out chain stores while exempting businesses like gas stations and theaters. Chain stores operate on very small profit margins and offer consumers the best products at the lowest prices. If this referendum passes, only wholesalers and other middle men will gain, not the consumer.
Endorsers: Bay W. Hays, Senator, 30th District; Paul A. Richie, Assemblyman, 79th Dist.

Election of November 8, 1938

PROPOSITION 1: Labor.
Type: Initiative Statute
Outcome: Rejected
Summary: Defines what constitutes lawful and unlawful picketing, boycotting, and display of banners. Prohibits the seizure of private property and interference with public highways, streets, wharves, docks, and other public places. Prohibits the use of abusive statements or threats of violence. Recognizes the right of employees to strike and bargain collectively. Provides for civil damages, criminal punishment, and penalties for violations. It repeals any law that conflicts with this one.
Arguments For: This will help build the best employment relations for all. It will promote peace by permitting peaceful picketing, pickets to peacefully persuade others to boycott, picketers to wear arm bands and carry banners. It also allows employees to organize and to strike at any time. It will prohibit interference in public places, mass picketing, picketing by outsiders, intimidation of employees, secondary boycotts, sit-down strikes, and "hot cargo"—

a union rule which forbids all union men to handle any commodity declared "unfair" by a union official.

Endorsers: Sanborn Young, Senator, 18th Dist., State Chairman of Calif. Comm. for Peace in Employment Relations; Alberta Gude Lynch, Pres., Business Women's Legislative Council; Alex Johnson, Secy.-Treas., Calif. Bureau Fed.

Arguments Against: This is not a fair regulation; it is designed to destroy labor organizations. It duplicates existing law. We need to enforce existing laws.

Endorsers: Edward D. Vandeleur; Ernest Besig; C.J. Haggerty.

PROPOSITION 2: Regulation of Pounds.
Type: Initiative Statute
Outcome: Rejected
Summary: Defines pounds and regulates their conduct. Prohibits the sale of animals in pounds for experimental purposes. This exempts kennels and buildings maintained on college premises or licensed medical research laboratories. Unclaimed and stray animals with no home available are to be put to death in a humane way.
Arguments For: This is a question of decency. Presently, "dog-bootleggers," in collusion with poundmasters, can sell animals to labs. With regulated pounds, strays are cleared from the streets and a place is provided where someone can take an animal he has found and where someone may find a lost pet.
Endorsers: A.L. Rosemont, Editor and Publisher, Western Kennel World; Vincent J. Garrity.
Arguments Against: This will prevent life-saving scientific research. Untold benefits have come from animal experimentation.
Endorsers: Rufus B. Von Kleinsmid, Pres., University of Southern Calif.; Ray Lyman Wilbur, Pres., Stanford University; P.K. Gilman, M.D., San Francisco.

PROPOSITION 4: Highway and Traffic Safety Commission.
Type: Initiative Statute
Outcome: Rejected
Summary: Creates a five-member Highway and Traffic Safety Commission appointed by the Governor with the consent of the Senate. Prescribes terms of office and salaries. It will take over duties of certain state agencies. The California Highway Patrol is transferred to the new Commission. Preserves existing civil service rights. The legislature can enlarge the Commission's power.

Arguments For: Having one commission will make the functions more efficient. The only agency to be abolished is the present State Highway Commission whose members have no fixed terms and serve at the pleasure of the governor. **Endorsers:** H.W. Keller, Vice Pres. and Chairman, Roads and Highways Comm., Automobile Club of So. Calif.; Francis Carr, Pres., Calif. State Automobile Assn.; Chas. A. Whitmore, Visalia, former Chairman, Calif. Highway Commission.

Arguments Against: It is a diversion of gas tax funds because $50,000 annually must be paid for high salaries, whereas the present Commission has no salary. Also, it is not a constitutional amendment. It takes the control of the distribution of highway funds from the people. Plus, the Commission serves for 10 years and can only be removed with a two-thirds vote of the Senate. Also, the current Commission is efficient and the new one is inexperienced, political, high-salaried, and long-term. **Endorsers:** Emil Gumpert, Gumpert and Mazzera, Counsel for Calif. Assn. of Highway Patrolmen.

PROPOSITION 5: Fishing Control.
Type: Initiative Statute
Outcome: Approved
Summary: Adds a new section to the Fish and Game Code. Prohibits the operation of fishing boats in state waters which deliver fish, wherever caught, to points beyond state waters, unless approved by the State Fish and Game Commission. The Commission can issue revokable licenses if someone is depleting a species. If violations occur, there can be penalties, seizures, and forfeitures.

Arguments For: This will offer protection against unregulated and destructive exploitation. Presently a large portion of fish used by floating reduction plants are caught within the three mile state water radius. **Endorsers:** Sanborn Young, Senator, 18th Dist.; C.R. Danielson, Past Pres., Assn. of Sportsmen of Calif.; Dr. Henry C. Veatch, Treas., Fish and Game Development Assn.; also endorsed by Fish and Game Commission, Governor, and Lt. Governor.

Arguments Against: The fish canning industry is trying to perpetuate its monopoly. **Endorsers:** W.B. Roby, Gen. Mgr., San Joaquin Valley Poultry Producers Assn., Porterville Calif.; James R. Lochhead, Secy., Fisherman's Produce Company, Monterey, Calif.; Lyman Henry, Attorney at Law, San Francisco, Calif.

PROPOSITION 10: Oil Leases on State-Owned Tidelands at Huntington Beach.
Type: Referendum
Outcome: Rejected
Summary: Referendum of the act, Chapter 304, Statutes 1937. Act provides for competitive bidding on 11 parcels of state-owned tideland at Huntington Beach for oil drilling. It states that no bid would be accepted unless it pays a royalty of 30% or more to the state when, in 30 days, 200+ barrels are produced with 10 wells per lease.
Arguments For the existing legislation, Against this referendum: This legislation provides protection for the state interest in oil resources in coastal tidelands, which have been depleted by drilling in privately-owned lands adjacent to state lands. The state will lease the lands via competitive bidders, and, if none are found, the state will drill for oil itself. This measure is vital to protecting a valuable source of revenue for the state.
Endorsers: Culbert L. Olson, Senator, 38th Dist., Los Angeles County; Harry C. Westover, Senator, 35th Dist., Orange County; J.C. Garrison, Senator, 22nd Dist., Stanislaus County.
Arguments Against the existing legislation, For this referendum: Our tourist business is the second largest in the state. This bill will ruin several miles of public beaches. Tideland drilling causes beach pollution. Revenues can be had through the license of littoral or slant drilling which does not damage the beaches.
Endorsers: Lynn O. Hossom, Attorney at Law, Chairman of the Fact Finding Comm. of the Long Beach Junior Chamber of Commerce, Harbor Commissioner, Legal Counsel of Associated Property Owners of Long Beach; James S. Farquhar, Editor/Publisher, Huntington Beach News; A.C. Peterson, Publisher, South Coast News, Laguna Beach, CA.

PROPOSITION 13: Revenue Bond Act of 1937.
Type: Referendum/Bond Act
Outcome: Rejected
Summary: Referendum on Chapter 51, Statutes 1937. The act created a Public Utilities Commission within any city or county rendering services to the public. It authorized the sale of revenue bonds to decrease costs of acquiring public utilities and extensions and improvements. It provided for production, distribution and sale of products and services of such public utilities and for payment of such bonds and interest.
Arguments For the existing legislation, Against this referendum: It allows for the paying of public improvements through the earnings of the improvements themselves. With revenue bonds it is possible to finance public improvements without mortgaging homes or farms.

Endorsers: George Sehlmeyer, Master, Calif. State Grange; Walter D. Wagner, Executive Secy., Irrigation Districts Assn. of Calif.; J. C. Garrison, Senator, 22nd Dist.

Arguments Against the existing legislation, For this referendum: This would abolish the two-thirds required vote of the people to approve public borrowings. Public bonds are private mortgages.

Endorsers: Mrs. Robert J. Burdette, Pasadena, Founder, Calif. Fed. of Women's Clubs; Glenn D. Willaman, Los Angeles, Secy., Calif. State Real Estate Assn.; Lewis M. Foulke, Gazelle, Siskiyou County, Pres., Common Property Taxpayers Assn. of Calif.

PROPOSITION 20: Taxation.
Type: Initiative Constitutional Amendment
Outcome: Rejected
Summary: Repeals limitation on ad valorem property taxes for state appropriations. Prevents the increased present assessed valuation of improvements and tangible personal property. Annually decreases tax rate and exempts same from taxes in nine years. Existing tax rate limitations become inoperative as necessary to offset reductions. Exempts from taxation $1000 of assessed improvements on land occupied by owner used as his home. Limits tax moratoriums to improved property in one parcel and ownership having assessed valuation not exceeding $5000. It also repeals specified sales, use and private car taxes. The rate of taxation on improvements and on tangible personal property shall not exceed 90% of the rate levied on land for the same year. Annually it shall be reduced 10% and after 10 years it shall be exempt.
Arguments For: This will repeal retail sales taxes. It will stimulate construction.
Endorsers: Jackson H. Ralston; Harry Ferrell; Noah D. Alper.
Arguments Against: This would require almost all revenues to be raised by taxes on land alone. Half of tax sources to local governments would be wiped out.
Endorsers: Mrs. James K. Lytle, Pres., Calif. Congress of Parents and Teachers; Frank Y. McLaughlin, 585 Bush Street; Vincent D. Kennedy, Managing Director, Calif. Retailers Assn.

PROPOSITION 24: Leasing State-Owned Tidelands for Oil Drilling.
Type: Referendum
Outcome: Rejected
Summary: Referendum on Chapter 832, Statutes 1937, an act that provides for competitive bidding on 11 parcels of state-owned tideland at Huntington Beach for oil drilling. It states that no bid would be accepted unless it pays

a royalty of 30% or more to the state when, in 30 days, 200+ barrels are produced with 10 wells per lease. Created a commission called the State Oil and Gas Commission, consisting of the Director of Finance, Director of Natural Resources, and State Controller, to secure development from said lands for the benefit of the state by advertising for bids and accepting only those that paid the state in excess of 30%. Leases would be of limited duration, and public access would not be impeded.

Arguments For the existing legislation, Against this referendum: None recorded.

Arguments Against the existing legislation, For this referendum: This is like the earlier proposition to establish tideland drilling in California. Five previous attempts have been rejected. It is needless destruction. Oil is the most menacing, far-reaching source of pollution. We must protect against it. Royalties are too high a price to pay for this destruction.

Endorsers: John H. O'Donnell, Member of the Assembly, 3rd Dist.; James S. Farquhar, Editor, Huntington Beach News; W.W. Crosby , Pres., San Diego County State Parks and Beach Assn.; and Giles B. Johnson, Pres., San Mateo County Fed. of Improvement Clubs and Assns.

PROPOSITION 25: Retirement Life Payments.
Type: Initiative Statute
Outcome: Rejected
Summary: Creates a State Retirement Life Payments Administrator appointed by the Governor from three named persons, to serve until 1940, when a successor will be elected for four years. Retirement compensation warrants are required and redemption stamps must be affixed to redeem warrants. This requires a weekly issuance of at least thirty one-dollar warrants during one's lifetime at age 50 years or older.

Arguments For: This will provide a new form of redeemable credit issued in $1 denominations. Real wealth will be doubled by the warrant system, so inflation in prices won't occur. It involves no taxes.

Endorsers: Petition Campaign Comm. for $30 a Week for Life Calif. State Pension Plan, Willis Allen, Campaign Director; Roy G. Owens, Engineer-Economist; Carl S. Kegley, Chief Counsel.

Arguments Against: It does not provide $30 per week to qualified individuals as it claims. They have to redeem them in excess of the face amount of the warrants. They are distributed to the wealthy and the poor, and this program would be wasted on the wealthy.

Endorsers: Daniel C. Murphy; Jefferson E. Peyser; Byron C. Hanna.

Election of November 7, 1939

PROPOSITION 1: Retirement Warrants.
Type: Initiative Statute
Outcome: Rejected
Summary: Requires the state to issue weekly at least thirty one-dollar warrants for life to persons over 50 years of age, redeemable in cash. Creates state banks to handle warrants. Requires $20,000,000 bond issue for initial capital. Administrator may propose amendments and call elections. The courts cannot interfere with administration. The warrants can be accepted at face value for payments of any licenses, tax fees, royalties, purchase of real or personal property, for rents, services, and debts. Banking services will be created for this.
Arguments in Favor: It will provide $30/week for life. It will increase business, eliminate the $500,000 daily cost of relief, provide security, have California taxes payable with warrants. It adds to the old-age pension, makes acceptance by public employees voluntary, and adjusts public employees' salaries quarterly. It exempts all warrant income and money income up to $3000 per year.
Endorsers: Roy G. Owens, Engineer-Economist; Retirement Life Payments Assn.
Arguments Against: Too much power would be conferred on a self-nominated administrator. For six months he isn't subject to recall. Warrants must circulate as money to serve their purpose, and retailers can't accept them at face value.
Endorsers: Mrs. James K. Lytle, Pres., Calif. Congress of Parents/Teachers; U. S. Webb, Former Atty. Gen. of Calif.; J. Ray Files, Los Angeles, Atty. at Law.

PROPOSITION 2: Chiropractors.
Type: Initiative Statute
Outcome: Rejected
Summary: Amends the Chiropractor Act. The Secretary of the Chiropractor Board shall devote full time to duties, with increased salary. Powers of the board would increase and education requirements of applicants for licenses would increase. Permits licensees to diagnose diseases and treat them without drugs. Licenses have an annual renewal fee and can be revoked. Licensees must report communicable diseases and sign birth and death certificates.
Arguments For: It would increase the educational requirements and allows for inspection. It does not burden taxpayers.
Endorsers: Stanley M. Innes, Past Pres.; Affiliated Chiropractors of Calif.; W.F. Morres, Member, State Board of Chiropractor Examiners; George E. Swanson, Pres., Affiliated Chiropractors of Calif., Alameda-Contra Costa Unit.
Arguments Against: No chiropractic educator was consulted when writing this amendment. We believe the training is adequate. The Board can set up a

"pay-off racket" because of the unusual powers conferred on it.   The amendment would retard chiropractic education and scientific progress.
Endorsers: T.F. Ratledge, D.C., Chairman, Legislative Comm., Calif. Chiropractic Assn; L.H. McLellan, D.C., Pres. of Palmer Standardized Chiropractors of Calif.

PROPOSITION 3: Personal Property Brokers.
Type: Referendum
Outcome: Approved
Summary: Amends the "Personal Property Brokers Act" (Chapter 952, Statutes 1939) that regulates business of brokers and personal property brokers, and requires their licensing. The act exempts banks, trust companies, building and loan associations, industrial loan companies, credit unions, or licensed pawnbrokers.   Administration is provided by the Corporate Commission, enforcing all fees, issuing and revoking licenses, conducting investigations, and making regulations. There are penalties for violations.
Arguments For the existing legislation, Against this referendum: The act was passed to stop loan shark personal property brokers. It protects the people by setting personal property loans at the lowest possible rate; the small borrower will be protected by the state Commissioner of Corporations.
Endorsers: Gov. Culbert I. Olson; Atty. Gen. Earl Warren; Legal Aid Societies of Calif.; Organized Labor of Calif.; Better Business Bureaus of Los Angeles, San Francisco, Oakland, Long Beach, San Diego, Sacramento, and San Jose; John F. Shelley, Senator, 14th Dist., San Francisco; Gerald J. O'Gara, Atty. at Law, Counsel for Better Business Bureau of San Francisco; Robert J. Bauer, General Manager, Better Business Bureau, Los Angeles.
Arguments Against the existing legislation, For this referendum: This act does not protect the small borrower. Also, not all the money lenders are loan sharks. Plus, this act does not require the licensing of every person or company in the business of making loans where a charge is made above our constitutional rate of interest. The bill only controls a portion of the business. The loan business should be competitive.
Endorsers: M.M. May, Los Angeles; V.G. Wise, San Francisco, Calif.; J.C. Earle, Los Angeles.

PROPOSITION 4: Personal Property Brokers.
Type: Referendum
Outcome: Approved
Summary: Amends the "Personal Property Brokers Act" (Chapter 1044, Statutes 1939), which regulates brokers, including personal property brokers, and requires them to be licensed. Loans of $300 or less are regulated.

Exempts certain businesses (listed on the previous referendum). Administration is provided by the Corporate Commission which can revoke/suspend licenses, collect fees, conduct investigations, and make regulations. There are penalties for violations.

Arguments For the existing legislation, Against this referendum: The act provides for the maximum rate at two and one-half percent per month on unpaid balance on first $100 and two percent on next $200. Most legitimate lenders favor this act.

Endorsers: Albert C. Wollenberg, Assemblyman, 27th Dist., San Francisco; Alexander Sheriffs, Atty. for Legal Aid Society of San Francisco.

Arguments Against the existing legislation, For this referendum: This is prohibition on small loans under $100.

Endorsers: M. M. May, Los Angeles; V. G. Wise, San Francisco, Calif.; J. C. Earle, Los Angeles.

PROPOSITION 5: Oil and Gas Control.
Type: Referendum of Legislative Act (Chapter 811, Statutes 1939)
Outcome: Rejected
Summary: The law under reconsideration creates an Oil Conservation commission that can limit and prorate the production of crude petroleum oil and natural gas, adopt regulations, and prescribe procedures in hearings and proceedings before the Commission. It would provide for court review. It would define legal/illegal oil (and products) with the illegal being impounded and sold, and monies deposited in the general fund. Penalties would be prescribed for violations. Charges would be made to well operators and royalty owners.

Arguments For the existing legislation, Against this referendum: It is a conservation measure to secure a controlled supply of reasonably priced oil and gas, and to end reckless waste. The control of the industry is placed in the hands of the people's representatives. It will guarantee to the people cheap gasoline, continued employment of oil workers, and adequate supplies of oil to the Navy. It will also help the small independent service station.

Endorsers: Culbert L. Olson, Governor of the State of Calif.; Wentworth H. Osgood, Lt. Commander, U.S. Navy, Inspector, Naval Petroleum Reserves; Maurice Atkinson, Assemblyman, 70th Dist.; Wills B. Wylis, Executive Secy., Retail Petroleum Dealers Assn.

Arguments Against the existing legislation, For this referendum: It would set up a three man commission with artificial control of oil production, with consequent higher prices to consumers. Monopolistic interests urge this bill. This is not a conservation measure.

Endorsers: Ralph C. Dills, Assemblyman, 69th Assembly Dist.; Seth Millington, Assemblyman, 4th Assembly Dist.; J. Frank Burke.

Election of November 5, 1940

PROPOSITION 5: Daylight Saving.
Type: Initiative Statute
Outcome: Rejected
Summary: Provides daylight saving time as standard time in California between the last Sunday in April and the last Sunday in September annually. This would provide the maximum usage of daylight hours. Daylight Standard Time would advance one hour ahead. This would repeal any conflicting legislation.
Arguments For: As with the one-third of the people in the U.S. already using Daylight Saving time, it provides more sunlight for people's leisure time. It will increase general health, create time for recreation. It will also increase business and industrial efficiency, and decrease traffic accidents.
Endorsers: Calif. Daylight Saving League, Allyn M. Suffens, Secy.
Arguments Against: People have voted against this measure before because they do not want it. There's no such thing as daylight savings. There are only 24 hours and to say that you can add an hour is absurd. California will be out of step if it accepts this because no place west of the Mississippi uses it. Keep California normal!
Endorsers: Thomas A. Maloney, Member of Assembly, 20th Dist., San Francisco County; C. J. Haggerty, Pres., Calif. State Fed. of Labor, Los Angeles; Gorden H. Garland, Speaker and Member of the Assembly, 38th Dist., Tulare and Kings Counties, Woodlake, Calif.; Ms. Thomas H. Richards, Pres., Calif. State Fed. of Women's Clubs, Chico, Calif.; Dr. James Whitcomb Brougher, Jr., Pastor, First Baptist Church, Glendale, Calif.; R.H. Taylor, Executive Secy., Agricultural Council of Calif., Sacramento.

Election of November 3, 1942

PROPOSITION 1: Prohibiting "Hot Cargo," "Secondary Boycott."
Type: Referendum
Outcome: Approved
Summary: The law under reconsideration declares unlawful Hot Cargo and Secondary Boycott; gives persons injured injunctions and damages. Hot Cargo is defined as an agreement resulting in employer's or employee's refusal to handle goods or perform services because of another employer's labor dispute or contract. Secondary Boycott is defined as an agreement to cease performing services or cause any employer loss to induce him to refrain from business with another employer because of the latter's dispute. The act is to be enacted on May 1, 1943 and to last for the duration of the period of the National Emergency.

Arguments For the existing legislation, Against this referendum: It is designed to prevent interruption of essential industry during the war emergency. It will secure workmen against industrial disputes. It will curb, for the duration, the abuse of excessive powers assumed by labor leaders. It is a patriotic measure. This will not interfere with the right of organized labor to strike or with collective bargaining, or with the practices of legitimate trade unionism.
Endorsers: W.P. Rich, Senator, 10th Dist.; Frank L. Gordon, Senator, 11th Dist.
Arguments Against the existing legislation, For this referendum: It is un-American and unconstitutional. It is an attempt by employers to cause discontent. This act would make it unlawful to refuse to work for an unfair or un-American employer. No one is exempt from the act.
Endorsers: C.J. Haggerty, Pres., Calif. State Fed. of Labor; Edward D. Vandeleur, Secy., Calif. State Fed. of Labor; J.W. Buzzell, Secy., Los Angeles Central Labor Council.

PROPOSITION 3: Basic Science Act.
Type: Initiative Statute
Outcome: Rejected
Summary: Creates a Board of Examiners in Basic Sciences, five members with prescribed qualifications to be appointed by the governor. In order to apply to Medical, Dental, Osteopathic, or Chiropractor Boards for licenses to practice the healing arts, a person must obtain a basic science certificate from the Board after a written examination. It exempts various professions, present licensees, and persons treating sicknesses by prayer. Fees and penalties with the fines are used to administer the act.
Arguments For: It does not affect the systems of healing now legally recognized in California. This act will help protect anyone injured.
Endorsers: Dr. Ray Lyman Wilbur, Chancellor, Stanford Univ.; Rufus B. Von Kleinsmid, Pres., Univ. of Southern Calif.; Tully C. Knoles, Pres., College of the Pacific.
Arguments Against: It will create another unnecessary board that overlaps the functions of the existing boards. $5,000 is earmarked from the General Fund to carry out this act, but taxpayers are already overburdened. It encourages the current bureaucratic trend and unrestricted control over the medical professions.
Endorsers: Public School Protective League, Emily W. Gregory, Executive Secy.

PROPOSITION 4: Personal Income Tax Laws.
Type: Initiative Constitutional Amendment

Outcome: Rejected

Summary: Amends Article XIII, Section 11 of the Constitution. States that no law imposing taxes on persons or their estates shall be valid unless approved by the majority of voters after the initiative proceedings or after it is passed by two-thirds of each house of the legislature. This repeals the 1935 Personal Income Tax Act, Chapter 329, Statutes 1935.

Arguments For: Why should you pay an unnecessary tax? The state personal income tax diverts money from the federal to state government, which diverts money from the war effort.

Endorsers: Leslie E. Burks, Executive Secy., San Francisco Real Estate Board; Isidore B. Dockweiler; Zack Farmer, Municipal Airport Commissioner; Mrs. Gertrude H. Rounsavelle, Parent-Teachers Assn. Leader and Educator; Donald J. Willson, Vice Pres., Calif. Fruit Exchange.

Arguments Against: It restricts the state's power to tax in accordance with the ability to pay. Also, the wealthy will be exempted.

Endorsers: Chris N. Jaspersen, Senator, 29th Dist.; John F. Shelley, Senator, 14th Dist.; J.C. Garrison, Senator, 22nd Dist.; George Sehlmeyer, Master, Calif. State Grange; Ray B. Wiser, Pres., Calif. Farm Bureau Fed.; Von T. Ellsworth, Director of Research Development and Legislative Representative, Calif. Farm Bureau Fed.; Helen Gahagan; Roy Cloud, State Executive Secy., Calif. Teachers Assn.

PROPOSITION 10: Reorganization of the Building and Loan Association.
Type: Indirect Initiative
Outcome: Rejected

Summary: Adds Article XVII to Building and Loan Association Act. Authorizes plans for rehabilitation, reorganization, consolidation, or merger of building and loan associations, and defines those affected. Consents and procedures are required. Plans must be fair and feasible. Specifies duties of the Building and Loan Commissioner. Legislation may amend or repeal the act.

Arguments For: This is a practical and inexpensive way by which Pacific States Savings and Loan Company may be reorganized. No plan may be operative unless approved by the court and it receives majority consent from the stockholders and shareholders, and two-thirds consent from investment certificate holders and creditors.

Endorsers: Robert S. Odell, Pres., Pacific States Savings and Loan Co.; Donzel Stoney, Vice Pres., Title Insurance and Guaranty Co.

Arguments Against: It is a special interest measure. It will allow for the reorganization for only a few to benefit. It gives stockholders an absolute veto. The financial institutions will no longer have governmental supervision. There is no public emergency for this act. No assurance is given to the savings of the investing public after reorganization, nor will there be supervision by the government. There is no evident need for reorganization.

Endorsers: Harley Hise, Building and Loan Commissioner; Brodie Ahlport, Special Counsel to the Building and Loan Commissioner; Geo. B. Campbell, Chairman, Legislative Comm. of the Calif. Savings and Loan League.

Election of November 7, 1944

PROPOSITION 9: Funds for Elementary Schools.
Type: Initiative Constitutional Amendment
Outcome: Approved
Summary: Increases the amount of revenue required to be raised and apportioned by the legislature for public elementary schools from 100% to 166 ⅔% of the total amount otherwise required to be spent by counties. Public day and evening secondary and technical school revenues raised would remain unchanged.
Arguments For: Without the increase in funding, there will be classrooms without teachers and closed schools. More revenue is needed due to the acute shortage of teachers, an increase of 1.5 million in state population, and many tax-poor districts. Prop 9 would increase funding from $60 to $80 per child, transfer cost from taxpayers to the state, and enable 1.5 million new residents to pay a fair share of the cost for California's education.
Endorsers: Charles Albert Adams, San Francisco; John F. Brady, Pres., State Council of Education; Arthur W. Brouillet, San Francisco; Dorothy D. Decker, Santa Ana, Pres., Calif. Fed. of Business and Professional Women Clubs, Inc.; Dr. Walter F. Dexter, State Supt. of Public Instruction, George A. Duddy, San Francisco, State Secy., Calif. State Aerie, Fraternal Order of Eagles; McIntyre Faries, Los Angeles; Mrs. John J. Garland, Menlo Park, Pres., Calif. Congress of Parents and Teachers; C. J. Haggerty, Secy.-Treas., Calif. State Fed. of Labor; Mrs. Alfred J. Mathebat, Alameda, Past National Commander, American Legion Auxiliary.
Arguments Against: California is already spending too much money on education—more than any other state. Not one school has closed due to money shortage. California teachers have the highest minimum salary. This proposition would freeze a minimum of $15 million per year into the constitution. It would provide no decrease in property taxes and an increase in state tax. Prior to the war, there was a surplus of teachers, and after the war a surplus will again exist.
Endorsers: Lee T. Bashore, Assemblyman, 49th Dist., Chairman, Comm. on Revenue and Taxation, Calif. State Legislature.

PROPOSITION 11: Retirement Payments, Gross Income Tax.
Type: Initiative Constitutional Amendment
Outcome: Rejected
Summary: Calls for payment of $60 monthly to those residents age 60 and over, or totally and permanently disabled, including those in the military services, or blind. Recipients prohibited from "gainful" employment and required to expend payments. Places a 3% gross income tax on pensions and organizations, except non-profit, to be distributed between the general fund and a special fund created for these payments. Repeals sales and use tax.
Arguments For: Proposition 11 provides a social insurance guarantee of $60 per month, which also acts to stimulate employment and business. It will help maintain property values, create postwar job opportunities, and eliminate the degrading characteristics of charity, case worker investigations, relatives' responsibilities, or pension deductions because of home ownership. It will repeal the sales tax since it is financed through a 3% gross income tax. Most citizens reaching 60 cannot support themselves. Recipients retiring will give jobs to returning veterans. Similar legislation has been successful in Hawaii for 10 years.
Endorsers: Dr. F. E. Townsend, B. G. Ran Kine[?], Wilford Howard, John C. Cuneo.
Arguments Against: The proposition is unfair to 650,000 young persons in the armed forces because they are unable to vote. It would increase gross taxes to $1 billion and hurt everyone. This is truly class legislation, since 90% of the money will go to 10% of the population. It would do away with public and state university claims on state revenue. It hurts the aged because it forces them to spend $60 in 30 days. California would lose $40 million per year from the federal government Old Age Security program. The Townsend Movement, which failed to get its plan through Congress, is trying to foist it on California voters.
Endorsers: George H. McLain, Chairman, Board of Trustees, Citizens' for Old Age Pensions.; Mrs. T. J. Garland, Pres., Calif. Congress of Parents and Teachers; Ray B. Wiser, Pres., Calif. Farm Bureau Fed.; Paul Cowgill, Pres., Calif. State Employees Assn.; Mrs. Curtis S. Albro, Pres, YMCA; Leland P. Reeder, Past Pres., Calif. Real Estate Assn.; Joseph Scott, Attorney, Los Angeles.

PROPOSITION 12: Right of Employment.
Type: Initiative Constitutional Amendment
Outcome: Rejected
Summary: Guarantees the right of employees to be free from interference from labor organizations. Employees can be hired whether they do or do not belong or pay to a union. Such interference by unions is to be declared unlawful, and

remedied by court action. Organized labor is defined as any organization that deals with employees concerning grievances, labor disputes, rates of pay, hours of employment, or conditions of work. This amendment would declare itself self-executing, and authorizes legislation to facilitate operation.

Arguments For: Without this amendment, young men returning from the war would find employment barred by union "tollgates." Without the passing of this proposition, persons would have to pay for the right to work and "housewives" would pay unions when they patriotically volunteered to increase our nation's food supply. Labor unions will only gain strength and dignity through the earned respect of society and the free allegiance of those who volunteer to join, attracted by wise and honest leadership.

Endorsers: C. Campbell, Citrus Grower, Ventura County, Chairman, Calif. Comm. for the Right to Work; James L. Beebe, Lawyer, Los Angeles; Byron C. Hanna, Lawyer, Los Angeles; Mark Holhouse, Dairyman, Los Altos; R. F. Schmeiser, Farmer, Fresno.

Arguments Against: A small minority of short-sighted employers are trying to sneak through a drastic change in the Bill of Rights of California. This proposition's purpose is to single out and destroy the basic American rights of freedom of speech, press, and assembly. Men are fighting to protect these rights, and they cannot vote on this amendment. It would decrease California's standard of living, wages, and state income. While undoing the work of generations of progressive legislation, it would decrease employment, increase chaos, and be in conflict with state and federal public policy. It disrupts California's harmony.

Endorsers: Anthony L. Noriega, Pres., Calif. State Fed. of Labor; C. J. Haggerty, Sec.-Treas., Calif. State Fed. of Labor; J. G. Thimmes, Pres., State CIO Council; M. C. Hermann, Quartermaster Adjutant, Dept. of Calif. Veterans of Foreign Wars; Walter L. Bachrodt, Supt., City Schools of San Jose.

Election of November 5, 1946

PROPOSITION 2: Greyhound Racing.
Type: Initiative Constitutional Amendment
Outcome: Rejected
Summary: Permits greyhound dog racing and parimutuel wagering in counties having a population over 175,000. Establishes a board that would license and regulate the racing and betting. Authorizes 74 racing days per year in Los Angeles County and in the San Francisco metropolitan area, 25 days in other counties. Provides that 8% of all sums wagered be retained by a parimutuel pool operator, 4% paid to fund for "pursuing claims of veterans" against citizens of this state and for veterans' rehabilitation. Also provides penalties for violating the provisions of the act.

Arguments For: With this amendment, greyhound racing under strict state supervision would raise over $1.5 million for veterans through the payment of 4% of the track wagers earned. This extra revenue would relieve overburdened taxpayers by shifting support of the veterans' welfare program from state tax sources to state-supervised racing. Present services for veterans are terribly underfunded for those who served us in the war and their suffering families. California agriculture would be stimulated by the increased attendance at state and county fairs caused by those eager to wager on fair-run races.

Endorsers: Charles P. Ash, Dept. Commander, Veterans of Foreign Wars; Dr. John L. Murphy, Past Commander, Post 93, American Legion; Lloyd F. Olsen, State Commander, Disabled American Veterans.

Arguments Against: Gamblers have tried to force their evil ways onto California's citizens in the past. Now, their greedy intentions are disguised in the name of our veterans. These gamblers are not interested in veterans' needs or even sport, for they could have dog racing right now without gambling. They want to cheapen the good name of those who offered their lives to keep America free. The bottom line in all this is those who support this proposition are only interested in gambling and the money made from it.

Endorsers: H. E. Dillinger, Senator, 9th Dist.; James W. Fifield, Jr., Pastor, First Congregational Church, Los Angeles.

PROPOSITION 3: Public Schools.
Type: Initiative Constitutional Amendment
Outcome: Approved
Summary: Establishes a minimum salary of $2,400 per year for teachers and increases state support to $120 per year for each pupil, $90 of which would be given to local school districts. Authorizes local authorities to determine the amount of money to be raised by school district taxes and prohibits transfer of any school or college to any authority not under the public school system.
Arguments For: California's population has increased by over two million in the past six years. California's public schools are swelling with students in need of supplies, rooms, and teachers. Proposition 3 would aid the state in its most serious time of need. The crisis is real and unmistakable, for enrollments are expected to double in eight years. The challenge to meet our children's needs can be met with this measure.
Endorsers: Roy W. Cloud, State Secy., Calif. Teachers Assn.; Mrs. Rollin Brown, State Pres., Calif. Congress of Parents and Teachers; Thomas J. Riordan, Past State Commander, American Legion.
Arguments Against: This measure is a questionable answer to the dilemma of public schools in a shameful state caused by public indifference. Teachers need to be paid more than $2,400 per year, but to constitutionally guarantee them this minimum salary would cause dire consequences in the future. If one

group of public employees is protected, soon all will cry for this "right." Something needs to be done about public education, but Proposition 3 is not the right "something."

2. Signers against: John Swan, Junior College Teacher and Attorney-at-Law, Member of Calif. State Senate, 1941-1945.

PROPOSITION 11: Fair Employment Practices Act.

Type: Initiative Statute

Outcome: Rejected

Summary: Declares that state policy should dictate that all persons have the right of equal opportunity in securing employment. Makes it unlawful to refuse to hire, to discharge, or to discriminate against any person on the basis of color, national origin, or ancestry. A commission would be established to prevent such unlawful practices by conciliation or by order or by education. Also provides a judicial review of commission's orders, and appropriates a sum for the commission.

Arguments For: This measure would further the cause of American Democracy, which rests on equality and opportunity. We must continue the unity and equality of job opportunity which helped in the war. Unless we maintain our "mass-purchasing power" we shall "revert back into the dark depression" of the 1930s. Every worker wants the right of a good job, and Proposition 11 would make it a civil right to be employed without discrimination. This does not restrict an employer; he may hire whom he chooses without discrimination playing a part in his decision. Let us not allow this war to be fought in vain.

Endorsers: Augustus F. Hawkins, Assemblyman, 62nd. Dist.; Leon H. Washington, Jr., Editor and Publisher, Los Angeles Sentinel; Herman Hill, Pacific Coast Editor, Pittsburgh Courier; Loren Miller, Lawyer, Los Angeles; Mrs. Betty Hill, Pres., Women's Political Study Club, Los Angeles; Rev. Hughbert H. Landram, San Francisco; Mrs. Sumner Spaulding, Los Angeles; George D. Collens, Jr., Assemblyman, 22nd Dist.; Mrs. Marjorie Pittman, San Jose; Daniel G. Marshall, Los Angeles.

Arguments Against: Religious, national, or racial intolerance is a matter of individual conscience that cannot be changed by legislative coercion. This measure would cause serious friction in the agricultural industry where farmers usually employ one minority group to avoid racial and nationality conflict between employees. In three states where such commissions have been established, there is no evidence that it accomplishes its purposes. This law would deprive the accused employer of a right to trial by jury.

Endorsers: George M. Breslin, Attorney, Los Angeles; W. J. Cecil, General Manager, Calif. Grape and Fruit Tree Assn., Fresno; Dr. james W. Fifield, Jr., Minister, First Congregational Church, Los Angeles; Francis V. Keesling, San

Francisco; Hal G. Hotchkiss, Realtor, San Diego; Ray B. Wiser, Pres., Calif. Farm Bureau Fed., Berkeley; Mrs. Alice Tanner Gardner, Los Angeles; Alfred J. Lundberg, Oakland; A. J. McFadden, Agriculturalist, Santa Ana; Mrs. Eugene M. Price, San Francisco.

Election of November 2, 1948

PROPOSITION 2: Local Control and Enforcement of Intoxicating Liquors.
Type: Initiative Constitutional Amendment
Outcome: Rejected
Summary: The county and city must regulate the presence of minors in licensed liquor premises and regulate lighting and sanitation on the premises. Unescorted women may be served liquor but only at a table. Collected state license fees shall be apportioned to the local government. Licenses for distilled spirits shall be based on population numbers.
Arguments For: It will promote social and moral welfare and temperance in the sale and use of liquors.
Endorsers: Ralph E. Swing, Senator, 36th Dist..
Arguments Against: This is a confusion measure used to take votes from Proposition 12. It would require unescorted women to be segregated. Also, fees are already turned over to the cities and counties; this was just inserted to give voters the idea that they will get something if they vote for this initiative.
Endorsers: H.E. Dillinger, Senator, 9th Dist.

PROPOSITION 3: Railroad Brakemen.
Type: Initiative Statute
Outcome: Approved
Summary: The Public Utilities Commission will name the number of brakemen to be used on railroad trains. Prohibits featherbed practices, employing more than is necessary.
Arguments For: It will remove the Excess Crew Law. Thirty-seven years ago it was a safety measure and now it has become featherbedding. Many progressive unions want to end this law.
Endorsers: Alfred W. Robertson, Former Chairman, Democratic State Central Comm., Santa Barbara; Ed Tickle, Former Chairman, Republican State Central Comm., Carmel; Mrs. Leiland Atherton Irish, Los Angeles Clubwoman; Thomas J. Riordan, Past State Commander, American Legion, San Francisco; William M. Jeffers, Former Pres., Union Pacific Railroad, Los Angeles; R.V. Garrod, Pres., Calif. Farmers, Inc., Saratoga; Joseph J. Deuel, Director, Calif. Farm Bureau Fed., Berkeley.

Arguments Against: All engineers and engine crewmen are opposed to this. The same potential dangers still exist and they need the extra crewmen still. Because of the war, there was a period with a No Full Crew Law and there was an enormous accident rate increase.

Endorsers: F.G. Pellett, State Representative, Trainmen's Brotherhood.

PROPOSITION 4: Aged and Blind Aid.
Type: Initiative Constitutional Amendment
Outcome: Approved

Summary: The maximum aid for the aged and blind will increase from $60 to $75 monthly. Lowers age and resident requirements for aged aid and increases income and property exemptions for the aged and blind. Makes the Director of the Department of Social Welfare an elective office. The aid program would be under state administration.

Arguments For: The high death rate of the aged keeps the cost of the program at a constant level. Old people will not move to California for the higher pensions, so any fears of this should be dispelled.

Endorsers: George H. McLain, Chairman, Citizens' Comm. for Old Age Pensions; Frank E. Gardner, Chairman Legislative Comm. of Calif. Blind; Myrtle Williams, Secy.-Treas., Calif. Inst. of Social Welfare; John W. Evans, Assemblyman, 65th Dist.; Gordon R. Hahn, Assemblyman, 66th Dist.

Arguments Against: It will freeze rates at their inflated levels and not allow for adjustments to the changing business cycles and economic conditions. This would be the first lien against all monies in the state treasury. It would destroy the present system of aid to the needy aged and blind. Plus, it will create a new state department to administer the act without repealing the present agencies, which will result in duplicating costs and increased taxes.

Endorsers: Ray B. Wiser, Pres., Calif. Farm Bureau Fed.; Arthur J. Will, Supt. of Charities, County of Los Angeles; William A. Pixley, Chairman of the Board, Property Owners Assn. of Calif., Inc.; James L. Beebe, Attorney at Law, Los Angeles.

PROPOSITION 6: Regulation of Commercial Fishing.
Type: Initiative Statute
Outcome: Rejected

Summary: Nets, traps and set lines are prohibited in commercial fishing in fish and game districts in which San Francisco Bay and tributary and connecting bays and streams are situated and are used as a recreational fishing area. Exempted from this are commercial fishing for crabs, clams, and oysters, and other named varieties. Exempts Clear Lake and Lake Almanor from the initiative. Repeals inconsistent provisions of the Fish and Game Code.

Arguments For: This initiative is for conservation and recreation.
Endorsers: George D. Difani, No. Calif. delegate for the Associated Sportsmen of Calif.
Arguments Against: It will harm the conservation of game fish and commercial fish in the waters affected. It will wipe out a long-standing industry in the state. It will lower the supply of fish and raise the prices for the consumers. There is no conservation need to restrict any phase of the fishery. There are no signs of overfishing or depletion.
Endorsers: Brayton Wilbur, Former Pres., San Francisco Chamber of Commerce; Bjorne Halling, Secy.-Treas., Calif. CIO Council; Theo Weissich, Pres., Eureka Chamber of Commerce; Vincent A. Davi, Mayor, City of Pittsburg. Recorded as Opposed: Pacific Marine Fisheries Comm., consisting of the Fish and Game Commissions of Calif., Oregon, and Washington.

PROPOSITION 12: Local Control of Intoxicating Liquors.
Type: Initiative Constitutional Amendment
Outcome: Rejected
Summary: Licenses for the sale of liquors, whether for consumption on or off the premises, are only valid when approved by the particular governing body within the city or county.
Arguments For: This provides for effective control by local authorities. It only affects retail liquor licenses, not the manufacturing licenses or manufacture, transportation, or possession. The current Board of Equalization has shown a lack of interest in local opinion. This would give the right to a local vote to each city or county.
Endorsers: Rufus B. von Kleinsmid, author.
Arguments Against: This is the forerunner to local prohibition; ordinances and resolutions can be adopted without regard to any state pattern. Liquor control should function on a statewide basis. Proposition 12 would jeopardize the manufacture, transportation, and distribution of liquor.
Endorsers: Thomas A. Maloney, Assemblyman 20th Dist., Speaker Pro Tempore; Walt L. Moreland, Pres., Southern Calif. Business Men's Assn.

PROPOSITION 13: Senate Reapportionment.
Type: Initiative Constitutional Amendment
Outcome: Rejected
Summary: States that counties shall be represented in the state Senate according to population, with a maximum of 10 senators per county. It would eliminate the present provision that no county shall have more than one Senate district. Reapportionment should change according to the 1940 census.

Election for all senators will occur in 1950, with one half to be elected every two years.

Arguments For: This will restore more representative government. Women, veterans, and taxpayers are now disenfranchised.

Endorsers: Jno W. Preston, Former Calif. State Supreme Court Justice; M.C. Hermann, Adjutant, Veterans of Foreign Wars, Dept. of Calif.; C.J. Haggerty, Secy.-Treas., Calif. State Fed. of Labor.

Arguments Against: This will destroy the balanced system of representation, "The Federal Plan," which gives big cities control of the Assembly but allows rural districts equal voices in the Senate.

Endorsers: Mrs. J.C. Bradbury, Pres., Calif. Fed. of Women's Clubs, Modesto; Mr. Rollin Brown, Los Angeles; Justus F. Craemer, Pres., Calif. Press Assn., San Francisco; Frank P. Doherty, Atty. at Law, Los Angeles; Thomas A.J. Dockweiler, Atty. at Law, Los Angeles; Richard Graves, Executive Secy., League of Calif. Cities, Berkeley; A.J. McFadden, Pres., Agricultural Council of Calif., Santa Ana; Garret McEnerney, II, Atty. at Law, San Francisco; Thomas J. Riordan, Past Department Commander, American Legion, San Francisco; W.P. Wing, Secy.-Manager, Calif. Wool Growers Assn., San Francisco.

PROPOSITION 14: Housing.
Type: Initiative Constitutional Amendment
Outcome: Rejected
Summary: A state Housing Agency would be created. The state would guarantee expenditures for subsidies to public housing authorities of a maximum of $25,000,000 annually. State bonds of up to $100,000,000 would be used to finance state loans to public housing authorities and private non-profit housing associations. The bond principal and interest would be paid from state tax revenues. It would also exempt local housing authority bonds from taxation.

Arguments For: Slums continue to grow as homeless families cannot afford new homes. It is the responsibility of the government to help the people obtain homes. 100,000 homeless families will be able to afford homes with this proposition.

Endorsers: Rt. Rev. Msgr. Thomas J. O'Dwyer, Chairman, Calif. Housing Initiative Comm.; John F. Shelley, Pres., Calif. State Fed. of Labor; Dr. Vada Somerville, Pres., Los Angeles Metropolitan Council of Negro Women; Sen. Chris N. Jespersen, Senator, San Luis Obispo County; Mrs. Horace Gray, Housing Consultant, League of Women Voters of Calif.

Arguments Against: This is no "cure-all" for the housing shortage. It would mean heavier taxes, reduced local power, and tax-free encroachment on revenue-producing private business for a fortunate few.

Endorsers: Frank P. Merriam, Former Governor of Calif., Long Beach; George L. Eastman, Hollywood; J.W. O'Sullivan, Chairman, Housing Comm., Department of Calif., AMVETS, Los Angeles; Milton J. Block, Sr., Pres., National Assn. of Home Builders, Los Angeles; Raymond M. Young, Manufacturer, Berkeley, Calif.; Carleton B. Tibbetts, San Marino, Calif.; Earl W. Smith, Chairman, Home Builders Council of Calif., San Francisco, Calif.; Ray D. Nichols, Oakland, Calif.; Joe D. Dickey, Fresno, Calif.; Harold C. Geyer, Monterey, Calif.; Frederick C. Dockweiler, Attorney, Los Angeles; Laguna Beach Chamber of Commerce.

PROPOSITION 15: Fish Nets.
Type: Initiative Statute
Outcome: Rejected
Summary: Amends the Fish and Game Code. Purse nets and round haul nets would be prohibited in ocean and tide waters south of the line extending due west from Point San Simeon in San Luis Obispo County. This would conserve the fish supply. It would be subject to limitations, and bait nets would be permitted for taking bait fish.
Arguments For: This would insure an adequate supply of fish for sportsmen and commercial fishermen. With this initiative, small fish can survive and propagate. It will only affect a small percentage of the commercial fishing industry.
Endorsers: Dr. A.R. Anderson, Pres., Southern Council of Conservation Clubs, Inc.
Arguments Against: This would be too far-reaching and would affect many workers.
Endorsers: Hugh M. Burns, State Senator, 30th Dist.; Joseph Scott, Vincent Thomas, Assemblyman, 68th Dist.; Irwin L. DeShelter, CIO Regional Director; Edward T. Cook; C.J. Haggerty, Secy.-Treas., Calif. State Fed. of Labor.

Election of November 8, 1949

PROPOSITION 2: Aged and Blind Aid.
Type: Initiative Constitutional Amendment
Outcome: Approved
Summary: Reinstates the plan of Old Age Security and Aid to the blind. The maximum monthly payments would be retained at $75 for the aged and $85 for the blind. Legislature can increase or decrease payments.
Arguments For: It would benefit the needy aged and blind. The state would remain committed to social justice.

Endorsers: Dr. Newel Rerry, Pres., Calif. Council for the Blind; Mrs. G.W. Luhr, Pres., Calif. Congress of Parents and Teachers; Ray B. Wiser, Pres., Calif. Farm Bureau Fed.; Ben C. Duniway, Pres., Calif. Assn. for Social Welfare; Mrs. Pauline T. Ploeser, Pres., League of Women Voters of Calif.

Arguments Against: Proposition 2 takes away all the benefits voted by the people last November [Proposition 4].

Endorsers: George H. McLain, Chairman Citizens' Comm. for Old Age Pensions; Frank E. Gardner, Chairman, Legislative Comm. for Calif. Blind; Charles Ohlson, Vice-Pres. Calif. Institute of Social Welfare; Mrs. Eva Scott, State Pres. American War Mothers; John F. Shelley, Pres., Calif. State Fed. of Labor.

PROPOSITION 12: Daylight Saving Time.
Type: Initiative Statute
Outcome: Approved
Summary: Provides for daylight saving time during a portion of each year. The standard time would be Pacific Standard Time. The time would advance one hour from the last Sunday in April to the last Sunday in September. Repeals conflicting laws.

Arguments For: California needs summertime daylight saving time. It will increase public health and business and employment. It tends to decrease juvenile delinquency. It reduces traffic accidents. It will aid in the battle against the perennial water shortage. The eastern part of the country already uses the system and we should be on the same system. 312,000 signatures were obtained for this measure.

Endorsers: Dr. Phillip W. Reames, Pres., Calif. State Jr. Chamber of Commerce; Mrs. Frederick N. Gregory, Pres., San Francisco Women's Legislative Council; Dr. Russell W. Starr, Pres., Vice Commander, Department of Calif. American Legion; Shepard Tucker, Pres., San Francisco Real Estate Board; Mrs. Lewis Allen Weiss, Civic and Women's organizations Leader.

Arguments Against: This proposition was overwhelmingly defeated in 1930 and 1940. Farmers are opposed because it will work against nature's law. Housewives' and railroads' schedules would be upset. It would decrease revenues for the motion picture industry. We can open businesses an hour early and close an hour earlier without changing clocks.

Endorsers: Charles E. Gibbs, Executive-Secy. Associated Farmers of Calif., Inc.

Election of November 7, 1950

PROPOSITION 1: Personal Property Taxation.

Type: Initiative Constitutional Amendment
Outcome: Rejected
Summary: The state and its political subdivisions cannot tax personal property, tangible or intangible. This shall not affect estate, inheritance, income, or other excise taxes.
Arguments For: California taxes the individual consumer more heavily than any other state. Consumer and income taxes support California's educational and welfare program. As a source of local revenue, personal property tax is negative.
Endorsers: James O. Stevenson, Dir., Los Angeles Bureau of Municipal Research; John C. Goff, Atty.; United Taxpayers, Inc.; Calif. Comm. for Repeal of Personal Property Tax.
Arguments Against: This will bring financial chaos to local governments. It would upset the state tax structure. To make up for the revenue loss, new or increased taxes would be necessary. This proposition would benefit a few at the cost of many. Personal property taxes do not hamper California's industrial growth.
Endorsers: Von T. Ellsworth, Director of Research and Legislative Representative, Calif. Farm Bureau Fed.; Arthur F. Corey, State Executive Secy., Calif. Teachers' Assn.; James L. Beebe, Chairman, State and Local Government Comm., Los Angeles Chamber of Commerce.

PROPOSITION 6: Legalizing and Licensing Gambling.
Type: Initiative Constitutional Amendment
Outcome: Rejected
Summary: Allows for wagering and gambling in licensed places. A five-member state commission will issue licenses and supervise the gambling. Includes a tax on money wagered, with revenue going to the pension and welfare fund for the aged and blind. The Horse Racing Board will have continued licensing authority.
Arguments For: It will help decrease taxes. Bookmakers would have to pay taxes like everyone else. It is a good law that will work.
Endorsers: Roy G. Owens, Vice-Pres., Pension and Taxpayers Union, Inc.; Glen S. Wilson, Former Townsend Plan National Field Representative; Aaron Sapiro, Attorney at Law.
Arguments Against: It will encourage big-time crime, civic corruption, and juvenile delinquency. The Commission is not subject to control by the governor or legislature.
Endorsers: Francis V. Keesling, Sr., Chairman, Californians Against the Gambling Combine; Mrs. Edward T. Walker, Pres., Calif. Congress of Parents and Teachers; Mrs. Chalmers McGaughey, Chairman, Southern Calif. Citizens Comm.

PROPOSITION 10: Public Housing Projects.
Type: Initiative Constitutional Amendment
Outcome: Approved
Summary: The electors must first vote in favor of a proposition before any low-rent housing project can be established by the state. Those eligible would be persons of low income, financed or assisted by the federal government or state public body. Exempted are projects that are contracts between the state public body and federal government.
Arguments For: This will give the people the right to vote on housing projects.
Endorsers: Earl Desmond, State Senator, Sacramento County; Frederick C. Dockweiler.
Arguments Against: It is unnecessary. It will increase taxes. California has an adequate statute already. The people already have adequate control and this will only slow down procedures.
Endorsers: Chris N. Jespersen, State Senator, 29th Dist.; C.J. Haggerty, Secy., Calif. State Fed. of Labor, A.F. of L.; Fletcher Bowron, Mayor of the City of Los Angeles.

Election of November 4, 1952

PROPOSITION 2: Public School Funds.
Type: Initiative Constitutional Amendment
Outcome: Approved
Summary: State support would be increased to $180 per year per student in public schools so that within each local school district students wouldn't receive less than $120. This would become effective July 1, 1953.
Arguments For: We need to provide good educational opportunity for the children. With pressures of inflation and the population, schools are only left with three choices to find more funds: (1) increase taxes, (2) cut school services, or (3) increase revenues from the broader state tax base to relieve pressures on homeowners. This would place more of the burden on the state rather than the taxpayer.
Endorsers: Mrs. P.D. Bevil, Pres., Calif. Congress of Parents and Teachers; Assemblyman Francis Dunn, Jr., Chairman, Assembly Comm. on Education, Calif. State Legislature; Arthur Corey, Executive Secy., Calif. Teachers Assn.
Arguments Against: We want to continue the present system. This proposition will stop the legislature from continuing to pass laws which have been alleviating the problem. The increased taxes proposed will give teachers higher salaries but they already have the highest in the nation.
Endorsers: Von T. Ellsworth, Ph.D., Director, Research Dept., Calif. Farm Bureau Fed.; A. C. Hardison, LL.D., Pres., Calif. Taxpayers Assn.

PROPOSITION 3: Taxation: Welfare Exemption of Non-profit School Property.
Type: Referendum
Outcome: Approved
Summary: The act under reconsideration would extend property tax exemption (called welfare exemption) to property used for schools of less than collegiate grade, owned and operated by nonprofit religious, hospital, or charitable organizations.
Arguments For the existing legislation, Against this referendum: This will help solve the shortage of schools in California. It will mainly affect grade schools and high schools, and schools for the blind, deaf-mute, crippled, palsied, and mentally retarded. Taxation of church-financed schools violates the traditional separation of church and state. Parents of non-tax-supported schools will still pay taxes for public schools.
Endorsers: Fleet Admiral Chester V. Nimitz, Regent, University of Calif.; C.J. Haggerty, Secy.-Treas., Calif. State Fed. of Labor; Adrien J. Falk, Past Pres., Calif. State Chamber of Commerce.
Arguments Against the existing legislation, For this referendum: This would add more millions to the already too large amount of private property exempt from taxation. Also, there is no limit to the extent of this proposed exemption. The parochial schools are competing with free public schools. Also, this measure violates the principle of separation of church and state. This should be voted against now because it was voted against twice before.
Endorsers: Charles Albert Adams, Former Member, State Board of Education, Founder of Public Schools Week; Henry W. Coil, Attorney-at-Law; Alfred J. Lundberg, Past Pres., Calif. State Chamber of Commerce.

PROPOSITION 10: Public Funds: Certain Expenditures Prohibited.
Type: Initiative Constitutional Amendment
Outcome: Rejected
Summary: Prohibits appropriation or expenditure of public money to California State Chamber of Commerce, any local Chamber of Commerce, County Supervisors Association, or private organization that tries to influence legislation. This is in effect retroactively and the Attorney General can take action to recover past money.
Arguments For: Money given to these sources is a misuse of funds. This proposition will stop these organizations playing politics with tax money.
Endorsers: Richard Richards, Chairman, Los Angeles Democratic County Central Comm.; John S. Borcome, Member and Former Chairman, Los Angeles Republican County Central Comm.; George McLain, Chairman, Calif. Institute of Social Welfare.

Arguments Against: This is purely a retaliatory measure. Projects carried on by these organizations with public funds would end.
2. **Endorsers:** Ralph Taylor, Executive-Secy., Agricultural Council of Calif.; John Home, Past Commander, American Legion, Department of Calif.; Walter Swanson, Vice-Pres. and General Manager, San Francisco Convention and Tourist Bureau.

PROPOSITION 11: Payment to Aged Persons
Type: Indirect Initiative
Outcome: Approved
Summary: Places the old age security program under state administration, eliminating county administration. Repeals relatives' responsibility requirements. The maximum of $75 for monthly payments would increase with the cost-of-living, with certain limits. There would be state payments up to $25 monthly for health services and up to $150 for funeral expenses. Property qualifications for recipients would be changed.
Arguments For: The elderly need relief from their misery and suffering. We need to honor our elderly (as God said to Honor thy Father and Mother).
Endorsers: Mrs. Amelia Mayberry, Pioneer Organizer of Calif. P.T.A. Age 88; Mrs. Eva Warring, 79-year-old Gold Star Mother; George McLain, Chairman, Calif. Institute of Social Welfare.
Arguments Against: This is too costly. This new burden would require higher taxes. Financially-able children should take care of their parents. We need our money for education.
Endorsers: L.A. Alesen, M.D., Pres., Calif. Medical Assn.; James L. Beebe, Chairman, State and Local Government Comm., Los Angeles Chamber of Commerce; Francis V. Keesling, Sr.

PROPOSITION 13: Elections: Prohibiting Cross-Filing.
Type: Indirect Initiative
Outcome: Rejected
Summary: No one can be a candidate or nominee of a political party for any office unless he has been registered as affiliated with such party for at least three months prior to filing nomination papers.
Arguments For: Cross-filing is a double-cross against the people. How can one person be both Republican and Democratic? It is political hypocrisy.
Endorsers: John B. Elliott, Chairman, Abolish-Cross Filing in Calif.; Edward H. Tickle, Chairman, Californians for Responsible Party Government.
Arguments Against: Cross-filing eliminates political boss control. This has strengthened the 2-party system, not weakened it. Cross-filing gives people a real voice.

Endorsers: James J. McBride, State Senator, Ventura County; Mrs. Mildred Prince, Past Pres., Pro-America of Calif.; Joseph Scott, Attorney.

Election of November 2, 1954

PROPOSITION 4: Aid to Needy Aged.
Type: Initiative Statute
Outcome: Rejected
Summary: Aid is increased to the aged who meet the requirements of the Welfare and Institution's Code. Maximum monthly will now be $100, and the legislature can only increase, not decrease this amount. These payments are to be regarded as the income of the recipient alone. The state Treasury would pay the state share.
Arguments For: California does not pay the highest aid. Statistics show the actual need is $101 per month, not $80. Many of the aged have experienced malnutrition because of this.
Endorsers: George McLain, Chairman, Calif. Institute of Social Welfare; John A. Despol, Secy.-Treas., Calif. Industries Union Council, CIO; George W. Ballard, State Representative, Calif. Legislative Board, Brotherhood of Railroad Trainmen.
Arguments Against: It will cost millions and threaten America's finest pension system. It will drain the already over-extended state treasury. Our payments are already one-third higher than the national average. This proposition is just another grab for political power by George McLain.
Endorsers: Mrs. G.W. Luhr, 3335 Freeman Road, Walnut Creek; Mr. Louis A. Rozzoni, First Vice-Pres., Calif. Farm Bureau Fed.; Mr. Joseph Scott, 1151 South Broadway, Los Angeles.

Election of November 6, 1956

PROPOSITION 4: Oil and Gas Conservation.
Type: Initiative Statute
Outcome: Rejected
Summary: Prohibits waste. Provides for unit operation of pools to increase ultimate recovery on agreements of three-fourths of the pool. The California Oil and Gas Conservation Commission will be created to prevent waste, including by limiting production. It will provide for wide spacing and pooling of spacing units in new pools.
Arguments For: Only 25% of oil is being recovered. This means fewer jobs and millions of dollars lost in taxes. We need to increase production to battle

against increasing gas prices, to safeguard against higher taxes, to increase employment, and for greater national security.

Endorsers: Brig. Gen. Warren T. Hannum (Ret.), Former Director of the State Dept. of National Resources, San Francisco; Roger Kent, Attorney, interested in conservation; Lewis Gough, Republican Comm., Past National Commander, American Legion, Los Angeles.

Arguments Against: Labor is against this proposition because it will mean unemployment, increased taxes, and increased gas prices. This is slick oil control legislation. The oil companies will profit tremendously. It will force us to rely on foreign oil too much.

Endorsers: Charles E. Robinson, Bakersfield, Secy., District Council No. 1, Oil, Chemical and Atomic Workers Union, AFL-CIO, Acting Chairman, statewide Union Labor Comm. vs. Proposition 4; Calif. Comm. Opposed to Oil Monopoly, W.H. Geis, Chairman, Los Angeles; Joseph F. Taylor, Rear Admiral, U.S.N. Ret., Los Angeles.

Election of November 4, 1958

PROPOSITION 16: Taxation of School Property of Religious and Other Nonprofit Organizations.
Type: Initiative Constitutional Amendment
Outcome: Rejected
Summary: Amends Section 1c of Article XIII of the State Constitution. States that property that is to be exempted will no longer include religious or private schools. It will only include schools for the blind, mentally retarded, or physically handicapped.

Arguments For: It would no longer allow exemptions for private or religiously controlled schools. Presently, we have a separation of church and state that must not continue. Also, public funds would no longer be diverted for private purposes.

Endorsers: Tully C. Knoles, Educator, Stockton; Dorothy H. Rogers, San Francisco; John A. Owen, Pres., Californians for Public Schools, Los Angeles.

Arguments Against: It will raise taxes. It punishes religious schools. It is un-American to tax schools. It is condemned by both political parties and the AFL-CIO. It threatens religious and educational freedoms.

Endorsers: Bert W. Levit, Immediate Past Pres., San Francisco Bd. of Education, Immediate Past Pres., Calif. State Boards Assn.; Justus F. Craemer, State Chairman, Citizens United Against Taxing Schools, Pres., Calif. Press Assn., Past Pres., Calif. Newspaper Publishers Assn.; The Rev. Kenneth W. Cary, Chairman, "Protestants United Against Taxing Schools," representing the Episcopal Dioceses in Calif.

PROPOSITION 17: State Sales, Use and Income Tax Rates.
Type: Initiative Statute
Outcome: Rejected
Summary: Sales and use tax would be reduced from 3% to 2%. Income tax rates would be changed to range from one-half of one percent on incomes under $5000, to 46% on incomes over $50,000. Legislature can only lower, not increase sales and use taxes. A change of income tax rates would be permitted only by a vote of the people. The sales and use tax will become effective January 1, 1959, and the income tax after December 31, 1957.
Arguments For: This measure will bring justice to the taxpayers who unfairly pay more than their share, shifting more of the tax burden to the wealthiest, who are currently under-taxed. It will protect the revenue of the state, and will meet the existing deficit in a just manner. Education is not threatened by this change. The revised income tax would offset losses from the sales tax.
Endorsers: Mrs. Anne Dippel, Mrs. Hazel Davis, Co-Chairmen, Citizens Comm. for Tax Equality; C.J. Haggerty, Secy.-Treas., Calif. State Fed. of Labor.
Arguments Against: This proposition would jeopardize education, welfare programs, veterans' programs, and, most of all, opportunity in California. The decrease in sales tax will mean a loss of $50 million this year, and as much as $200 million per year within five years. The new income tax rates will drive people and businesses from the state, jeopardize the state's credit, and require additional property taxes.
Endorsers: Richard Owens, Calif. Farm Bureau Fed.; James Musatti, Secy.-Treas., Calif. State Chamber of Commerce; Arthur F. Corey, Gen. Mgr., Calif. Teachers Assn.

PROPOSITION 18: Employer-Employee Relations.
Type: Initiative Constitutional Amendment
Outcome: Rejected
Summary: Adds Section 1-A to Article I of the Constitution. Employers and employee organizations are prohibited from entering into collective bargaining which establishes membership in a labor organization or payment of dues as a condition of employment. Each person should be allowed to voluntarily join a labor organization. Rights shall not be affected because of non-membership or membership. If anyone is denied employment because of non-membership, damages may be sought.
Arguments For: It would protect workers against unfair practices of employers and union officers. Union membership would be made voluntary.
Endorsers: Arthur E. Simpson, Member, Local 770, Retail Clerks Union; August E. Sommerfield, Former Steward, Local 170, Sheetmetal Workers Union, Calif. Coordinator, Comm. for Democracy in Labor Unions; Howard

B. Wyatt, Member, Local 626, Teamsters Union, Executive Secy., Comm. for Democracy in Labor Unions.

Arguments Against: Registered opposition: Pres. Eisenhower, Adlai Stevenson, Vice Pres. Nixon, Chief Justice Earl Warren, Governor Goodwin J. Knight, Congressman Clair Engle, Attorney General Edmund G. Brown, U.S. Senator Thomas Kuchel, Lt. Governor Harold Powers, late Senator Robert A. Taft of Ohio.

Endorsers: Benjamin H. Swig, Pres., Fairmont Hotel Co, San Francisco; Charles J. Smith, Director, District 38, United Steelworkers of America, Los Angeles; C.J. Haggerty, Secy.-Treas., Calif. State Fed. of Labor.

Election of November 8, 1960

PROPOSITION 15: Senate Reapportionment.
Type: Initiative Statute
Outcome: Rejected
Summary: Establishes and apportions 40 Senatorial Districts. All senators would be elected in 1962, with one half of the senators to be elected every 2 years thereafter. Districts would be made according to population, area, and economic affinity. After each federal census, districts may be reapportioned.
Arguments For: We do not have enough senators to adequately represent our rapidly growing population.
Endorsers: Frank G. Bonelli, Chairman, Board of Supervisors, Los Angeles County; Mrs. Leiland Atherton Irish, Civic Leader; James L. Beebe, Chairman, State and Local Government Comm., Los Angeles Chamber of Commerce.
Arguments Against: It is a reckless State Senate-packing scheme.
Endorsers: J.F. Sullivan Jr., Chairman, Californians Against Proposition No. 15; George W. Milas, Immediate Past Chairman, Republican State Central Comm.; Joseph L. Wyatt Jr., Pres., Calif. Democratic Council.

Election of November 6, 1962

PROPOSITION 23: Senate Reapportionment.
Type: Initiative Constitutional Amendment
Outcome: Rejected
Summary: Fifty Senatorial Districts would be established (instead of forty). Elections for Senators would occur in 1962, with one half of all to be elected every two years. Additional districts would be allocated to single county districts based on population. Boundaries shall be fixed by the legislature in 1963. Following each federal census, districts can be reapportioned according to population, area, and economic affinity.

Arguments For: Protect your voting rights! Endorsed by: San Francisco Examiner, Los Angeles Herald-Examiner, Los Angeles Times, Pres. John F. Kennedy, Governor Edmund G. Brown, Ex-Vice Pres. Nixon.

Endorsers: Frank G. Bonnelli, Supervisor, Los Angeles County; John W. Quimby, Executive Secy.-Treas., San Diego County, Central Labor Council; Felix S. LeMarinel, Orange County, Past Pres., Calif. State Junior Chamber of Commerce.

Arguments Against: It was poorly drafted. Urban areas are already protected by the governor and Assembly. All interests are already effectively represented by the California legislature. Urban areas are well represented in the Senate already.

Endorsers: John A. Murdy, Jr., Senator from Orange County, 35th Dist.; Joseph A. Rattigan, Senator from Sonoma County, 12th Dist.; Jerome R. Waldie, Antioch, Majority Leader, Calif. State Assembly.

PROPOSITION 24: Subversive Activities.
Type: Initiative Constitutional Amendment
Outcome: Rejected
Summary: Communist and subversive organizations are denied political party status and tax exemption. Members of these organizations cannot hold public office or be employed by the state. Teachers and employees of public educational institutions are required to answer Congressional Committee inquiries about their affiliation to these organizations.

Arguments For: The Communist Party should be outlawed. California is a prime target for the Communist Party.

Endorsers: Louis Francis, Member of Calif. Legislature, 25th Assembly Dist., San Mateo County; Judge Byron J. Walters, Los Angeles County; Malcolm Champlin, Past State Commander, American Legion, Calif. Department, and Ex-FBI Agent.

Arguments Against: Extremists would have the power to destroy our liberty. It would destroy legal protection of the innocent. The amendment is unnecessary because we already have laws controlling Communists.

Endorsers: Governor Brown and Richard Nixon. Joseph A. Ball, Lawyer; John Anson Ford, Chairman, Calif. Fair Employment Practices Comm. and former Chairman, Los Angeles County Board of Supervisors; Rt. Rev. James A. Pike, J.S.D., Bishop of the Episcopal Diocese of Calif.

Election of November 3, 1964

PROPOSITION 14: Sales and Rentals of Residential Real Property.
Type: Initiative Constitutional Amendment

Outcome: Approved

Summary: The state cannot deny anyone the right to decline to sell, lease, or rent residential property to anyone he chooses. This does not include property owned by the state or transient lodging accommodations by hotels or similar public places.

Arguments For: This would allow owners to choose buyers and renters without state or local government interference. This right was lost with the Rumford Act of 1963 when the owner could not refuse to sell or rent based on race, color, religion, national origin, or ancestry.

Endorsers: L.H. Wilson, Fresno, Calif., Chairman, Comm. for Home Protection; Jack Schrade, State Senator, San Diego County; Robert L. Snell, Oakland, Calif., Pres., Calif. Apartment Owners Assn.

Arguments Against: This proposition is a deception. It would destroy all existing fair housing laws. It would deny millions the right to buy a home. It is not legally sound. It is bigotry. It is a threat to the economy.

Endorsers: Rev. Dr. Myron C. Cole, Pres., Council of Churches in Southern Calif.; Most Reverend Hugh A. Donohoe, Bishop, Catholic Diocese of Stockton; Stanley Mosk, Attorney General of Calif.

PROPOSITION 15: Television Programs.

Type: Initiative Statute

Outcome: Approved

Summary: Subscription television business is prohibited. Television programs transmitted to home television sets will be free of charge. This is not applicable to community, hotel, or apartment antenna systems, or non-profit educational systems.

Arguments For: You will be forced to pay what you now get for free unless this act is passed. Preserve your right to free television.

Endorsers: Don Belding, Chairman, Citizens' Comm. for Free-TV, Director, Eversharp Corp., Financial Corporation of America; Mrs. Fred S. Gerri Teasley, Vice Chairman, Citizens' Comm. for Free-TV and Radio-TV Chairman, Calif. Fed. of Women's Clubs; George Johns, Executive Secy., San Francisco Central Labor Council.

Arguments Against: Vote NO and it will ensure better TV programming. It will not affect commercial TV. This proposition will only serve the theater owners.

Endorsers: S.L. Weaver, Jr., Pres., Subscription, TV, Inc.; Ralph Bellamy, Acting Pres., Fair Trial for Pay TV Council; Ralph Clare, Secy., Joint Council of Teamsters of Southern Calif.

PROPOSITION 16: Lottery.

Type: Initiative Constitutional Amendment
Outcome: Rejected
Summary: A state Lottery Commission is created, as well as a state lottery with monthly drawings. The Commission will issue only one license to a corporation for ten years to conduct the lottery. 74% of the money will go to public education and 26% to the Commission and prizes.
Arguments For: It will help lower taxes. It will help aid the schools without burdening taxpayers. Instead of money going to Las Vegas or to the Irish Sweepstakes, we can keep it in California.
Endorsers: Robert W. Wilson, Proponent of Initiative; Tessie Smith, Proponent of Initiative; Virginia Crawford, Proponent of Initiative.
Arguments Against: The private corporation would get 13% of the proceeds. The promoters are using education to sell the scheme. Lotteries are a tax on the poor.
Endorsers: Laughlin E. Waters, State Chairman, Former State Legislator, and Former U.S. Attorney; Don Fazackerley, Co-Chairman, No. Calif., Former San Francisco Police Commissioner; Eugene W. Biscailuz, Co-Chairman, So. Calif., Past Pres., State Peace Officers Assn.

PROPOSITION 17: Railroad Train Crews.
Type: Initiative Statute
Outcome: Approved
Summary: Declares a state policy on manning trains. Award No. 282 of the Federal Arbitration Board shall be effective in California. No law shall prevent a railroad from manning trains in accordance with federal legislation. Would repeal initiative provisions on crews for certain trains like freight, mixed, and work.
Arguments For: It would provide for the gradual elimination of firemen on 90% of freight trains as they are no longer necessary. It repeals outmoded "excess crews" laws and allows for real collective bargaining procedures.
Endorsers: Senator Hugh M. Burns, D, Fresno, Pres. Pro Tem, Calif. State Senate; John F. McCarthy, State Senator, 13th Dist.; Dr. Muriel B. Duncan, Los Angeles State Women's Club Leader.
Arguments Against: The present law protects the general public. There would no longer be a state or federal agency controlling the safe manning of trains.
Endorsers: James L. Evans, Chairman, Brotherhood of Locomotive Firemen and Enginemen, AFL-CIO, State Legislative Board; G.W. Ballard, State Representative, Brotherhood of Railroad Trainmen, AFL-CIO.

Election of November 8, 1966

PROPOSITION 16: Obscenity.
Type: Initiative Statute
Outcome: Rejected
Summary: Obscene matter and conduct are prohibited. Obscenity is redefined and procedures are given for prosecution. It is a felony to conspire to violate obscenity laws. Obscene matter may be seized to determine its character. Obscenity cases would be tried by a jury.
Arguments For: This will protect the children. Our present law is too weak and leads to publishers and distributors avoiding any prosecutions. 600,000 Californians have signed petitions to have this initiative placed on the ballot.
Endorsers: Chaplain E. Richard Barnes, Captain, U.S. Navy (Ret.), Assemblyman, 78th Dist.; Lloyd Wright Sr., Past Pres., American Bar Assn.; Jay Kaufman, Ph.D, Consulting Psychologist.
Arguments Against: This amendment is drastic, badly written, and unconstitutional. It would not protect works of art and literature.
Endorsers: Directors of No. Calif. Council of Churches; Calif. Library Assn.; City Attorney of San Diego; Bishop Donald Harvey Tippett, Pres., No. Calif. Council of Churches; Charles Warren, Assemblyman, 56th Dist., Calif. Legislature; Martha Boaz, Past Chairman, Comm. on Intellectual Freedom, American Library Assn.

Election of November 5, 1968

PROPOSITION 9: Taxation. Limitations on Property Tax Rate.
Type: Initiative Constitutional Amendment
Outcome: Rejected
Summary: Reduces ad valorem taxes on property to an amount no greater than one percent of its market value. As of July 1, 1969, the total annual taxes levied on property for any fiscal year, when added to ad valorem special assessments for the immediately prior fiscal year, could not exceed one percent of the market value of the property, to provide for the total cost of property-related services, except for the payment of bonds.
Arguments For: This measure will lower property taxes, which have doubled in the last 15 years, by an average of fifty percent. It removes school and welfare costs from property taxes; after 1973, property tax monies can only be used for financing property-related services, plus bonds and long-term lease charges. A property tax is a good tax only if it is limited to services which enhance and maintain the value of a property. This benefits not only property owners, but tenants as well, since higher property taxes mean higher rents. Legislators will have five years to look for alternative sources for additional money.

Endorsers: Philip E. Watson, Assessor, Los Angeles County; David N. Robinson, Past Pres., Calif. Real Estate Assn.; Everett C. McKeage, Former Judge of the Superior Court of Calif., Co-Chairman, Citizens Comm. for Property Tax Limitation, Inc.

Arguments Against: This measure will reduce taxes for a few huge landowners, landlords, and apartment house owners, and will mean heavier taxes for most Californians. It prohibits expenditures for schools and welfare services, while making no provision for revenue replacement. Public schools, which derive fifty percent of their budgets from property taxes, would be severely hurt. Its limitation on bond financing could destroy the state water project. Other state taxes would have to be sharply increased.

Endorsers: Robert C. Brown, Exec. Vice-Pres., Calif. Taxpayers Assn.; Jack Rees, State Exec. Secy., Calif. Teachers Assn.; Joseph Diviny, Vice-Pres., International Brotherhood of Teamsters.

Election of June 2, 1970

PROPOSITION 8: Taxation for Schools and Social Welfare.
Type: Initiative Constitutional Amendment
Outcome: Rejected
Summary: Provides educational revenue from sources other than property taxes. It specifies that an amount of not less than 50% of the cost for public schools, exclusive of capital outlay and federal funds, be provided by sources other than property taxes. Also specifies that 90% of the costs for social welfare services be provided by outside sources. The homeowners property tax exemption would be increased from $750 to $1,000. If this measure is passed, additional financing from state sources in the amount of $1,130,000 would be required. The educational system is defined as kindergarten, elementary, high schools, technical schools, and community colleges. The measure does not provide for sources of revenue; therefore the legislature would be forced to seek alternative ways to finance education.

Arguments For: Reduction of property taxes. Makes no change in the present level of welfare support. It does not increase total welfare cost. It only requires the legislature to fund new county programs mandated by the state legislature. Proposition 8 grants relief immediately

Endorsers: Margaret L. Lemmer, Pres., Calif. Teachers Assn.; Sig Sanchez, Pres., County Supervisors Assn. of Calif.

Arguments Against: State income or sales taxes could increase. State property taxes will not decrease. There are no cost controls. Teachers will press for salary increases. Rich school districts will get richer and poor ones will get poorer. The school board will bypass state mandated rates through loopholes.

This measure assumes needs never change. The state will take away decision making on many issues from local government.

Endorsers: Robert C. Brown, Executive Vice-Pres., Calif. Taxpayers Assn.; Mrs. Edward Rudin, Pres., League of Women Voters of Calif.

Election of November 2, 1970

Proposition 10: Interest Rate Limitation.
Type: Referendum Constitutional Amendment
Outcome: Rejected
Summary: Eliminates Section 22 of Article XX of the state constitution, which provides for a maximum interest rate of ten percent on all loans in excess of $100,000. Exempts from this section loans made by savings and loans, industrial loan companies, credit unions, banks, pawnbrokers, personal property brokers, and certain agricultural non-profit cooperatives. The legislature is authorized to provide, by statute, maximum rates of interest and other compensation charges for loans made by these exempt organizations.

Arguments For the existing legislation, Against this referendum: This measure will generate new sources of revenue and relieve pressure on property taxes. There is an urgent need to bring new capital into California; thirty states have no such restrictions, and California cannot compete with its current ceilings. Low rates cause tight money, and are particularly hurtful to the construction industry. The legislature is still permitted to set justifiable interest rates, as allowed by market conditions.

Endorsers: Paul Priolo, Assemblyman, Chairman, Elections and Constitutional Amendments Comm.; Joseph Kennick, State Senator; Art Linkletter, Entertainer, State Chairman, YES on Prop. 10.

Arguments Against the existing legislation, For this referendum: The measure eliminates protection against usury. Current provisions place no restrictions on banks that do business with the consumer.

Endorsers: William Campbell, Assemblyman, 50th Dist.

Election of June 6, 1972

Proposition 9: Environment.
Type: Initiative Statute
Outcome: Rejected
Summary: Establishes permissible compositions for fuel. Calls for shutting down plants violating air quality standards. Imposes restrictions on leasing and extraction of oil and gas from tidelands or submerged lands, or on—shore

areas within one mile of the mean high tide line, and prohibits construction of atomic-powered electric generating plants for five years. Establishes restrictions on the manufacture, sale, and use of pesticides; prohibits enforcement officials from having conflicting interests; provides for relief by injunction and mandate to prevent violations; and imposes penal sanctions and civil penalties.

Arguments For: This measure amends and reinforces state laws, and requires performance, conformance, and compliance. It will clean our beaches and waters, and require that state polluters and automobile manufacturers meet state standards. It will create new jobs, better health, and a stronger economy. It will save the state more than $4 billion per year from environmentally-caused medical problems, consumer costs, and material damage.

Endorsers: William M. Bennett, Member, Calif. State Board of Equalization, Attorney; Fortney H. Stark, Jr., Pres., Security National Bank; Hijinio Romo, URW-131, AFL-CIO.

Arguments Against: The measure would set back environmental improvement and would hurt California's economy. It would take many years and a great deal of money to build refineries that could produce the called-for fuel in quantity. Our transportation system would cease to operate, and the resultant shift from buses to automobiles would cause even greater pollution. Massive unemployment would occur. It would ban pesticides for which there are no known substitutes. The ban on construction of nuclear power plants removes the only current source of clean energy.

Endorsers: Joseph J. Diviny, Pres., Calif. Teamsters Legislative Council; Myron W. Doornboos, Pres., So. Council of Conservation Clubs, Inc.; J. E. McKee, Professor of Environmental Engineering.

Election of November 7, 1972

PROPOSITION 14: Property Tax Limitation.
Type: Initiative Constitutional Amendment
Outcome: Approved
Summary: Establishes ad valorem property tax rate limitations for all purposes except payment of designated types of debts and liabilities. Eliminates property tax for welfare purposes, limits property tax for education, and requires state funding of these functions from other taxes. Increases sales, cigarette, distilled spirits, and corporation taxes. Decreases state taxes on insurance companies and banks, and local sales and use taxes. Requires severance tax on extraction of minerals and hydrocarbons. Requires two-thirds vote of legislature to increase designated taxes. Restricts new exemptions from property tax to those approved by election. Financial Impact: A net ascertainable decrease in revenues to state and local government in excess of $1,233,000,000.

Arguments For: Reduces homeowner property taxes by 40%, will curtail rent increases, and will raise corporate taxes while leaving personal income taxes unchanged. Prohibits property taxes to pay for welfare. Prohibits property taxes on household furnishings and personal effects. Eliminates tax exemptions currently held by banks and corporations. People have lost their homes and young people cannot afford housing because of increased property taxes. Ensures a minimum of $825 per pupil allocated towards education, more than is provided today. The major beneficiaries of this proposal are homeowners and renters—not large landowners. The opponents do not admit to special interest loopholes that currently exists for insurance companies, apartment house complexes, stocks, bonds, etc.

Endorsers: Phillip E. Watson, Assessor, Los Angeles County; Joseph B. Carnahan, Pres., Calif. Real Estate Assn.; Allan Grant, Pres., Calif. Farm Bureau Fed.

Arguments Against: This means higher taxes for the average citizen; taxes will be shifted from the large landowners to homeowners and renters. This cuts back vital funds from fire and police protection, schools, transit, and other important government services. Assessors can retain the power to increase the market value of your home, which would wipe out property tax savings in a few years. Property taxes will not be reduced until 1977, while increased consumer taxes will begin immediately. Landlords are not required to pass on their savings to tenants. Sales taxes will go up 40% and other consumer taxes as much as 100%. Among organizations representing Proposition 14 are large corporations and wealthy landowners. Business and non-residential property accounts for over 70% of the property taxes. Proposition 14 would damage our educational system. Public transit will be adversely affected.

Endorsers: Dr. Norman Topping, Chairman, Californians Against Higher Taxes, Chancellor, University of Southern Calif.; Wilson Riles, Supt. of Public Instruction; Mrs. Walter Schuiling, Pres., League of Women Voters.

PROPOSITION 15: State Employee Salaries.
Type: Initiative Constitutional Amendment
Outcome: Rejected
Summary: Requires State Personnel Board, University of California Regents, and State University and College Trustees semiannually to determine prevailing rates in private and public employment for services comparable to those performed by state employees, to set salaries and benefits necessary to equal prevailing rates. The recommendations must be included in governor's budget, cannot be reduced or eliminated except by two-thirds vote of legislature, and are not subject to governor's veto. Provides for written agreements and arbitration between state and employees on other employer-employee relation matters. Financial Impact: Indeterminable but potential major cost increase.

Arguments For: Put an end to work stoppages in critical areas such as education, hospitals, and law enforcement. Limit state salaries so that the average prevailing pay rates in the private sector are paid. Give fair pay adjustments to civil servants. Give civil servants collective bargaining rights. **Endorsers:** Yvonne Brathwaite, Assemblywoman, 63rd Dist.; Edwin L. Z'Berg, Assemblyman, 9th Dist.; Cornelius G. Dutcher, San Diego Business Leader **Arguments Against:** There would be automatic increases in salaries and benefits for employees of the state of California in the budget presented to the state legislature. It also would remove the governor from participating in decisions on the amount of money to be made available for salary and benefit increases for state employees. This violates the principal of checks and balances by eliminating the governor as head of the executive branch in participating in establishing salaries and benefits for state employees. This would reduce a governor's power to veto salary and benefit increases in the budget, which is a basic part of our constitutional system. Collective bargaining should not be frozen into the constitution. It would be better to make it part of statutory law which can be more readily changed. This proposition specifies binding arbitration as the only means of resolving disputes, which is not limited to the interpretation of the contractual agreement.
Endorsers: Mrs. Nita Ashcraft, Pres., Calif. State Personnel Board; Stephen P. Teale, State Senator, 3rd Dist.; Frank Lanterman, Assemblyman, 47th Dist.

PROPOSITION 16: Salaries, California Highway Patrol.
Type: Initiative Constitutional Amendment
Outcome: Rejected
Summary: Requires state Personnel Board to: (1) Determine maximum salary for each class of policeman or deputy sheriff in each city and county within state, (2) adjust salaries of uniformed members of highway patrol to at least the maximum rate paid policemen or deputy sheriffs within comparable classes, and (3) report annually to governor on its determinations and adjustments. Requires governor to provide in budget for full implementation of these determinations and adjustments. These budget provisions can be modified or stricken only by two-thirds vote of legislature, voting solely on this issue. Financial Impact: indeterminable but potential major cost increase.
Arguments For: This provides salary parity without an increase in taxes. Annual salary adjustment would be based on a periodic salary survey conducted by the state personnel board and approved, reduced, or rejected by the legislature as part of the annual budget act. Forty-eight other agencies of law enforcement receive higher salaries than the highway patrol. This proposition would ensure that the highway patrol officers are paid a salary equal to other police officers who perform similar duties.

Endorsers: Kenneth B. Anderson, Sergeant, CHP, Pres., Cal Assn. of Highway Patrolmen; Ralph L. Schiquone, Executive Manager, Cal. Assn. of Highway Patrolmen.

Arguments Against: This would automatically raise the salary of state traffic officers to match the highest paid salary to any policeman or deputy sheriff in the state. It would continue escalating the cost of government. It would be difficult for the legislature to limit the salary increases. This would remove a governor's ability to reduce or veto this item to protect the taxpayers' interests. This will lead to dissatisfaction and unrest for other groups of employees who do not receive the same favored treatment. This gives preferential treatment to one group of citizens and erodes the constitutional system of checks and balances.

Endorsers: Mrs. Nita Aschcraft, Pres., Calif. State Personnel Board; Stephen P. Teale, State Senator, 3rd Dist.; Frank Lanterman, Assemblyman, 4th Dist.

PROPOSITION 17: Death Penalty.
Type: Initiative Constitutional Amendment
Outcome: Approved
Summary: Amends California constitution to provide that all state statutes in effect February 17, 1972, requiring, authorizing, imposing, or relating to the death penalty are in full force and effect, subject to legislative amendment or repeal by statute, initiative, or referendum. Provides that death penalty provided for under those state statutes shall not be deemed to be, or constitute, infliction of cruel or unusual punishment within meaning of California constitution, nor shall such punishment for such offenses be deemed to contravene any other provision of the California constitution. Financial Impact: None.

Arguments For: If this proposition passes, the California Supreme Court's ruling that the death penalty is unconstitutional will be overruled. This will allow the legislature to follow the guidelines of the U.S. Supreme Court allowing the death penalty. The death penalty serves as a deterrent to crime. Capital punishment is an appropriate penalty for certain crimes. Our legal system has safeguards which ensure a fair trial to every person charged with murder regardless of his wealth, education, or race.

Endorsers: George Deukmejan, State Senator, 37th Dist.; S.C. Masterson, Judge, Superior Court; John W. Holmdahl, State Senator, 8th Dist.

Arguments Against: We must be concerned with preventing instead of revenging crime. Killing is not the answer to the death problem; most civilized countries no longer use the death penalty. Stopping executions has not led to more murders. Most murders are committed in passion by people who do not think about penalties. The death penalty aggravates the crime problem by wasting resources needed to fight crime. Death row uses a lot of resources that could instead be used to rehabilitate criminals. It is cheaper to imprison a person for life than to execute him. Murderers imprisoned for life are not quickly released. The process of sentencing a person to execution is arbitrary. **Endorsers:** Edmund G. "Pat" Brown, Former Governor of Calif.; Erwin Loretz, Pres., Calif. Probation, Parole, and Correctional Association; Bill Cosby.

PROPOSITION 18: Obscenity Legislation.
Type: Initiative Statute
Outcome: Rejected
Summary: Amends, deletes, and adds Penal Code statutes relating to obscenity: defines nudity, obscenities, sadomasochistic abuse, sexual conduct, sexual excitement, and other related terms. Deletes "redeeming social importance" test. Limits "Contemporary Standards" test to the local area. Creates misdemeanors for selling, showing, producing, or distributing specified prohibited materials to adults or minors. Permits local governmental agencies to separately regulate these matters. Provides for county jail term and up to $10,000 fine for violations. Makes sixth conviction of specified misdemeanors a felony. Creates defenses and presumptions. Permits injunctions and seizures of materials. Requires speedy hearing and trial. Financial Impact: None.
Arguments For: States have a right to provide for children an environment conducive to their healthy emotional and moral development. Recent experience indicates California's obscenity laws are inadequate. This measure eliminates the exposure of children to pornography, which often cripples their emotional development. It eliminates a vague requirement in the law which states that for material to be obscene it must be without any redeeming social importance. It will allow legal authorities to more effectively eliminate pornography, and allow local communities to have control over pornographic materials.
Endorsers: John L. Harmer, State Senator, 21st Dist.; Woodruff J. Deem, Dist. Atty., Ventura County; Homer E. Young, Pornography Specialist, Federal Bureau of Investigation (Retired).
Arguments Against This would be a drastic form of censorship, affecting material in books, newspapers, motion pictures, sculpture, paintings, and records. It would abolish the protection given to recognized works of art and literature. California already bans obscenity to the extent constitutionally permissible. This proposition is so broad that it would make it a crime to exhibit a photograph that shows the nude or nearly nude body. An identical proposition of this nature was soundly defeated by the people of this state in 1966. This could spawn hundreds of new censorship laws. It empowers cities and countries to pass censorship laws going beyond those in the initiative. This proposition strangles basic freedoms of speech and press.

Endorsers: Father Charles Dollen, Library Director, University of San Diego; Rt. Reverend Richard Millard, Suffragan Bishop to Calif. Episcopal Bishop of San Jose; Charles Warren, Assemblyman, 56th Dist.

PROPOSITION 19: Marijuana Initiative.
Type: Initiative Statute
Outcome: Rejected
Summary: Removes state penalties for personal use. Proposes a statute which would provide that no person eighteen years or older shall be punished criminally or denied any right or privilege because of his planting, cultivating, harvesting, drying, processing, otherwise preparing, transporting, possessing, or using marijuana. Does not repeal existing, or limit future, legislation prohibiting persons under the influence of marijuana from engaging in conduct that endangers others. Financial Impact: none.

Arguments For: This proposition does not legalize the sale or encourage the use of marijuana. It recognizes the responsibility of government to maintain criminal penalties for activity under the influence of marijuana which may endanger others. The recommendation to legalize marijuana has come from Pres. Nixon's Commission on Marijuana, the Los Angeles County Grand Jury, the National Institutes of Mental Health, and the American Medical Association Drug Comm. Many sources agree that marijuana is not addictive and does not harm the body. Decriminalization is the best solution to changing people's behavior without destroying them. This proposition would save Californians hundreds of millions of dollars each year currently wasted on the needless arrest, prosecution, and jailing of otherwise innocent and law abiding citizens. Distortion of the dangers of marijuana leads young people to disbelieve the truth about heroin, amphetamines, and other dangerous drugs.

Endorsers: Joel Fort, M.D., Public Health Specialist and Criminologist, former consultant on drug abuse for the World Health Organization; Mary Jane Fernandez, Educator.; Gordon S. Brownell, J.D., former Member of White House Staff (1969-1970).

Arguments Against: The content of marijuana is tetrahydrocannabinol; very little research has been done on this chemical. One dangerous aspect of THC is progressive loss of inhibitions, distortion of judgement, distortion of space and time relationships, and abnormal alteration of all the senses. Marijuana is unpredictable because no quality controls are maintained. The chemistry of alcohol and tobacco is readily understood and their effects are generally predictable. The statement that marijuana is not physically addicting is misleading. Even one marijuana trip is dangerous because marijuana is the vehicle for crossing the psychological barrier to drug abuse. Liberalization of marijuana laws would be the green light for even more drug abuse. No civilized nation in the world permits the sale and use of marijuana by law.

India and Nigeria are examples of countries that have gone from legalization of marijuana to abolishing it.
Endorsers: H.L. Richardson, State Senator, 19th Dist.; Dr. Harden Jones, Ph.D., Professor of Medical Physics and Physiology, Asst. Director of Donner Laboratory, U.C. Berkeley.

PROPOSITION 20: Coastal Zone Conservation Act.
Type: Initiative Statute
Outcome: Approved
Summary: Creates State Coastal Zone Conservation Commission and Six Regional Commissions. Sets criteria for and requires submission of plan to legislature for preservation, protection, restoration, and enhancement of environment and ecology of coastal zone, as defined. Establishes permit area within coastal zone as the area between the seaward limits of state jurisdiction and 1,000 yards landward from the mean high tide line, subject to specified exceptions. Prohibits any development within permit area without permit by state or regional commission. Prescribes standards for issuance or denial of permits. Act terminates after 1976. This measure appropriates five million dollars for the period 1973 to 1976. Financial Impact: Cost to state of $1,250,000 per year plus undeterminable local government administrative costs.
Arguments For: The measure provides direct participation by the people in coastal planning; the commissions will comprise an equal number of citizens and elected officials. Public hearings will be held, and conflicts of interest will be prevented. California's beaches will be protected from corporate exploitation, and will be more available to all. It will stimulate growth of the $4.2 billion annual tourist industry and make new jobs. This will lead to a fair statewide plan for balanced development of our coast. It ensures that authorized construction will have no substantial adverse environmental effect. Homeowners can make minor repairs without any more permits than currently needed. The legislature can amend the act if necessary.
Endorsers: John V. Tunney, U.S. Senator; Donald Grunsky, State Senator; Bob Moretti, Assemblyman, Speaker, Calif. State Assembly.
Arguments Against Proposition 20 would impose an appointed super-government to control the destinies of almost 3½ million people. The California coastline is not endangered. Proposition 20 is a power grab by those who would bypass the democratic process. There will be a $25,750,000 loss in revenues if this passes, as values in the coastal zone are reduced. We will lose millions of dollars and thousands of jobs in needed development projects, and experience delay of needed ocean front and beach recreational projects. There will be a loss of local control of local affairs, and of property rights as private land use is denied. The elitists who will grab our coastline will continue to pursue the mountains, lakes, and streams for their own purposes. There will

be a threat of increased power shortages and possible brownouts because of delays in construction of new power generating plants.

Endorsers: James S. Lee, Pres., State Building and Construction Trades Council of Calif.; George Christopher, former Mayor of San Francisco; John J. Royal, Exec. Secy.-Treas., Fishermen's and Allied Workers Union, I.L.W.U.

PROPOSITION 21: Assignment of Students to Schools.

Type: Initiative Statute

Outcome: Approved

Summary: Adds section to Education Code providing: "No public school student shall, because of his race, creed, or color, be assigned to or be required to attend a particular school." Repeals section establishing policy that racial and ethnic imbalance in pupil enrollment in public schools shall be prevented and eliminated. Repeals section which (1) establishes factors for consideration in preventing or eliminating racial or ethnic imbalances in public schools; (2) requires school districts to report numbers and percentages of racial and ethnic groups in each school; and (3) requires districts to develop plans to remedy imbalances. Financial Impact: None.

Arguments For: This proposition will preserve your right to have your children attend schools in your neighborhood. It repeals the law that states it is the declared policy of the legislature that racial and ethnic imbalances in pupil enrollment shall be prevented and eliminated. This would eliminate the section of the Education Administration Code relating to attendance areas and practices, which has created legal chaos for school districts. Forced integration destroys the neighborhood school concept, while at the same time using tax dollars needed to upgrade our educational standards.

Endorsers: Floyd L. Wakefield, Assemblyman, 52nd Dist.; Dr. Robert Peterson, County Superintendent of Schools, Orange County; Ken Brown, Pres., Solano County Board of Education

Arguments Against: Passage of this proposition will encourage court-ordered busing. Its language has been declared unconstitutional unanimously by the U.S. Supreme Court. Local districts will not be able to adequately solve educational inequalities, so court ordered busing will take place. If the current guidelines are followed, planning can take place and busing can be avoided. This proposition does not remove local control. The current law allows local districts to identify problems and allow for long range discussion and solution.

Endorsers: John Cimolino, Pres., Calif. School Boards Assn.; Mrs. Erna Schuilling, Pres., League of Women Voters; William J. Bagley, Assemblyman, Marin and Sonoma Counties.

PROPOSITION 22: Agricultural Labor Relations.

Type: Initiative Statute
Outcome: Rejected
Summary: Sets forth permissible and prohibited labor relations activities of agricultural employers, employees, and labor organizations. Makes specified types of strikes, picketing, and boycotts unlawful. Defines unfair labor practices. Creates Agricultural Labor Relations Board with power to certify organizations as bargaining representatives, conduct elections therefor, prevent unfair labor practices, and investigate and hold hearings relating to enforcement of act. Board's orders are reviewable and enforceable by courts. Interference with Board's performance of duties, or commission of defined unlawful acts is punishable by fine and/or imprisonment. Financial Impact: Cost increase to state of $600,000 a year.
Arguments For: There exists a need for an Agricultural Labor Relations Law. Agriculture is a significant part of our economy but there are no reasonable rules for agricultural relations. Consumers will be protected as prices and the food supply will no longer be affected by strife between farmers and farm worker unions. Farmers would have the right to organize and bargain collectively through representatives of their own choosing. Workers who are fired or discriminated against would be protected and can receive back pay. Farmers would be protected from unfair union tactics, and would be assured of the right to manage and work on their own farms. This would be a peaceful way of settling disputes through legal procedures instead of costly and wasteful strikes.
Endorsers: Joy G. Jameson, Farmer; Mrs. Joyce Valdez, Housewife; Rennick J. Harris, Rancher.
Arguments Against: Proposition 22 destroys the progress that farm worker unions have made. It would outlaw the processes that have enabled farm worker unions to be successful. This proposition is being financed by giant agribusiness corporations that are attempting to serve their own interests. Proposition 22 takes away from farm workers the right to vote in representation elections. Seasonal workers would not be fairly represented in a vote under the provisions. The constitutional right to help farm workers will be taken away. This is the first step towards anti-labor legislation in industries other than agriculture.
Endorsers: Cesar E. Chavez, Director, United Farm Workers, AFL-CIO; Rev. Wayne (Chris) Hartmire, Director, Calif. Migrant Ministry; John F. Henning, Executive Secy.-Treas., Calif. Labor Fed., AFL-CIO.

Election of November 6, 1973

PROPOSITION 1: Tax and Expenditure Limitations.
Type: Initiative Constitutional Amendment

Outcome: Rejected

Summary: Limits state expenditures: restricts use of defined surplus revenue to tax reductions, refunds, or emergencies. Constitutionally eliminates personal income tax for lower income persons, reduces others' 1973 tax up to 20%, and reduces subsequent year rates seven and one-half percent. Requires two-thirds legislative vote for new or changed state taxes. Limits local property tax rates. Requires state funding of new programs mandated to local governments, with tax and expenditure limit adjustments when functions are transferred. Allows local tax rate and expenditure limit increases upon voter approval. Summary of legislative analyst's analysis: $170,000,000 annual reduction in state tax revenues and probable undeterminable future revenue reductions; reduction in projected state program expenditures of estimated $620,000,000 in first year to $1,366,000,000 in fourth year, and increasing thereafter, with probable substantial offsetting cost and tax increases to local government. The initiative provision exempting certain low income persons from income taxes and granting a one-time 20% credit on 1973 income taxes for all taxpayers has been accomplished by legislation passed August 23, 1973, granting low income persons exemptions and granting others a 1973 tax credit ranging from 20% to 35%.

Arguments For: Permanent cuts can be put into the state constitution to place a lid on local property taxes, give taxpayers an ongoing tax cut, and provide a reasonable restraint on the overall growth of the state tax burden. This measure will prevent future state programs such as education and the environment from ever having to be reduced below the current level of services. it requires that any future tax surpluses be returned to the people in the form of tax reductions, unless used to meet emergency situations. This proposition prevents the state from shifting service costs to local government without paying for them, and prohibits a tax increase except by a vote of the people.

Endorsers: John Conlon, Supervisor, Ventura County; Mack J. Easton, Pres., Calif. Taxpayers Assn.; Verne Orr, Director, Department of Finance, State of Calif.

Arguments Against The offer of reducing taxes by imposing expenditure limitations is false. Expenditure ceilings elsewhere in the country have meant deteriorating public services and more costly methods of financing state and local government. The proponents' claim that services will not be cut is based on past trends and questionable assumptions about future growth. This proposition would force increases in local taxes. The rebate enacted by the legislature lowers the base on which future limitations must be calculated. This measure makes no provision for adjusting the expenditure limitation if costs of programs now financed by the federal government are shifted to the state. It places a heavier burden on low and middle income people.

Endorsers: Evelyn P. Kaplan, Pres., League of Women Voters of Calif.

Election of June 4, 1974

PROPOSITION 9: Political Reform Act of 1974.
Type: Initiative Statute
Outcome: Approved
Summary: Provides for regulation of campaign and ballot expenditures; the registration of political lobbyists, and a limitation on their campaign contributions; a prohibition against public officials participating in a decision in which they have financial interest. It requires candidates to file disclosure statements, and reforms the ballot to present measures in a manner that the voter can understand. These measures would be overseen by a new Fair Political Practices Commission. It would raise state and local costs $500,000 for 1974-5, and from $1,360,000 to $ 3,210,000 each year thereafter.
Arguments For: It is time for politicians to be honest and to answer to the people and not paid interests. Big businesses, such as oil companies, write the laws with the politicians they control, and the taxpayers pay for the cost of these new laws. In light of the Watergate and related scandals, it appears evident that more politicians are dishonest than Senator Bradley thinks. This measure would, contrary to Senator Bradley's belief, encourage better candidates and build faith in our government once again.
Endorsers: Joyce A. Koupal, Los Angeles County Energy Commission, Director, Peoples Lobby Inc.; Richard B. Spohn, Attorney, Coordinator, Ralph Nader's California Citizen Action Group; Michael H. Walsh, Attorney, Chairman, California Common Cause.
Arguments Against: Most of the issues here have been grossly exaggerated. If corruption was a common as the opposition believes, there would be continual scandals. This measure would not, however, stop dishonesty. The provision for candidates to report contributions 12 days prior to the election will only result in their waiting until the last eleven days to collect the large sums. The result of this measure would be to discourage honest, educated people from seeking office, in its removal of faith and trust in our leaders.
Endorsers: Senator Clark L. Bradley, 14th Senatorial Dist.

Election of November 5, 1974

PROPOSITION 17: Wild and Scenic Rivers.
Type: Initiative Statute
Outcome: Approved
Summary: Includes two portions of the Stanislaus River into the Wild and Scenic Rivers Act of 1972. It would prevent the construction of flood control facilities except for those needed to protect lives and property. Flood control

facilities could not adversely affect the designated sections of the river, except under extreme circumstances, and only for a limited amount of time.

Arguments For: This river is irreplaceable in the scenic, ecological, and educational values it holds. The Army Corps of Engineers, which would build the proposed dam, has admitted that a dam of one-fifth the size would adequately control flooding. The dam will not provide us with a significant increase in water nor will it provide a significant increase in hydroelectric power. In addition, the proposed reservoir will not increase the recreational capabilities of the area significantly, as the opposition claims.

Endorsers: Dennis Vierra, State Dir., Friends of the River; Joyce Kouple, L. A. County Energy Comm.; Marge Mobley, Dir., Calaveras County Chamber of Commerce.

Arguments Against: The supporters of this measure have misled the public with mistaken facts. The water rights approved by the board would affect only a small area and only in a part of summer. These rights will eliminate only a small whitewater rafting area for a very small number of rafters and rafting companies. In return, they will provide improved recreational benefits; improved salmon fishing and spawning; the preservation of much of the river's scenic shoreline, as well as protecting human life and the flora and fauna; and the conservation of water and a cheap source of clean energy.

Endorsers: John Hertle, Pres., Stanislaus River Flood Control Assn.; Alexander Hildebrand, Member, Sierra Club, Director, South Delta Water Agency.

Election of June 8, 1976

PROPOSITION 15: Nuclear Power Plants.
Type: Initiative Statute
Outcome: Rejected
Summary: After one year, this proposition prohibits nuclear power plant construction and operation of existing plants at more than 60% of the original licensed core power level. This applies unless federal liability limits are recovered. After 5 years, it requires derating of existing plants by 19% annually unless the legislature confirms their safety. Small scale medical or experimental nuclear reactors are permitted. The Governor must publish and review evacuation plans of plants. $800,000 is appropriated from the General Fund to an advisory group. If operations of the plant are reduced or halted, utilities will experience losses in their investments. Electrical costs to consumers may also increase. Local property taxes will be affected accordingly.
Arguments For: It will ensure California the best possible standards of safety. In case of atomic disaster, Californians will be compensated. Industry's claims

of safety will be tested in public hearings. The proposition requires the industry to develop a plan to store waste materials safely.

Endorsers: Harold C. Urey (Nobel Laureate), Physics Prof. Emeritus, University of Calif., San Diego; John Knezevich, Pres., International Brotherhood of Electrical Workers, AFL-CIO, Local #1969; Kent Gill, Pres., The Sierra Club.

Arguments Against: They are only using emotional slogans and not facts. We need more energy sources, not fewer. A shutdown will cause serious economic problems. We need nuclear energy to fill the gap. A shutdown would mean an increase in utility bills, increase of air pollution because of an increase in burning oil, and increased dependence on foreign oil.

Endorsers: Dr. Robert Hofstadter, Nobel Laureate, Physics, Stanford University; Dr. Ruth P. Yaffe, Prof. of Chemistry, San Jose State University; Dr. Jack Edward McKee, Prof. of Environmental Engineering; Calif. Institute of Technology.

Election of November 2, 1976

PROPOSITION 13: Greyhound Dog Racing.
Type: Initiative Statute
Outcome: Rejected
Summary: A Greyhound Racing Commission is established to license and regulate the conduct of greyhound races. First time license applicants pay $50,000. It is renewable for three-year periods unless revoked. Pari-mutuel method of wagering is allowed with monies going to the Greyhound Racing Fund.

Arguments For: The public should decide if it wants greyhound races. It would aid high school athletics, day care centers, senior citizens, the handicapped, cancer and heart research, juvenile delinquency prevention, and bilingual education. It will create jobs and not cost taxpayers. No dogs will be killed after racing, but retirement farms will be created.

Endorsers: Robert M. Karns, M.D.; Michael S. McFarland, Pres., Calif. Assn. of Animal Control Officers; James S. Lee; Pres., State Bldg. & Const. Trades Council of Calif.

Arguments Against: It will provide no tax relief. Promoters will pocket our money. It will bring more crime, more government spending, and damage to California communities. George Hardie (the promoter) will get a monopoly on dog racing in California. Plus, it is inhumane treatment of animals.

Endorsers: Wilson Riles, Supt. of Public Instruction, State of Calif.; Peter J. Pitchess, Sheriff of Los Angeles County; Pete Wilson, Mayor of San Diego, Pres., League of Calif. Cities.

PROPOSITION 14: Agricultural Labor Relations.
Type: Initiative Statute
Outcome: Rejected
Summary: Makes technical amendments to maintain status quo under the 1975 Act except for requiring new appointments to the Agricultural Labor Relations Board. Additional amendments require access for union organizers to property of employers to campaign, and a minimum of 50 percent of employees to petition for decertification of union. Allows the Board to award damages to unfair labor practices. Requires the board to make a list of employees who wish to petition for elections.
Arguments For: Last year workers were given the right to vote in agribusiness. There were no longer strikes, only elections. Agribusiness lost most of the elections and now is demanding changes in the law. The workers are going directly to the people to permanently guarantee their right to vote.
Endorsers: Cesar Chavez, Pres., United Farm Workers of America, AFL-CIO; Mervyn Dymally, Lt. Gov. of Calif.; Richard Alatorre, Member of the Assembly, 55th Dist., Coauthor, Agricultural Labor Relations Act.
Arguments Against: This labor law is not workable. Consumers, workers and employers will suffer if this passes. It is an inflexible law. It is financially irresponsible. It is blank check financing.
Endorsers: Kenneth L. Maddy (R), Member of Assembly, 30th Dist.; John Garamendi (D), Member of Assembly, 7th Dist.; Harry Kubo, Pres., Nisei Farmers League.

Election of June 6, 1978

PROPOSITION 13: Tax Limitation.
Type: Initiative Constitutional Amendment
Outcome: Approved
Summary: Limits ad valorem taxes on real property to one percent of value except to pay indebtedness approved by voters. The 1975-6 assessment rates are used. Limits annual increase in value. Reassessment is provided after a sale or transfer. To increase revenues, a two-thirds vote is required by the legislature. No new state taxes are allowed. Local government taxes are possible with a two-thirds vote of electors. This will result in annual losses of local government property tax revenues.
Arguments For: One percent is still enough to pay for government services. This does not decrease property taxes, and it will not decrease vital services.
Endorsers: Howard Jarvis, Chairman, United Organizations of Taxpayers; Paul Gann, Pres., Peoples Advocate; John V. Briggs .
Arguments Against: Nearly two-thirds of the relief will be to business property and landlords. Local control will be transferred to state and federal

bureaucracies. No tax relief is provided for renters. New taxes will be needed to preserve critical services. School budgets will be cut. Income taxes will be increased. It will invite economic and governmental chaos.

Endorsers: Stated opposition: League of Women Voters, Calif. Taxpayers Assn., Los Angeles Chamber of Commerce, League of Cities, County Supervisors Assn., Calif. Retailers Assn.

Signed: Houston I. Flournoy, Dean, Center for Public Affairs, USC, former State Controller; Tom Bradley, Mayor, City of Los Angeles; Gary Sirbu, State Chairman, Calif. Common Cause.

Election of November 7, 1978

PROPOSITION 5: Regulation of Smoking.
Type: Initiative Statute
Outcome: Rejected
Summary: Declares that smoking in enclosed areas is detrimental to nonsmokers. With some exceptions, smoking is prohibited in enclosed public places, places of employment, and educational and health facilities. Restaurants must make nonsmoking areas. Legislature may amend if consistent with this statute. Penalties are imposed for violations. Signs must be posed for nonsmoking areas, which will require modest costs to the government. If smoking is reduced it will decrease health costs. This is referred to as the "Clean Indoor Air Initiative."

Arguments For: It will protect everyone's rights. Studies show that second-hand smoke can be quite dangerous. It will save tax dollars and reduce business costs. It does not restrict tobacco sales and it does recognize the right to smoke.

Endorsers: Nicholas P. Krikes, M.D., Pres., Calif. Medical Assn.; Carol Kawanami, P.H.N., Pres.-Elect, Calif. Lung Assn.; Justin J. Stein, M.D., Pres., American Cancer Society, Calif. Div.

Arguments Against: It will cost taxpayers millions because of installing signs plus law enforcement and court costs. Costs will also be added because of the need to construct smoke-proof walls. Shopkeepers will be deprived of the right to decide if they want smoking allowed on their property.

Endorsers: Houston I. Flournoy, Dean, USC, Center for Public Affairs; Katherine Dunlap, Co-Chairman, Californians for Common Sense; Peter J. Pitchess, Sheriff, County of Los Angeles.

PROPOSITION 6: School Employees. Homosexuality.
Type: Initiative Statute
Outcome: Rejected

Summary: School employees can be brought up on charges if they advocate, solicit, impose, or encourage sex acts defined in the Penal Code between persons of the same sex. If they are determined unfit for service, they can be fired by a process of two-stage hearings, findings, and judicial review.

Arguments For: Homosexual teachers are imposing their own brand of non-morality on the children. We encourage the removal of anyone promoting homosexual behavior. A small militant group of homosexuals is trying to impose its lifestyle on the majority.

Endorsers: John V. Briggs, State Senator, 35th Dist.; Dr. Ray Batema, Pastor, Central Baptist Church; F. La Gard Smith, Prof. of Law.

Arguments Against: Teachers are not promoting homosexuality in classrooms. It is a bad law and will cause trouble in the community. This proposition would legislate intolerance and harassment. It will invade the private lives of school employees. Don't institute witch hunts!

Endorsers: James McKaskle Murphy, San Francisco Police Commissioner; Raoul Teilhet, Pres., Calif. Fed. of Teachers, AFT, AFL-CIO; Edmund D. Edelman, Los Angeles County Supervisor, 3rd Dist.

PROPOSITION 7: Murder. Penalty.
Type: Initiative Statute
Outcome: Approved
Summary: Expands and changes the criteria for first degree murder. Minimum sentence from life to 25 years-to-life. The penalty is also increased for second degree murder. Parole is prohibited until service of 25 to 15 year terms, subject to good-time credit. During punishment stage, the death penalty is authorized. Special circumstances of death or life imprisonment without the possibility of parole.

Arguments For: We need a tough death penalty policy to protect us from ruthless killers.

Endorsers: John V. Briggs, State Senator, 35th Dist.; Donald H. Heller, Attorney at Law, former Federal Prosecutor; Duane Lowe, Pres., Calif. Sheriffs' Assn., Sheriff of Sacramento County.

Arguments Against: No law can guarantee the automatic execution of all convicted murderers. The present law is not weak and ineffective.

Endorsers: Maxine Singer, Pres., Calif. Probation, Parole and Correctional Assn.; Nathaniel S. Colley, Board Member, National Assn. for the Advancement of Colored People; John Pairman Brown, Board Member, Calif. Church Council.

Election of November 6, 1979

PROPOSITION 13: Limitation of Government Appropriations.
Type: Initiative Constitutional Amendment
Outcome: Approved
Summary: Appropriation limits are made on state and local government entities based on appropriation of the past fiscal year. Changes are required because of adjustments in the cost of living and population. Appropriations can be changed by the electorate. There will be some reimbursement of local governments for new programs or higher levels of services mandated by the state. Revenues received in excess of appropriations to be returned by revision of tax rates.
Arguments For: It will preserve the gains of Proposition 13. It will guarantee that state tax surpluses are returned to the taxpayer. State and local governments will have to limit their budgets. Services will not have to be cut. It is supported by nearly one million voter signatures.
Endorsers: Paul Gann, Coauthor, Proposition 13; Carol Hallett, Member of the Assembly, 29th Dist., Assembly Minority Leader; Leo T. McCarthy, Member of the Assembly, 18th Dist., Speaker of the Assembly.
Arguments Against: This is not a cure-all. It will not eliminate government waste or user fees. The government won't be able to respond to emergencies without severe penalty. This is not a tax reform. It will cripple economic growth.
Endorsers: Jonathan C. Lewis, Executive Director Calif. Tax Reform Assn.; Susan F. Rice, Pres., League of Women Voters of Calif.; John F. Henning, Executive Secy.-Treas., Calif. Labor Fed., AFL-CIO.

Election of June 3, 1980

PROPOSITION 9: Taxation. Income.
Type: Initiative Constitutional Amendment
Outcome: Rejected
Summary: Taxes measured by income imposed under the Personal Income Tax Law shall not exceed fifty percent of those rates in effect for the 1978 taxable year. The legislature must provide a system to adjust personal income tax brackets to reflect annual changes in the California Consumer Price Index. This will decrease state income tax revenues. It will decrease $3 billion in state aid to local school districts and state payments to cities.
Arguments For: It will cut your state income tax by 49% or more, to 1978 levels. The business inventory tax is eliminated altogether. Tax cuts are good for the economy. New jobs are created. It will help fight inflation. It will decrease taxes mostly for those with the lowest income.

Endorsers: Howard Jarvis, Chairman, Calif. Tax Reduction Movement; Dr. Arthur Laffer, Prof. of Economics, USC; Bob Wilson, Democratic State Senator, 39th Dist..

Arguments Against: It is an irresponsible scheme to give huge tax breaks to the wealthy at our expense. It is a poorly designed proposition and is outdated. Who is going to replace millions of dollars cut from the state? Services will be cut also. Plus, it does not close a single tax loophole. The privileged will receive most of the tax break. Other taxes are not cut and will only have to increase to meet the demands on the state.

Endorsers: Everett V. O'Rourke, Chairman, Calif. Legislative Comm., American Assn. of Retired Persons; National Retired Teachers Assn.; Anthony Ramos, Executive Secy., Calif. State Council of Carpenters; Freda Thorlaksson, Pres., Calif. State PTA.

PROPOSITION 10: Rent.

Type: Initiative Constitutional Amendment
Outcome: Rejected
Summary: Rent control will become a matter of local government concern. It will only be imposed by the vote of the people through enactment of local ordinances. No state-enacted rent control is allowed. Annual rent increases are based on the Consumer Price Index. A Commission will be created to resolve any grievances involving rent increases. Certain rental units are exempted from rent control. No landlord retaliation for the exercise of tenant's rights is allowed.

Arguments For: Californians need to be protected from rent gouging and unjustified eviction. This proposition establishes standards to which local rent control ordinances must comply. This proposition will stimulate construction, create jobs, and return competition to the rental marketplace. It is fair to both sides. Statewide control would be prohibited and only local control would be allowed.

Endorsers: James S. Lee, Pres., State Building and Construction Trades Council, AFL-CIO; Dixon Arnett, Vice-Pres., Public Affairs Research, Claremont Men's College; Jack Flanigan, Executive Dir., Calif. Housing Council.

Arguments Against: This proposition does nothing for renters. It will eliminate existing protection of renters. It will also eliminate local control and force all to conform to universal procedures. Rents would be higher and there would be no construction. It prevents a local government from acting to protect its citizens. It will create unnecessary local bureaucracy. The sponsors of this proposition are landlords.

Endorsers: Tom Bradley, Mayor, City of Los Angeles; David A. Roberti, State Senator, 23rd Dist., Senate Majority Leader; Raoul Teilhet, Pres., Calif. Fed. of Teachers, AFL-CIO.

PROPOSITION 11: Taxation. Surtax.
Type: Initiative Statute
Outcome: Rejected
Summary: Levies a 10% surtax on the business income from California sources of energy businesses that obtain, process, distribute, or market oil, gas, coal, or uranium. A tax credit of fifty cents per dollar is allowed for investment in California after January 1, 1979 to increase production of crude oil. Proceeds of surtax will go to bus and rail services, and to develop other transportation fuels. Surtax cannot be passed on to the consumer.
Arguments For: Tax big oil! Their profits are too large and our gas prices keep going up. This proposition only affects the big oil companies, not those earning less than $5 million per year. It will save energy because money will go to alternative sources. It will create new jobs and save cities by creating convenient public transit. It will help California businesses. It will not create a new bureaucracy. Oil companies are not spending money to research alternatives, so we need to.
Endorsers: Edmund G. Brown Jr., Governor; Dianne Feinstein, Mayor of San Francisco; Bill Press, Chairman, Citizens to Tax Big Oil.
Arguments Against: It would affect small companies and those not involved solely in energy. It would place money in bureaucracies instead of private industries exploring new energy sources. The tax would go beyond excess profits to the business income tax, and it is unclear if it will affect gross or net income. This proposition is just a political scheme.
Endorsers: Milton Friedman, Nobel Laureate, Hoover Institute, Stanford University; Kirk West, Executive Vice-Pres. Calif. Taxpayers Assn.; Morris S. Frankel, Pres., Calif. Independent Producers Assn.

Election of November 4, 1980

PROPOSITION 10: Smoking and No-Smoking Sections.
Type: Initiative Statute
Outcome: Rejected
Summary: Smoking and No-Smoking sections are provided in enclosed public places, employment places, health facilities, clinics, and educational facilities. Does not affect outdoor areas or private residences. Signs must be posted. Fines of $15 are set per violation. Allows for enactment of further legislation. It will create a minor cost to local and state governments.

Arguments For: Nonsmokers are being harmed by smokers. Millions will be saved because of a decrease of smoking-induced illness. A distance between smokers and nonsmokers will protect the latter without inconveniencing the former. Mr. Pitchess and Mr. Flournoy were misquoted on the last proposition and state that they are for the current legislation.

Endorsers: Sponsored by: Amer. Cancer Society, Lung Assn., Heart Assn., and Calif. Medical Assn.

Signed by: Raymond L. Weisberg, M.D., Pres., American Cancer Society, Calif. Division; Diane E. Watson, State Senator, 30th Dist., Vice Chair, Senate Health Comm.; Peter E. Pool, M.D., Pres., American Heart Assn. of Calif.

Arguments Against: There are hidden taxpayer costs. This is an overkill approach to a minor social annoyance. It will affect the Health Department budget and the local police and court budgets.

Endorsers: Houston I. Flournoy, Former State Controller; Peter J. Pitchess, Sheriff, County of Los Angeles; David Bergland, Pres., Californians Against Regulatory Excess.

Election of June 8, 1982

PROPOSITION 5: Gift and Inheritance Taxes. (Proponent Miller)
Type: Initiative Statute
Outcome: Approved*
Summary: Repeals existing statutes governing gift and inheritance taxes. Prohibits gift and inheritance taxes. Reestablishes state "pickup" tax on decedents' estate at rates set by the Internal Revenue Code. Legislature will collect and administer this tax. It will decrease state inheritance and gift tax revenues and will save the state $6 million annually in administrative costs.

Arguments For: It will completely eliminate inheritance and gift taxes. It affects mainly the middle class who have enough taxes already. The initiative may not be reversed without being resubmitted to a vote of the people.
Endorsers: David E. Miller.
Arguments Against: Even when there is a tax liability, it can be deferred 10-15 years. The federal estate tax is changing and within 5 years will only affect the wealthiest. The repeal of inheritance tax is tax relief for the wealthy. It will mean a loss of $400 million to the state per year. Surviving spouses are now excluded from paying tax, and 65% of heirs pay no tax under the current law. The inheritance tax seeks to prevent the concentration of wealth in a few families.
Endorsers: Kenni Friedman, Pres., League of Women Voters of Calif.; Chris Adams, Pres., Calif. State PTA; Thomas G. Moore, Pres., Calif. Gray Panthers.
(Proposition 6 received more votes than Proposition 5.)

PROPOSITION 6: Gift and Inheritance Taxes. (Proponent Rogers)
Type: Initiative Statute
Outcome: Approved
Summary: Same as Proposition 5, above.
Arguments For: It is a cruel and unfair tax. Middle class families are already strapped when paying for burial services. With the tax abolished, the economy will improve and jobs will be created. Proposition 6 is superior to Proposition 5 because it not only repeals the taxes, but prohibits their reenactment under a different name. But, both propositions (5 and 6) can be passed without hurting one another. The inheritance tax does not redistribute the wealth, and it affects primarily middle and low income Californians.
Endorsers: Calif. Farm Bureau; Calif. Chamber of Commerce; Calif. Assn. of Life Underwriters; Don Rogers, Member of the Assembly, 33rd Dist.; Alfred E. Alquist, State Senator, 11th Dist., Chairman, Senate Finance Comm.; Carol Hallett, Member of the Assembly, 29th Dist.
Arguments Against: No properties are being confiscated and no children are being robbed. New laws have eased the impact on the average family. If the tax is repealed, it will only relieve the wealthy. The tax is proportional to the amount inherited. Fifty percent of this proposed tax break will go to only 5.7% of beneficiaries.
Endorsers: Kenni Friedman, Pres., League of Women Voters of Calif.; Chris Adams, Pres., Calif. State PTA; Thomas G. Moore, Pres., Calif. Gray Panthers.

PROPOSITION 7: Income Tax Indexing.
Type: Initiative Statute
Outcome: Approved
Summary: Personal income tax brackets are adjusted annually by applying an "inflation adjustment factor" based on the California Consumer Price Index. This is called "indexing." Financially, this would reduce revenue going to the state.
Arguments For: This will make sure inflation will not increase tax rates. The wealthy already have indexing. Taxpayers should not face tax increases solely caused by inflation.
Endorsers: Howard Jarvis, Chairman, Index the Income Tax Comm.; Mike Curb, Lt. Governor; Paul Carpenter, State Senator, 37th Dist.
Arguments Against: Your tax bracket rate is already higher than your actual rate. The wealthiest only pay 3.3% to 7.2%. Under indexing, the progressive tax system will end. It will also cause great revenue losses resulting in drastic cuts in public services. Indexing is regressive.

Endorsers: Kent A. Spieller, Chairman, Californians for a Fair Index; John M. Bachar, Prof. of Mathematics, Calif. State University, Long Beach; Peter L. Coye, Member, Calif. Tax Reform Assn.

PROPOSITION 8: Criminal Justice.
Type: Initiative Statute and Constitutional Amendment
Outcome: Approved
Summary: Amends the Constitution and enacts statutes concerning procedural treatment, sentencing, release, and other matters for the accused and convicted. Provisions are included regarding restitution to victims, right to safe schools, exclusion of relevant evidence, bail, use of prior felony convictions for impeachment purposes or sentence enhancement, abolishing defense of diminished capacity, use of evidence regarding mental disorder, proof of insanity, notification and appearance of victims at sentencing and parole hearings, restricting plea bargaining, youth authority commitments, and other matters. The fiscal effect of this measure cannot be determined with any degree of certainty.
Arguments For: The people need to take decisive action against violent crime. We need the criminal justice system to protect the innocent. We need to bring violent crime under control. Free people should not have to live in fear. This measure will result in more convictions.
Endorsers: Mike Curb, Lt. Governor; George Deukmejian, Atty. General; Paul Gann, Proponent, Victims' Bill of Rights.
Arguments Against: It will take away everyone's right to bail. It would allow strip searches of minor traffic offenders. Proposition 8 will undermine new laws by adding confusing language. It will not allow criminals to testify against each other. Extra court hearings will be needed but no money is being provided. This is not a carefully written, tough, constitutional law. It will just create endless appeals and chaos in the legal system.
Endorsers: Richard L. Gilbert, Dist. Atty., Yolo County; Stanley M. Roben, Dist. Atty., Santa Barbara County; Terry Goggin, Member of the Assembly, 66th Dist., Chairman, Comm. on Criminal Justice.

PROPOSITION 9: Water Facilities Including a Peripheral Canal.
Type: Referendum
Outcome: Rejected
Summary: The act under reconsideration designates additional facilities including a canal as units of the Central Valley Project. Certain items must be specified, including feasibility, environmental impact, design, construction, operation, financing, and protection and enhancement of fish and wildlife. The

Water Resources Department must contract with delta agencies regarding users' rights, water quality, and benefit payments.

Arguments For the existing legislation, Against this referendum: It will help assure water supplies. It is a comprehensive water management and conservation measure. It will not require any new taxes. It will ensure jobs, save water, provide facilities to transport water, guarantee water to Northern California first to provide protection against drought, assure adequate irrigation water, guarantee water quality protection, and protect wildlife and rivers.

Endorsers: Loren L. Lutz, D.D.S., Chairman of the Board, Calif. Wildlife Fed.; Gordon W. Miller, Chairman of the Board, Calif. Water Resource Assn., Chief Engineer, Retired, Sonoma County Water Agency; Ruben S. Ayala, State Senator, 32nd Dist., Chairman, Agriculture and Water Resources Comm.

Arguments Against the existing legislation, For this referendum: Those who will mainly benefit are the oil companies and land developers. The project will never pay for itself. No agency can complete such a project. It will also damage the environment in the San Francisco Bay and Delta areas. It will result in the loss of water quality and quantity.

Endorsers: Lorell Long; John Thurman, Member of the Assembly, 27th Dist., Chairman, Assembly Agricultural Comm.; David Miller, Chairman, Californians for Responsible Government.

PROPOSITION 10: Reapportionment. Congressional Districts.

Type: Referendum

Outcome: Rejected

Summary: The act under reconsideration revises the boundaries of the forty-three Congressional districts and adds two new districts.

Arguments For the existing legislation, Against this referendum: This is a legislative expression of the will of the people. It is a fair, just, and equitable plan. It gives added representation to growing areas of the state. It provides protection of voting rights for minorities. The Republicans are against giving up any control and therefore are against this redistricting plan.

Endorsers: Richard Alatorre, Member of the Assembly, 55th Dist., Chairman, Assembly Elections and Reapportionment Comm.; John F. Henning, Executive Secy.-Treas., Calif. Fed. of Labor, AFL-CIO; Carl Jones, Senior Citizen Representative.

Arguments Against the existing legislation, For this referendum: This plan is unfair and blatantly partisan. It eliminates healthy electoral competition. This plan will only help a handful of politicians. This year's Congressional reapportionment will just increase the raw political power of politicians who drew new districts at the expense of ideal goals. They do not link voters with shared interests and they try to eliminate two-party competition.

Endorsers: Gerald R. Ford, former President of the United States; Robert Kane, Retired Justice, California Court of Appeals; T. Anthony Quinn, former member, Calif. Fair Political Practices Comm.

PROPOSITION 11: Reapportionment. Senate Districts.
Type: Referendum
Outcome: Rejected
Summary: The act under reconsideration revises the boundaries of the forty Senatorial districts and adopts provisions imposing time and other limitations on redistricting court challenges.
Arguments For the existing legislation, Against this referendum: Senatorial districting is fair and gives you better representation. The public was involved in this plan and it is fair to both parties. Big money is trying to stop you from voting yes to this plan. Two-thirds of the Senate voted yes on this proposition. And, don't be fooled, this has nothing to do with keeping the 70-year right of initiative and referendum.
Endorsers: Edmund G. "Pat" Brown, Sr., Former Governor of Calif.; Nathaniel S. Colley, Sr., Western Regional Counsel, NAACP; Joseph Montoya, State Senator, 26th Dist.
Arguments Against the existing legislation, For this referendum: Legislative power brokers are trying to assault your right to fair elections. Vote no to oddly shaped districts and gerrymanders.
Endorsers: Gerald R. Ford, former Pres. of the United States; Sandra R. Smoley, Sacramento County Supervisor; Donna Richardson, Mayor of San Mateo.

PROPOSITION 12: Reapportionment. Assembly Districts.
Type: Referendum
Outcome: Rejected
Summary: The act under reconsideration revises the boundaries of the eighty Assembly districts and adopts other provisions relating to redistricting and placing an initiative or referendum on the ballot.
Arguments For the existing legislation, Against this referendum: Under this law, all Californians are properly represented. It is one person-one vote. It also reflects the testimony of groups and individuals representing the diversity of California.
Endorsers: Richard Alatorre, Member of the Assembly, 55th Dist.; Edmund G. "Pat" Brown, Sr., Former Governor of Calif.; Dianne Feinstein, Mayor, City and County of San Francisco.
Arguments Against the existing legislation, For this referendum: The plan is riddled with errors. It ignores natural communities, fragments cities and

counties, and plays political games with your right to fair representation. The California Poll finds 80% of voters disapprove of our reapportionment process. This plan was drawn to protect incumbents.

Endorsers: Gerald R. Ford, former Pres. of the United States; Robert F. Kane, retired Justice, Calif. Court of Appeals; Shirley N. Pettis, retired Congresswoman.

Election of November 2, 1982

PROPOSITION 11: Beverage Containers.
Type: Initiative Statute
Outcome: Rejected
Summary: Beverage containers sold after March 1, 1984 must have a refund value of not less than five cents. That value must be stated on the container. Dealers and distributors must pay the refund. Redemption centers must be established. Manufacturers may not require a deposit from a distributor on a nonrefillable container. Violation is punishable by a fine. This statute will help reduce litter cleanup costs and solid waste disposal costs.
Arguments For: This works in other states. It will help decrease California's litter problem. It will save tax dollars for cleaning up the litter. It will conserve energy and natural resources. It will create more jobs.
Endorsers: Richard B. Spohn, Director, Calif. Dept. of Consumer Affairs; Chris Adams, Pres., Calif. State PTA; D. Bill Henderson, Secy.-Treas., Southwestern States Council of the United Food and Commercial Workers, AFL-CIO.
Arguments Against: It is a worthwhile idea but a bad law. The increased costs incurred from handling empties are passed on to the consumer. The initiative goes too far, costs too much, and will increase the use of fuel and water. Prices will increase. It will also cause sanitation problems from beverage residue.
Endorsers: Cass Alvin, Member, State Solid Waste Management Board; Barbara Keating-Edh, Pres., Consumer Alert, Captain, President's Transition Team, Consumer Product Safety Commission; John Hay, Executive Vice-Pres., Calif. Chamber of Commerce; Donald Beaver, Pres., Calif. Grocers Assn.; Gary Peterson, Co-founder, Calif. Resource Recovery Assn., Pres., Ecolohaul Recyclers.

PROPOSITION 12: Nuclear Weapons.
Type: Initiative Statute
Outcome: Approved
Summary: Identifies peoples' concern about the danger of nuclear war, and states findings and declarations regarding this. Requires the Governor to write

the President of the United States to request that the United States and Soviet Union halt testing, production, and further deployment in a verifiable way.

Arguments For: No one wins in a nuclear war. A freeze of the arms race is the first step in preventing a war. The risk of accidental war is increasing and without a freeze the arms race will continue.

Endorsers: Dr. Owen Chamberlain, Prof. of Physics and Nobel Laureate; Homer A. Boushey, Brigadier General, USAF, Retired; John H. Rubel, Former Asst. Secy. of Defense.

Arguments Against: The Soviet Union is involved in the largest weapons buildup ever. A freeze would undercut the United States' bargaining position, and ensure a Soviet advantage.

Endorsers: Admiral U.S. G. Sharp, USN, Retired, Co-chair, Comm. for Verified Arms Reduction—"No" on the Freeze; Robert Garrick, Former Deputy Counselor to Pres. Reagan, Co-chair, Comm. for Verified Arms Reduction—"No" on the Freeze.

PROPOSITION 13: Water Resources.

Type: Initiative Statute

Outcome: Rejected

Summary: Adds provisions to the Water Code, requiring the development and implementation of specified water conservation programs. Allows for wildlife and recreation in streams. Specifies conditions for water storage and use of the Stanislaus River and New Melones Dam.

Arguments For: California needs a statewide solution to its water problem. This measure will end wasteful and inefficient uses of water in California, and will protect Californians from a serious water crisis. It will protect remaining streams and rivers, and create new jobs.

Endorsers: Scott E. Franklin, Chairman, Calif. Water Commission; Jeanne G. Harvey, State Water Director, League of Women Voters of Calif.; A. Alan Post, former Legislative Analyst, State of Calif.

Arguments Against: This radical solution will make the problem worse. It penalizes urban water users. The state bureaucracy will dictate water policy decisions. It benefits fish first and people/food last. It places your water rights in the hands of appointed bureaucrats. It will also increase water rates substantially. It will encourage costly and lengthy court battles over water supplies.

Endorsers: John Thurman, Member of the Assembly, 27th Dist., Chairman, Assembly Comm. on Agriculture; Shirley Chilton, Pres., Calif. Chamber of Commerce; Henry Voss, Pres., Calif. Farm Bureau Fed.

PROPOSITION 14: Reapportionment by Districting Commission or Supreme Court.

Type: Initiative Constitutional Amendment
Outcome: Rejected
Summary: Repeals the legislature's power over reapportionment and establishes a Districting Commission that specifies boundaries for Senate, Assembly, Equalization Board, and Congressional Districts. Sets criteria for districts. Plans must be adopted for the 1984 elections. Provides for open meetings, procedures, public hearings, and judicial review.
Arguments For: The legislature has been redrawing districts to increase its political power. We want to take reapportionment out of the hands of the legislature. The Commission assures fair representation. New districts will only be based on population. The Commission will not cost more money.
Endorsers: Gerald Ford, former Pres. of the U.S.; Donall Wright, former Chief Justice, Calif. Supreme Court; Susan Rouder, Chair, Calif. Common Cause.
Arguments Against: This is an ill-conceived scheme that attacks the right to vote by referendum against any future gerrymanders. The Commission will be made up of elitists. If you do not like what the legislature is doing now, at least you have two remedies: elect someone else or support a referendum to repeal a law. This would only create a state bureaucracy. This type of Commission has failed in almost every state that tried it.
Endorsers: Jess M. Unruh, State Treas., former Speaker, State Assembly; David Roberti, State Senate, 23rd Dist., Pres. pro Tempore; Willie Lewis Brown, Jr., Member of the Assembly, 17th Dist., Speaker of the State Assembly.

PROPOSITION 15: Guns.
Type: Initiative Statute
Outcome: Rejected
Summary: Requires all concealable firearms to be registered by November 2, 1983. Makes registration information confidential. Restricts the legislature from banning ownership of shotguns, long rifles, or registered handguns. Limits the number of handguns in circulation. Violation penalties are imposed.
Arguments For: This measure is needed to fight street crime. It protects home guns and attacks street guns. It is not a ban. We need to curb handgun violence.
Endorsers: Peter J. Pitchess, Sheriff Emeritus, County of Los Angeles; John J. Norton, Chief of Police, Foster City, Pres. of the Calif. Police Chiefs Assn.; Cornelius P. Murphy, Chief of Police, City of San Francisco; Joseph D. McNamara, Chief of Police, City of San Jose; William B. Kolender, Chief of Police, City of San Diego.
Arguments Against: We already have registration. The freeze on future sales is misguided. It will create an elite class with a special property right to own

a gun. We need to enforce real criminal laws. This measure diverts funds away from fighting crime. Criminals will just ignore the initiative.
Endorsers: Carol Ruth Silver, Supervisor, City and County of San Francisco; Richard K. Rainey, Sheriff, Contra Costa County; Robert L. Fusco, Pres., Calif. Wildlife Fed.

Election of June 5, 1984

PROPOSITION 24: Legislature: Rules, Procedures, Powers, Funding.
Type: Initiative Statute
Outcome: Approved
Summary: Membership on the Senate and Assembly Rules Committees shall consist of members from the two largest parties, with the largest party having a one-vote majority. Membership on other committees shall be proportional to partisan composition in each house. The committees approve, by two-thirds vote, rules, committee establishment, appointments by the Speaker, and disbursement of funds. The legislature's support appropriations are decreased by 30% and future support appropriations are limited.
Arguments For: A few powerful bosses pick the committee. This proposition will cut the legislature's spending on itself by 30% and impose reasonable future increases. It establishes guidelines for the legislature's conduct.
Endorsers: Paul Gann.
Arguments Against: Since 1986, the average annual growth in legislative spending has been less than the growth rate in state spending for all other government programs. This is not a real reform. The initiative propagates minority control. The proposal won't achieve the needed honest legislative reform. It guarantees government by the tyranny of a minority.
Endorsers: Robert T. Monagan, Representative, former Speaker; Leo T. McCarthy, Lt. Governor; John K. van de Kamp, Atty. Gen.

Election of November 6, 1984

PROPOSITION 36: Taxation.
Type: Initiative Constitutional Amendment
Outcome: Rejected
Summary: Adds restrictions on real property taxation, enacts new tax measures, and charges fees. The imposition of new taxes based upon real property ownership, sale, or lease is prohibited. Other taxes can only be increased by two-thirds vote of the legislature for state taxes and two-thirds vote of electorate for local taxes. Provides refunds to assessed value inflation adjustments. This would become operative August 15, 1983.

Arguments For: Because of loopholes, taxes have increased without voter approval. Proposition 36 makes sure that taxes can only be raised by a two-thirds vote. This will protect Proposition 13, which has saved taxpayers billions of dollars.

Endorsers: Howard Jarvis, Author, Proposition 13, Chairman, Calif. Tax Reduction Movement; Paul Gann, Coauthor, Proposition 13; Dr. Arthur B. Laffer, Prof. of Economics, Presidential Economic Advisor.

Arguments Against: It is unfair to taxpayers. It will open new loopholes. Don't jeopardize educational progress. It is unfair to new businesses because they are forced to pay higher taxes. This is a tax redistribution scheme.

Endorsers: Richard P. Simpson, Calif. Taxpayers' Assn.; Bill Honig, State Supt. of Public Instruction; Bobette Bennett, Pres., Calif. PTA; John Hay, Calif. Chamber of Commerce; Kenneth S. Carnine, American Assn. of Retired Persons.

PROPOSITION 37: State Lottery.
Type: Initiative Constitutional Amendment and Statute
Outcome: Approved
Summary: Allows for the establishment of a state lottery and prohibits casinos. Fifty percent of the revenue must be returned as prizes, 16% maximum used for expenses, 34% minimum for public education. Monies distributed on an equal per capita basis for K-12, Community Colleges, State Universities and Colleges, and the University of California.

Arguments For: It would provide money for public education. Local control is assured. It will be run honestly and will be tightly controlled. Lotteries are fun and voluntary. It will be played predominantly by the middle-class. Organized crime will not invade California.

Endorsers: Gail N. Boyle, Pres., San Diego Teachers Assn.; Nancy J. Brasmer, Pres., Calif. School Employees Assn.; Ed Fogla, Immediate Past Pres., Calif. Teachers Assn., former Chairman, NEA National Tax Limitation Task Force; Rev. George Walker Smith, Pastor, Christ United Presbyterian Church, San Diego, Calif., Past Pres., National School Boards Assn.; Joseph D. McNamara, Police Chief, City of San Jose; Harold S. Dobbs, Attorney-at-Law, former Supervisor, City and County of San Francisco;.

Arguments Against: It will not solve our educational problems. It provides no tax relief. It is an unstable source of funds. It will add a new layer of bureaucracy. For every one dollar, fifty cents will end up in the promoters' hands. Other states with lotteries see that it breeds crime.

Endorsers: John van de Kamp, Atty. General; Robert Presley, State Senator, 36th Dist., Chairman, Senate Select Comm. on Children and Youth; Bobette C. Bennett, Pres., Calif. State PTA.

PROPOSITION 38: Voting Materials in English Only.
Type: Initiative Statute
Outcome: Approved
Summary: The Governor must write a letter to the President, the U.S. Attorney General, and Congress expressing the wish that voting materials be printed in English only.
Arguments For: In 1975, Congress approved legislation to have voting materials printed in foreign languages. This encourages the idea that a full life in the U.S. can be achieved without competence in English. Foreign language ballots create tensions among neighbors. These ballots are also costly and are discriminatory.
Endorsers: S.I. Hayakawa, Ph.D., U.S. Senator, 1977-82; J. William Orozco, Businessman; Stanley Diamond, Chairman, Calif. Comm. for Ballots in English.
Arguments Against: Almost half of the voting population didn't vote in the last election. Proposition 38 supporters attack an evil that does not exist. Bilingual ballots have been successful in America. The Voting Rights Act protects all citizens from voting discrimination. We need to protect the precious right to vote. Hispanics and Asians want to learn English to integrate. Having a ballot in other languages encourages assimilation through participation.
Endorsers: Robert Matsui, Member of Congress; Esteban Edward Torres, Member of Congress; Don Edwards, Member of Congress.

PROPOSITION 39: Reapportionment.
Type: Initiative Constitutional Amendment and Statute
Outcome: Rejected
Summary: New criteria are established to reapportion Senate, Assembly, Congressional, and Equalization Districts for the 1986 elections and after each decennial census. A new commission, consisting of eight former appellate justices, is created to adopt reapportionment plans. Plans are subject to referendum and Supreme Court review.
Arguments For: It will take reapportionment away from the legislature, ending the conflict of interest. Legislators no longer can advance their personal ambitions. This proposition will ensure absolute fairness.
Endorsers: Colleen Conway McAndrews, Member, Calif. Fair Political Practices Commission, 1977-83; Sandra R. Smoley, former Pres., County Supervisors Assn. of Calif.; Dr. George C. S. Benson, Prof. of Political Ethics; John T. Hay, Pres., Calif. Chamber of Commerce; Paul Gann.
Arguments Against: This will not save taxpayers money. They are lying to you about fair, non-partisan redistricting. This is a continuation of the same backroom political fight. Reapportionment is supposed to be every 10 years,

but we have already had it twice in the 1980s. Proposition 39 has no accountability to the people.

Endorsers: John K. van de Kamp, Atty. General; Daniel H. Lowenstein, former Chairman, Fair Political Practices Commission; Janet Levy, Co-chair, White House Conference on Aging Implementation Comm.

PROPOSITION 40: Campaign Contribution Limitations. Elective State Offices.

Type: Initiative Statute

Outcome: Rejected

Summary: Limits contributions to elective state office candidates. Individuals are limited to contributions of $1,000 per candidate, $250 per party or PAC, with $10,000 maximum to all candidates, parties, and political action committees. Party and PAC contributions are limited to $1,000 per candidate. Candidates may expend personal funds without limit. Provides limited public funding for candidates to match the opposition's personal funds.

Arguments For: We need to reform how campaigns are funded. Now 90%+ of funds are raised outside the districts involved. We need to preserve representative democracy. This will end contributions by special interests. Candidates cannot transfer funds to each other or to different accounts. Only candidates facing unfair competition will receive public funds.

Endorsers: Ross Johnson, Calif. State Legislator, Chairman, Comm. for Fair Campaign Finance.

Arguments Against: It does not limit spending. It favors wealthy candidates. It spends tax money on campaigns. Only a wealthy candidate can offer a realistic challenge. It limits contributions but not campaign spending. This makes money more difficult to raise. It helps protect incumbents.

Endorsers: Henry J. Voss, Pres., Calif. Farm Bureau Fed.; Dean A. Watkins, Past Chairman, Calif. Chamber of Commerce; Richard P. Simpson, Executive Vice Pres., Calif. Taxpayers' Assn.

PROPOSITION 41: Public Aid and Medical Assistance Programs.

Type: Initiative Statute

Outcome: Rejected

Summary: The Public Assistance Commission is created to survey medical assistance programs. Expenditures for benefits are limited to the national average expenditure. Increase in expenditures must be approved by a majority vote of the legislature. State expenditure would be decreased and county expenditure increased.

Arguments For: California has the most expensive welfare system in the U.S. Programs will be cut for the young and healthy. The welfare program is not working. We need a higher priority on education and transportation. The younger recipients will have to work.

Endorsers: Ross Johnson, Calif. State Legislator, Chairman, Californians to Halt Excessive Welfare Spending.

Arguments Against: It cuts medical aid to the elderly and disabled. It cuts foster care programs, and eliminates almost all employment and workfare programs. It cuts assistance to all. Medical aid is cut by 25%.

Endorsers: Ray Uzeta, Pres., Calif. Assn. of the Physically Handicapped; Rev. John Deckenbach, Pres., Calif. Church Council; Mary Jane Merrill, Pres., League of Women Voters of Calif.; Clifford W. Holliday, Pres., Calif. Congress of Seniors; Susan Gambini, Pres., Calif. State Foster Parent Assn.; Richard E. White, Pres., Easter Seal Society of Calif.

Election of June 3, 1986

PROPOSITION 51: Multiple Defendants Tort Damage Liabiliity.
Type: Initiative Statute
Outcome: Approved
Summary: Under existing law, tort damages awarded a plaintiff in court against multiple defendants may all be collected from one defendant. That defendant may seek reimbursement from the others. This measure limits the liability for non-economic damages to that portion of damages that is equal to the party's share of the fault. Non-economic is defined as pain and suffering. The court still requires one defendant to pay full economic damages if the other parties cannot pay their share.

Arguments For: This is the Fair Responsibility Act. It is unfair to force someone to pay for damages that are someone else's fault. In this case, the city often must foot the bill. This proposition protects both victims and taxpayers.

Endorsers: Richard Simpson, Calif. Taxpayers' Assn.; Donnetta Spink, Pres., Calif. State, PTA; Elwin E. Ted Cooke, Pres., Calif. Police Chiefs Assn.; Kirk West, Pres., Calif. Chamber of Commerce; Pat Russell, Pres., League of Calif. Cities, Pres., Los Angeles City Council; Leslie Brown, Pres., County Supervisors Assn. of Calif., Supervisor, Kings County.

Arguments Against: It will not lower taxes or insurance rates. It is an attempt by insurance companies to avoid paying victims for injuries. The current system works and is fair. This proposition solves nothing.

Endorsers: Pat Cody, DES Action; James E. Vermeulen, Founder and Executive Director, Asbestos Victims of America; Harry M. Snyder, Regional Director, Calif. Consumers Union of U.S., Inc.

Election of November 4, 1986

PROPOSITION 61: Compensation of Public Officials, Employees, Individual Public Contractors.
Type: Initiative Constitutional Amendment and Statute
Outcome: Rejected
Summary: The Governor's annual salary is set at $80,000 and other constitutional officers salaries are set at $52,500. Maximum compensation of elected or appointed employees and public contractors are set at 80% of the Governor's salary. A vote of the people is needed to increase salaries. Sick leave and vacation cannot be accrued from one calendar year to another. The salaries and benefit-related reductions would amount to $125 million.
Arguments For: We need to limit public salaries. Elected officials want no limits and want pay raises, and the voter currently has no say in the matter. This proposition would cut spending without cutting services.
Endorsers: Paul Gann.
Arguments Against: This will cost taxpayers $7 billion. Removing the ability to accumulate sick leave and vacation will encourage absenteeism. It will negatively affect our progress toward excellence in education. This is not about pension reform. It would cut government services. It has an unfair salary limit.
Endorsers: Jack Boling, Calif. Highway Patrol; Linda Broder, Pres., League of Women Voters of Calif.; Bill Honig, State Supt. of Public Instruction.

PROPOSITION 62: Taxation: Local Governments and Districts.
Type: Initiative Statute
Outcome: Approved
Summary: Statutes are enacted relative to new and increased taxation by local governments and districts. Imposition of special taxes must be approved by two-thirds of the voters. Imposition of general taxes will need the approval of two-thirds of the legislative body and approval by the electorate. Provisions are included governing conduct of elections. Restricts the use of revenues and has restrictions on specified types of taxes. Voters must approve to continue taxes imposed after August 1985.
Arguments For: It will guaranteee your right to vote on any tax increase. This will affect both new and existing tax increases.
Endorsers: Howard Jarvis, Author of Proposition 13, Chairman, Calif. Tax Reduction Movement; Paul Carpenter, Democrat,, State Senator, 33rd Dist.; John J. Lynch, Deputy Assessor, Los Angeles County.
Arguments Against: The proposition is poorly written. This is not a constitutional amendment, so it left out charter cities. It will also cost millions in extra interest costs. It interferes with local control. It would prevent local

governments from meeting critical local needs. Voters already can restrict local taxes.

Endorsers: Ted Cooke, Pres., Calif. Police Chiefs Assn.; Bill Teie, Pres., Calif. Fire Chiefs Assn.; Roy Ulrich, Calif. Common Cause; Linda Broder, Pres., League of Women Voters of Calif.; Lenny Goldberg, Executive Director, Calif. Tax Reform Assn.; Daniel A. Terry, Pres., Federated Firefighters of Calif.

PROPOSITION 63: Official State Language.
Type: Initiative Constitutional Amendment
Outcome: Approved
Summary: Provides for English to be the official state language.   The legislature must enforce this provision by appropriate legislation.
Arguments For: It strengthens our common bond in California through the English language. This is the way to overcome language conflicts and ethnic separatism. Assimilation is constructive. In the melting pot, the common thread that tied all together was and is the English language.
Endorsers: S.I. Hayakawa, Ph.D., U.S. Senator, 1977-82; J. William Orozco, Businessman; Stanley Diamond, Chairman, Calif. English Campaign; Frank Hill, Member of the Assembly, 52nd Dist.
Arguments Against: This will make English the only language in California. It does nothing positive to increase English proficiency. It discourages people from assimilating because it will isolate them. Don't breed intolerance and divisiveness.
Endorsers: The Honorable Dianne Feinstein, Mayor, San Francisco; Art Torres, State Senator, 24th Dist.; State Council of Service Employees; John van de Kamp, Atty. General; Willie L. Brown Jr., Speaker, Calif. State Assembly; Daryl F. Gates, Chief, Los Angeles Police Department.

PROPOSITION 64: AIDS.
Type: Initiative Statute
Outcome: Rejected
Summary: Declares AIDS an infectious disease and that a carrier of HTLV-III virus is in an infectious condition. Both are required to be placed on the list of reportable diseases maintained by the director of Department of Health Services. Both are subject to quarantine statutes and regulations.
Arguments For: It will protect the public from AIDS. AIDS is out of control. It is the gravest public health threat. You have the right to be protected from all contagious diseases, including AIDS. Today, public health authorities cannot be informed about who is spreading the virus.
Endorsers: Khushro Ghandhi, Calif. Director, National Democratic Party Comm. and Member-elect, Los Angeles County Democratic Party Central

Comm.; John Gauerhoz, M.D. FCA, Fellow, College of American Pathologists; William B. Dannemeyer, Member of Congress, 39th Dist.; Gus S. Sermos, former Centers for Disease Control Public Health Adviser with AIDS Program in Florida; Nancy T. Mulian, M.D., Burbank.

Arguments Against: This would hinder the ability to treat and cure AIDS. No one contracts AIDS by casual contact. This proposition will only create panic. The fear of quarantine would make people reluctant to be tested. It would cost millions to isolate these people.

Endorsers: Helen Miramontes, R.N., M.S., CCRN, Pres., Calif. Nurses Assn.; C. Duane Daimer, Pres., Calif. Hospital Assn.; Gladden V. Elliott, MD, Pres., Calif. Medical Assn.; Ed Zschau , Member of Congress, 12th Dist.; Alan Cranston, U.S. Senator.

PROPOSITION 65: Restriction on Toxic Discharges into Drinking Water; Requirement of Notice of Persons Exposed to Toxics.
Type: Initiative Statute
Outcome: Approved
Summary: Those doing business cannot expose individuals to chemicals known to cause cancer. The governor will publish lists of such chemicals. Civil penalties can be sought. If illegal discharge is being done, that information must be disclosed to the local Board of Supervisors and health officer.

Arguments For: This would keep chemicals out of the drinking water. Private citizens would be able to enforce these laws in court. Our toxic laws are not tough enough. It will apply equally to all businesses.

Endorsers: Ira Reiner, Dist. Atty., Los Angeles County; Art Torres, State Senator, 24th Dist., Chair, Senate Toxics and Public Safety Management Comm.; Penny Newman, Chair, Concerned Neighbors in Action, Stringfellow Acid Pits; Arthur C. Upton, M.D., former Director, National Institutes of Health; Norman W. Freestone, Jr., Farmer, Visalia; Albert H. Gersten, Jr., Businessman, member, Little Hoover Commission;

Arguments Against: Proposition 65 is filled with exceptions. It exempts the biggest polluters and limits funds to enforce the law. It undermines California's toxic law. This is a simplistic response to a complex issue. It unfairly targets farmers.

Endorsers: Edward R. Jagels, Dist. Atty., Kern County; Michele Beigel Corash, former General Counsel, U.S. EPA; Cathie Wright, Member of Assembly, 37th Dist., Member, Assembly Comm. on Environmental Safety and Toxic Materials; Dr. Bruce Ames, Chairman, Dept. of Biochemistry, University of Calif., Berkeley; Henry Voss, Pres., Calif. Farm Bureau; Alice Ottoboni, Ph.D., Toxicology Staff Toxicologist, Calif., Dept. of Health Services.

Election of June 7, 1988

PROPOSITION 68: Legislative Campaigns. Spending and Contribution Limits. Partial Public Funding.
Type: Initiative Statute
Outcome: Approved
Summary: Limits political contributions to state legislative candidates to $1,000 by individuals, $2,500 by organizations, and $5,000 by political action committees. The Campaign Reform Fund is established and individuals may contribute up to $3 annually. If candidates receive specified threshold contributions from other sources and meet requirements, they may receive limited matching funds from the Campaign Reform Fund. Penalties are provided for violations. (*Parts of this measure were automatically invalidated by Proposition 73 on the same ballot, which received more votes. The remainder was invalidated by a decision of the California Supreme Court on Nov. 1, 1990.*)
Arguments For: Vote for honesty and integrity in government. Limit campaign spending. We cannot afford a government controlled by special interests. Money is corrupting the democratic process. This measure does not raise taxes. Proposition 68 lets you voluntarily contribute.
Endorsers: Carol Federighi, Pres., League of Women Voters of Calif.; Raoul Teilhet, Administrative Director, Calif. Fed. of Teachers; Daniel Lowenstein, Professor, UCLA School of Law, former Chairman, Calif. Fair Political Practices Comm.; Geoffrey Cowan, Chair, Common Cause of Calif.; John K. van de Kamp, Atty. Gen., State of Calif.; Bill Honig, Supt. of Public Instruction, State of Calif.; Edmund G. "Pat" Brown, former Governor and Atty. Gen.; Consumers Union; So. Christian Leadership Conference; *et al.*
Arguments Against: It is a badly flawed proposition. Politicians can use special interest contributions to qualify for matching funds. Politicians want your tax money to pay for their campaigns.
Endorsers: John Keplinger, former Exec. Dir., Calif. Fair Political Practices Commission; Alice Huffman, Pres., Comm. to Protect the Political Rights of Minorities; Lewis K. Uhler, Pres., National Tax Limitation Comm.

PROPOSITION 69: AIDS.
Type: Initiative Statute
Outcome: Rejected
Summary: Aids is declared an infectious, contagious disease. People diagnosed as having AIDS or carrying the HTLV-III virus must be placed on a list kept by the Department of Health Services. Each person is subject to quarantine. The Health Services Department must protect the public from Aids.

Arguments For: AIDS is out of control. The present policy is a disaster. Certain steps must be taken to protect the public. It is being treated as a "civil rights" issue instead of a public health issue.

Endorsers: Khushro Ghandhi, Calif. Director, National Democratic Party Comm. and Member, Los Angeles County Democratic Party Central Comm.; John Grauerholz, M.D., FCAP, Fellow, College of American Pathologists; Lyndon H. Larouche, Jr., Candidate for the 1988 Democratic Party Presidential nomination.

Arguments Against: The proposition only spreads misinformation and falsehoods. AIDS is not passed by casual contact. We cannot allow our public health policy to be dictated by extremists with no medical training. This proposition is almost identical to the measure we defeated in 1986. The fear of quarantine would make people reluctant to be tested.

Endorsers: Laurens White, M.D., Pres., Calif. Medical Assn.; Marilyn Rodgers, Pres., Calif. Nurses Assn.; C. Duane Dauner, Pres., Calif. Assn. of Hospitals and Health Systems.

PROPOSITION 70: Wildlife, Coastal and Parkland Conservation Bond Act.
Type: Initiative Statute/Bond Act
Outcome: Approved
Summary: Bonds are issued at $776,000,000 to provide funds for acquisition, development, rehabilitation, protection, or restoration of park, wildlife, coastal, and natural lands. Funds from bond sales would be administered by the California Department of Parks and Recreation, Wildlife Conservation Board, and State Coastal Conservancy. Provisions are contained in case of other conservation bond acts.

Arguments For: It will protect our lands for generations. We will lose our natural heritage if we do not take steps now. It will provide permanent benefits for all. It will cost Californians less than $2 per year from existing taxes.

Endorsers: Alan Cranston, U.S. Senator; Pete Wilson, U.S. Senator; Leo McCarthy, Lt. Governor; John K. van de Kamp, Atty. Gen. of Calif.; Gerald R. Ford, former Pres. of the U.S.; Deane Dana, Chairman, Los Angeles County Board of Supervisors.

Arguments Against: Millions of dollars of pet projects are added in exchange for campaign contributions. Proposition 70 is based more on special interest priorities than public need. It would jeopardize funds in other areas. It is the most expensive park bond proposal ever. Less than 10% is actually allocated to development.

Endorsers: Steve Peace, Member of the Assembly, 80th Dist., Member, Assembly Comm. on Water, Parks, Wildlife (ACWPW); Chris Chandler, Member of the Assembly, 3rd Dist., Member, ACWPW; John W. Ross, Executive Vice Pres., Calif. Cattlemen's Assn.; Trice Harvey, Member of the Assembly, 33rd Dist., Member, ACWPW; Henry J. Voss, Pres., Calif. Farm Bureau Fed..

PROPOSITION 71: Appropriations Limit Adjustment.

Type: Initiative Constitutional Amendment
Outcome: Rejected
Summary: Tax revenues of state and local government are limited. It allows for cost of living and population changes.
Arguments For: We all want government spending to be restricted by strong limits and to have state and local government spending limits be updated. Unless we update the limit, $23 billion in cuts will be made from current service levels. Spending limits should reflect the California Consumer Price Index. This proposition is supported by many coalitions and is not a special interest piece of legislation.
Endorsers: Bill Honig, State Supt. of Public Instruction; Carol J. Federighi, Pres., League of Women Voters of Calif.; Josephine D. Barbano, American Assn. of Retired Persons, Calif.; John K. van de Kamp, Atty. Gen.; John Sonneborn, Chair, Calif. Commission on Aging; Craig Meacham, Pres., Calif. Police Chiefs Assn.
Arguments Against: They want to raise taxes and this will all help special interest groups. This measure gives the legislature a blank check to spend it on whatever it likes. The "Gann Limit" [Proposition 13, 1979] was designed to limit government spending and taxation. The "Gann Limit is flexible but firm.
Endorsers: Paul Gann, Proponent of "Gann Spending Limit"; John Hay, Past Pres., Calif. Chamber of Commerce; Tom Mezger, Yolo County Taxpayers Assn., Lewis K. Uhler, Co-Chairman, Californians Against Higher Taxes, and Pres., National Tax Limitation Comm.; Wm. Craig Stubblebine, Von Tobel Professor of Economics, Claremont McKenna College.

PROPOSITION 72: Emergency Reserve. Dedication of Certain Taxes to Transportation. Appropriation Limit Change.

Type: Initiative Constitutional Amendment
Outcome: Rejected
Summary: Three percent of the total state General Fund budget must be included in reserve for emergencies and economic uncertainties. Revenues will be derived from state sales and use taxes on motor vehicle fuels. Requires two-thirds vote of legislature or majority vote of voters before fuel tax can be raised. Fuel tax revenues are excluded from appropriation limit.
Arguments For: The Gann limit formula permits the state budget to grow with the rate of inflation and population. This proposition is along the same lines.

The new taxes will go to highways. Every dollar removed from the General Fund will be replaced by surplus tax revenues.

Endorsers: Paul Gann, Pres., People's Advocate; Joel Fox, Pres., Howard Jarvis' Calif. Tax Reduction Movement; Doris Allen, Assemblywoman, 71st Dist.

Arguments Against: This will be a disaster for schools and taxpayers. The developers will get new highways at the expense of schools, seniors, and law enforcement.

Endorsers: Ed Foglia, Pres., Calif. Teachers Assn.; Richard Peterson, Pres., Calif. School Boards Assn.; Mary Anne Houx, Pres., Calif. Fire Chiefs Assn.; Bill Honig, State Supt. of Public Instruction; Helen H. Lindsey, Pres., Calif. State PTA; Tom Noble, Pres., CHP.

PROPOSITION 73: Campaign Funding. Contribution Limits. Prohibition of Public Funding.
Type: Initiative Statute
Outcome: Approved
Summary: Contributions to candidates for public office are limited to $1,000 by individuals, $2,500 by political action committees, and $5,000 by political parties. Stricter local limits are permitted. Gifts and honoraria are limited to $1,000 each year. Transfer of funds between candidates is prohibited. Newsletters sent at the public's expense are prohibited. Public funds cannot be used for the purpose of seeking elective office. (*The contribution limits and certain other parts of this measure were invalidated by a U. S. District Court decision in September 1990.*)
Arguments For: Too much money is being spent on campaigns these days. Currently there are no limits to the amount of contributions. This is reform without giving tax money to politicians. Proposition 68 gives a blank check to politicians including extremists.
Endorsers: Joel Fox, Pres., Calif. Tax Reduction Movement; Dan Stanford, former Chairman, Fair Political Practices Commission, 1983-85; Quentin L. Kopp, State Senator, 8th Dist., Independent, San Francisco and San Mateo Counties; Joseph B. Montoya, State Senator, 26th Dist., Democrat, Los Angeles County; Ross Johnson, Member of the Assembly, 64th Dist., Republican, Orange County.
Arguments Against: This proposition was written by incumbents. It is not reform; its main support is special interest lobbyists and politicians. Proposition 73 does nothing to limit campaign spending or reduce the influence of the special interests. You cannot limit campaign spending without any public financing. Proposition 73 is a trick to defeat the real campaign reform, Proposition 68.

Endorsers: Carol Federighi, Pres., League of Women Voters of Calif.; Lucy Blake, Exec. Dir., Calif. League of Conservation Voters; John K. van de Kamp, Atty. Gen., State of Calif.; Walter Zelman, Exec. Dir., Calif. Common Cause, Roy Ulrich, Chairman, Calif. Tax Reform Assn.; Tom K. Houston, former Chairman, Calif. Fair Political Practices Commission.

Election of November 8, 1988

PROPOSITION 95: Hunger and Homelessness Funding.
Type: Initiative Statute
Outcome: Rejected
Summary: A public corporation is created to disburse funds to counties, subdivisions of the state, and nonprofit organizations for emergency and transitional services for the hungry and homeless, and for low-income housing. Funding will come from fines for violating existing laws relating to housing and food preparation, and bonds secured by the revenue from these fines.
Arguments For: Hunger and homelessness is unacceptable in California. Proposition 95 will provide a range of services for these people. Most of these people are victims of circumstance. Monies from fines will help these people. Proposition 95 is cost-effective and comprehensive; it will not use tax dollars or create a new big bureaucracy. This proposition enjoys strong nonpartisan support.
Endorsers: Conway H. Collis, Member, State Board of Equalization, proponent on behalf of Californians Working Together to End Hunger and Homelessness; Valerie Harper, Actress, Advocate for the Hungry and Homeless; Rev. Joseph A. Carroll, Pres., St. Vincent de Paul-John Kroc Center; Tom Bradley, Mayor, Los Angeles; William Campbell, State Senator, 31st Dist.; Robert W. Stringham, Pres., Calif. Assn. of Food and Drug Officials.
Arguments Against: Proposition 95 is ineffective, unfair, and wasteful. It will create a new bureaucracy and burden local taxpayers. It would single out small businesses for fines. It does not deliver services such as job training and placement, which are desperately needed. There are also hidden costs for taxpayers. It is a well-meaning, but misguided proposal.
Endorsers: Jeff Palsgaard, Pres., Calif. Environmental Health Assn.; Stanley Kyker, Executive Vice Pres., Calif. Restaurant Assn.; Don C. Beaver, Pres., Calif. Grocers Assn.; Trice Harvey, Member of the Assembly, 33rd Dist., Registered Sanitarian.

PROPOSITION 96: Communicable Disease Tests.
Type: Initiative Statute
Outcome: Approved

Summary: Requires courts, criminal and juvenile, upon finding probable cause to believe bodily fluids were transferred, to order those charged with sex offenses or assaults on peace officers, firefighters, or medical personnel, to provide blood to be tested for AIDS and AIDS-related conditions. Specified persons will be notified about the results. Medical personnel in correctional facilities must report inmate exposure to such diseases and notify personnel who come in contact with such inmates.

Arguments For: This is a victim's rights measure and a public health measure. It is constitutional and nondiscriminatory. It will offer peace of mind to know if one has been exposed to AIDS.

Endorsers: Sherman Block, Sheriff, Los Angeles County; Monroe Richman, M.D., Commissioner, Los Angeles County Commission on AIDS; Ed Davis, State Senator, 19th Dist.

Arguments Against: It is a wasteful, unnecessary measure which responsible public health and law enforcement authorities oppose. AIDS is not transmitted by casual contact. Proposition 96 is not limited to those sexually assaulted or being stuck by a needle, but applies to everyone accused of crimes. It is an unnecessary, heavy-handed approach to the AIDS epidemic. This will only spread ignorance about AIDS. Any person accused of sex-related crimes can be tested without consent.

Endorsers: Michael Hennessey, Sheriff, City and County of San Francisco; Robert J. Melton, M.D., M.P.H., Pres., Health Officers' Assn. of Calif.; Marcus A. Conant, M.D., Chairman, Calif. Dept. of Health Services, Task Force on AIDS, 1983-88.

PROPOSITION 97: State Occupational Safety and Health Plan.
Type: Initiative Statute
Outcome: Approved
Summary: Federal law permits states to enforce occupational safety and health standards in the private sector. In 1987, the governor withdrew this plan and its funding. This measure budgets funds for the plan and requires steps to be taken to prevent withdrawal of federal approval, or, if withdrawn, to require submission of a new plan. Other changes are made.

Arguments For: Many associations, such as the Lung Assn., League of Women Voters, Calif. Medical Assn., Sierra Club, and Calif. Labor Federation want to restore the job safety program. In 1973, the plan was known as California-OSHA (Occupational Safety and Health Administration). In 1987, it was eliminated and replaced by an inferior OSHA plan. The state plan was better because it dealt with cancer prevention, toxic contamination, inspections of hazards and accidents, close regulation of dangerous occupations, and prosecution. It does not waste any tax dollars.

Endorsers: John F. Henning, Executive Secy.-Treas., Calif. Labor Fed., AFL-CIO; Michael Paparian, State Director, Sierra Club of Calif.; Laurens P. White, M.D., Pres., Calif. Medical Assn.; Carol Federighi, Pres., League of Women Voters of Calif.; Hewitt F. Ryan, M.D., Pres., Calif. Society of Industrial Medicine and Surgery; Ira Reiner, Dist. Atty. of Los Angeles County.

Arguments Against: The federal program is not inferior. It gets the job done with experience and common sense. Proposition 97 asks for taxpayers to pay for a service they already fund with their federal taxes. We need to cut government waste and duplication.

Endorsers: George Deukmejian, Governor; Robert Stranberg, Chief, State Division of OSHA; John Hay, former Pres., Calif. Chamber of Commerce.

PROPOSITION 98: School Funding.
Type: Initiative Constitutional Amendment and Statute
Outcome: Approved
Summary: Amends the state Constitution by establishing a minimum level of state funding for school and community college districts. Adds provisions to Education Code requiring excess funds to be used solely for instructional improvement, and requiring schools to report student achievement, drop-out rates, expenses, progress toward decreasing class size and teaching loads, classroom discipline, curriculum, quality of teaching, and other school matters. Contains other provisions. (*The funding aspects of this measure were made less absolute by legislative constitutional amendment, Proposition 111, June 1990.*)

Arguments For: It is a well-thought out plan for California's schools. We need to reestablish public education as a first priority in this state. Take school financing out of politics. Proposition 98 only guarantees schools as much money as they received in the last year. It does not raise taxes.

Endorsers: Ed Foglia, Pres., Calif. Teachers Assn.; Helen H. Lindsey, Pres., Calif. State PTA; Bill Honig, State Supt. of Public Instruction; Ray Tolcacher, Pres., Assn. of Calif. School Administrators.

Arguments Against: It will do nothing to improve the quality of California education. Bigger budgets do not necessarily mean better schools. Education is already California's top budget priority. Since 1982, schools have received a 78% increase in funding while student enrollment has risen only 14%. Proposition 98 would throw away reasonable limits on state spending.

Endorsers: George Deukmejian, Governor; George Christopher, Chairman, Calif. Commission on Educational Quality; Richard P. Simpson, Executive Vice Pres., Calif. Taxpayers' Assn..

PROPOSITION 99: Cigarette and Tobacco Tax. Benefit Fund.
Type: Initiative Constitutional Amendment and Statute

Outcome: Approved
Summary: Imposes an additional tax of one and one-fourth cents on cigarette distributors. Taxes are also imposed on other tobacco distributors, equal to the combined rate of tax imposed on cigarettes. The State Board of Equalization must determine the rate annually. Money raised will be used for treatment, research of tobacco-related diseases, school and community health education programs about tobacco, fire prevention, environmental conservation, and damage restoration programs. Revenues are not subject to appropriations limits.
Arguments For: A 25-cents tax will be placed on each pack of cigarettes and will guarantee strong antismoking programs in our schools. The tobacco companies will lose money with the program. Bootlegging will not become an issue.
Endorsers: Sponsors: American Cancer Society, American Lung Assn. and American Heart Assn.
Signers: Jesse Steinfeld, M.D., Surgeon General, Retired; Neil C. Andrews, M.D., Pres., American Cancer Society, Calif. Division; Patricia A. Schufferle, Regional Director, The Wilderness Society, Calif./Nevada Region; John van de Kamp, Atty. Gen., State of Calif.; Carol Kavanami, Immediate Past Pres., American Lung Assn.; Richard V. Loya, Coordinator, Calif. Assn. of School Health Educators and Health Teachers.
Arguments Against: This proposition invites serious crime. It provides a potential new cash source for street gangs and other criminals. It will single out and penalize the behavior of one group of people who are breaking no laws, and will unfairly burden lower-income Californians. It will give the medical industry millions. It is designed to pay off its promoters.
Endorsers: Paul Gann, Pres., The People's Advocate; Vincent Calderon, National Chairman, Latino Peace Officers Assn.; William Baker, Member of the Assembly, 15th Dist., Vice Chairman, Ways and Means Comm.; Richard Floyd, Member of the Assembly, 53rd Dist., Chairman, Governmental Organizational Comm.

PROPOSITION 100: Insurance Rates, Regulation.
Type: Initiative Statute
Outcome: Rejected
Summary: Provides minimum 20% decrease, from January 1, 1988 levels, in certain automobile insurance rates for good drivers. Companies must insure any good driver in counties where they sell auto insurance. There must be a 20% minimum good driver differential. Funds auto fraud investigations and prosecutions. Consumers will get comparative insurance prices. Discrimination, price-fixing, and unfair practices are prohibited. The Insurance Consumer Advocate is established. Provisions in other propositions are canceled.

Arguments For: This proposition guarantees real, long-term reform and rate reduction. It was written by consumers. Rates have skyrocketed by over 40%. It will not let drunk drivers or insurance companies off the hook. It gives good drivers a 20% discount. It is supported by a diverse coalition—MADD, Congress of Calif. Seniors, Common Cause, League of Calif. Cities, Consumer Federation of America, National Insurance Consumer Organization. Your rate will be determined by your record.

Endorsers: Patricia Ramirez, State Administrator, MADD; Carl Jones, Director, Congress of Calif. Seniors; John van de Kamp, Atty. Gen. of Calif.; Steven Miller, Pres., Insurance Consumer Action Network; J. Robert Hunter, Jr., Pres., NICO; Stephen Brobeck, Exec. Dir., Consumer Fed. of America.

Arguments Against: This is a lawyer initiative. Thousands of minor accidents would have to be litigated. It will raise rates for two-thirds of drivers by 22%. The increase would be due to abolishing rating factors such as the safety record of your neighborhood. Banks will also be allowed to risk your assets by moving into the insurance business. Proposition 100's rate reduction is illusionary and temporary.

Endorsers: Henry J. Voss, Pres., Calif. Farm Fed.; Ed Davis, State Senator, 19th Dist., Vice Chair, Senate Judiciary Comm.; Betty Smith, former Chair, Calif. Democratic Party.

PROPOSITION 101: Auto Accident Claims and Insurance Rates.
Type: Initiative Statute
Outcome: Rejected
Summary: Bodily injury and uninsured motorist rates are decreased to 50 percent of level of October 31, 1988 or 1987 (whichever is lower), adjusted for medical inflation. Recovery for non-economic losses (pain/suffering) is limited to 25 percent of economic losses. Attorney contingent fees cannot be greater than 25 percent of economic losses. Not applicable to survival, wrongful death actions, or actions involving serious injury.

Arguments For: It would decrease rates by one-third for motorists. It will decrease incentives for attorneys to act as ambulance chasers. This proposition stops fraud. It lowers insurance rates and protects consumer rights.

Endorsers: Richard Polanco, Member of the Assembly, 55th Dist., Chair, Consumers for Lower Auto Insurance Rates; John Seymour, State Senator, 35th Dist., Orange County; Mike Roos, Member of the Assembly, 46th Dist., Assembly Speaker pro Tem, Los Angeles; Don Roth, Orange County Supervisor; May Shotwell, Seniors Advocacy Services.

Arguments Against: This proposition was drafted and supported by insurance companies. It will cost taxpayers money. Proposition 101 only applies to two portions of your premium and it can raise the rest as much as it wants.

Endorsers: John van de Kamp, Atty. Gen., State of Calif.; Edward V. Roberts, former Dir., Calif. State Dept. of Rehabilitation; Pres., World Institute on Disability; Harry M. Snyder, Dir., West Coast Regional Office, Consumer Union of U.S., Inc., Publisher, Consumer Reports magazine.

PROPOSITION 102: Reporting Exposure to AIDS Virus.
Type: Initiative Statute
Outcome: Rejected
Summary: Requires doctors, blood banks, and others to report patients whom they believe to be infected by or tested positive for AIDS to local health officers. Restricts confidential testing. Those testing positive must be reported. Health officers must notify the person's spouse, sexual partners, and others possibly exposed. No longer prohibits the use of the AIDS virus tests for employment or insurability. Those giving blood with the knowledge of having AIDS are committing a felony.
Arguments For: This does not call for quarantine. It calls for reporting so AIDS can be prevented. You will not be tested for AIDS by your employer without your consent. It will keep insurance rates down. Reporting is good public health policy.
Endorsers: Warren L. Bostick, M.C., former Pres., Calif. Medical Assn., UCI, former Pres., American Society of Clinical Pathologists; Laurence J. McNamee, M.D., Pres., Calif. Physicians for a Logical AIDS Response, Member, Los Angeles County Medical Assn. Comm. on AIDS; Paul Gann, Pres., People's Advocate, Inc.; Larimore Cummins, M.D., Chairman, Santa Cruz County Medical Society, AIDS Task Force, former Pres., Santa Cruz County Medical Society; William E. Dannemeyer, U.S. Congressman, Calif.
Arguments Against: Proposition 102 is a public health nightmare and a fiscal disaster. It would not enhance confidentiality. Anonymous testing has reduced the rates of new infections. Insurance costs would be shifted to the taxpayers. This would only make the epidemic worse. It is extreme and irrational. It will create a climate of fear and authorize witch hunts. Proposition 102 will affect all those who have positive AIDS antibody tests, which are not always accurate.
Endorsers: Leo McCarthy, Lt. Governor; Laurens P. White, M.D., Pres., Calif. Medical Assn.; Robert J. Melton, M.D., MPH, Pres., Health Officers' Assn. of Calif.; Marilyn Rodgers, Pres., Calif. Nurses Assn.; Tom Bradley, Mayor, City of Los Angeles.

PROPOSITION 103: Insurance Rates, Regulation, Commissioner.
Type: Initiative Statute
Outcome: Approved

Summary: Mandates minimum 20 percent rate decrease from November 8, 1987 levels for auto and property/casualty insurance. Rates are frozen until November 8, 1989 unless the company is threatened with insolvency. Thereafter, all eligible must be offered a good-driver policy with a 20 percent differential. Any rate changes must be approved by an elected Insurance Commissioner. Auto premiums must be determined primarily by the driving record. Discrimination, price-fixing, and unfair practices by insurance companies are prohibited. The Commissioner must provide comparative pricing information. Insurance activities by banks are authorized.

Arguments For: This is the voter revolt to cut insurance rates. It is written and paid for by consumers. It will allow the people to elect a Commissioner. There are no loopholes or fine print. The insurance companies are countering with Proposition 104 (No-fault), but this will actually raise rates. In Proposition 101, reductions only affect one area of premiums, and the rest can be raised. Insurance companies are also funding Proposition 106, which restricts your right to quality legal counsel. Proposition 103 is written by consumers and it will save everyone 20%. It bases your rates on your driving record and not where you live.

Endorsers: Ralph Nader, Consumer Advocate; Harvey Rosenfield, Chair, Voter Revolt to Cut Insurance Rates/Proposition 103.

Arguments Against: This will result in government interference in the insurance system. Your rates will go up because you will have to subsidize motorists in high-risk areas. Drunk drivers who have not lost their licenses can qualify for good-driver discounts. A massive bureaucracy is not the answer. An elected Commissioner will have enormous power, an "insurance czar."

Endorsers: Alister McAlister, former Chair, Assembly Finance and Insurance Comm.; Ed Davis, State Senator, 19th Dist.; Kirk West, Pres., Calif. Chamber of Commerce; William Campbell, State Senator, 31st Dist., Chairman, Joint Legislative Budget Comm.; David Davreaux, Author, Consumers' Guide to Auto Insurance.

PROPOSITION 104: Auto and Other Insurance.
Type: Initiative Statute
Outcome: Rejected
Summary: No-fault insurance is established for auto accident injuries. Victims can only recover from the responsible party beyond the no-fault limits. No recovery is allowed for non-economic injuries except in specified cases. Rates for certain coverages are decreased 20% for two years. Cancels Propositions 100, 101, and 103. Restricts future insurance regulation legislation. Arbitration of disputes over insurers' claims practices is required. Agents and brokers are prohibited from discounting. The Insurance Commissioner can prosecute fraudulent claims. Plaintiffs' attorney contingency fees are limited.

Arguments For: It truly reforms the system. It decreases the costs that have been driving rates up: high legal costs, fraud, and the burden of protecting ourselves against uninsured motorists. It guarantees a repayment of claims, and saves taxpayers money by reducing court cases. 90% of all accident claims would be covered by basic no-fault benefits. Proposition 104 offers permanent reductions.

Endorsers: Dianne Feinstein, former Mayor of San Francisco; Alfred F. Federico, Pres., Calif. State AAA; Pat Nolan, Member of the Assembly, 41st Dist., Assembly Minority Leader; Richard V. Robison, Pres., SoCal Auto Club; Betty Smith, former Chair, Calif. Democratic Party; Jim Nielsen, State Senator, 4th Dist., Vice Chair, Senate Insurance Claims and Corporations' Comm.

Arguments Against: This measure was written and paid for by insurance companies. It will not reduce rates but raise them. Proposition 104 is against real insurance reform. Insurance companies can continue their anti-competitive behavior: discounts can't be offered, consumers can't challenge unfair rates, and rate reduction only affects part of the premium. It will also make it harder for drivers to make insurance companies pay fully for a legitimate claim.

Endorsers: Harvey Rosenfield, Chair, Voter Revolt to Cut Insurance Rates/Proposition 103; Ralph Nader, Consumer Advocate.

PROPOSITION 105: Disclosures to Consumers, Voters, Investors.
Type: Initiative Statute
Outcome: Approved
Summary: Requires: (1) advertisers' warnings regarding disposal of toxic household products with exceptions, (2) notices regarding coverage limits and insurance offeror's identity on insurance policies to supplement Medicare, (3) disclosures in nursing home contracts and ads regarding access to State Ombudsman and facility violation information, (4) initiative and referendum campaign committees to disclose contributors, (5) disclosures by corporations selling stocks in state as to whether or not they are doing business in South Africa. Fines are issued for violations. (*Invalidated by the state Court of Appeals on 11 Feb. 1990, for violating the constitutional provision limiting initiatives to one subject only.*)

Arguments For: This is the consumer right-to-know initiative. We need truthful advertising. It does not stop companies from doing business, it just requires them to tell the truth. It will protect the consumer without creating an expensive bureaucracy.

Endorsers: Jim Rogers, Pres., Consumers United for Reform; Lois McKnight, Dir., Nursing Home Ombudsman Program of Contra Costa County, Member, Board of Directors, East Bay Elder Abuse Prevention Consortium; Bill Shireman, Exec. Dir., Californians Against Waste, Chairman, ECCO-Environmental and Commerce Coalition; George Sandy, Pres., Congress of

Calif. Seniors; Ken McEldowney, Exec. Dir., Consumer Action; Margaret Byrne, Administrator, Bay Area Advocates for Nursing Home Reform.

Arguments Against: Proposition 105 is covering too many diverse issues. This proposition has confused household safety and health with truth in advertising issues. The California Waste Management Board is already acting on the household hazardous waste issue.

Endorsers: Jim Caudill, Household Products Disposal Council.

PROPOSITION 106: Attorney Fees Limit for Tort Claims.
Type: Initiative Statute
Outcome: Rejected
Summary: Places a limit on the amount of contingency fees an attorney may collect for representing a plaintiff in connection with a tort claim. The fee may not be greater than 25 percent of the first $50,000 recovered, 15 percent of the next $50,000, and 10 percent of $100,000 and above. The court may reduce the fee if it is not reasonable and fair.

Arguments For: It will limit fees and secure more money for victims. Currently attorneys collect up to 40%. Injured victims will not find it difficult to find proper legal representation. Don't believe trial lawyers when they claim they cannot work for less money.

Endorsers: Tom McClintock, Member of the Assembly, 36th Dist., Vice Chairman, Assembly Judiciary Comm.; Alan F. Shugart, Chairman of the Board and CEO, Seagate Tech; John Fleming, Univ. of Calif., Law Professor; Jerry Eaves, Member of the Assembly, 66th Dist.; James Nielsen, State Senator, 4th Dist.; Regis McKenna, Chairman of the Board and CEO, Regis McKenna, Inc.

Arguments Against: The present system allows victims to pay lawyers only if they win. This measure does not restrict fees that insurance companies pay their lawyers, so they get the best. This is an insidious insurance industry-sponsored initiative. It obscures the real issues—insurance reform and accountability. This initiative will not save you money.

Endorsers: Ralph Nader, Consumer Advocate; Heather Bechtel Maurer, Exec. Dir., Asbestos Victims of America; Gene Patterson., Exec. Dir., National Victim Center; Judith Rowland, Exec. Dir., Calif. Center on Victimology; Tom Bradley, Mayor of Los Angeles.

Election of June 5, 1990

PROPOSITION 115: Criminal Law.
Type: Initiative Constitutional Amendment and Statute
Outcome: Approved

Summary: Makes significant changes in criminal law and the judicial procedures for criminal cases. Gives accused no greater rights than those under U.S. Constitution. Expands definition of first-degree murder, and number of crimes permitting capital punishment. Prohibits preliminary hearings after a grand jury indictment, and allows the use of hearsay evidence in preliminary hearings. Changes rules for disclosure of information. (*The section of this measure requiring state courts to follow U.S. Supreme Court rulings, rather than state decisions on specified constitutional rights, was ruled unconstitutional by the California Supreme Court in December 1990, on the basis that it was a "revision," rather than a simple amendment, to the state constitution, and therefore could not be accomplished by an initiative.*)

Arguments For: Politicians have failed to enact tough anti-crime laws. This proposition will speed up the court process for criminal trials. It will greatly increase the sentencing for torture, and improve the death penalty law, making it less vulnerable to court interference.

Endorsers: Pete Wilson, U. S. Senator; Calif. District Attorneys Assn.; Collene Thompson Campbell, Chair, Memory of Victims Everywhere (M.O.V.E.); William G. Plested, M.D., Pres., Calif. Medical Assn.; Women Prosecutors of Calif.

Arguments Against: This proposition is too broad and complicated, and it takes away our right of privacy. It threatens a woman's right to make a personal decision relative to abortion. The privacy of medical records and of religious and sexual practices are threatened. It will require millions of dollars in new taxes, and great congestion in the courts.

Endorsers: Robin Schneider, Exec. Dir., Calif. Abortion Rights Action League (CARAL); Shirley Hufstedler, former Judge, U. S. Court of Appeals, former Secy. of Education; W. Benson Harer, Jr., M.D., Chairman, Dist. 9, American College of Obstetricians and Gynecologists; Michael G. W. Lee, Pres., San Francisco Bar Assn.; William R. Robertson, Exec. Secy.-Treas., Los Angeles County Fed. of Labor; Linda M. Tangren, State Chair, Calif. National Women's Political Caucus.

PROPOSITION 116: Rail Transportation Bond Act.
Type: Initiative Statute/Bond Act
Outcome: Approved
Summary: Authorizes general obligation bond issue of $1.99 billion, primarily for passenger and commuter rail systems. Money to be allocated to state and local agencies according to a grant process. Just over $1 billion to be used for commuter and intercity rail projects, and $728 million to be used for urban rail transit and local rail projects.

Arguments For: This measure will reduce traffic congestion, help improve air quality, conserve energy, and protect the environment. It will benefit every county in California and will not require an increase in taxes.

Endorsers: John Van de Kamp, Atty. Gen. of Calif.; Pete Wilson, United States Senator; Lawrence D. Odle, Pres., Calif. Air Pollution Control Officers Assn.; Carole Wagner Vallianos, Pres., League of Women Voters of Calif.; Claudia Elliott, Chair, Sierra Club of Calif.; Dianne Feinstein, former Mayor of San Francisco.

Arguments Against: This measure will not clean the air or improve transportation. It will take money from needed programs in education, health care, etc., including worthwhile transportation programs. Rail transportation is too expensive; California should, instead, expand bus service, ridesharing programs, and bicycle and pedestrian amenities, using existing streets and highways.

Endorsers: Dr. Martin Wachs, Prof. of Transportation Planning, UCLA Grad. School of Architecture and Urban Planning; Ryan Snyder, Urban Planner/Transportation Specialist.

PROPOSITION 117: Wildlife Protection
Type: Initiative Statute
Outcome: Approved
Summary: Establishes Habitat Conservation Fund, receiving $30 million annually from existing environmental funds and the general fund. The Fund's monies will be appropriated to specified agencies for wildlife protection, particularly the acquisition of deer and mountain lion habitat. Prohibits taking of mountain lions.

Arguments For: Hundreds of plant and animal species are in danger of extinction in California. This measure will help stop this extinction. It outlaws the trophy hunting of mountain lion, and will help maintain wetlands. The money will be spent under careful supervision. The proposition is endorsed by "every major conservation organization" [seven specified].

Endorsers: John Van de Kamp, Atty. General; Ed Davis, State Sen., 19th Dist., former Police Chief, City of Los Angeles; Richard Katz, Member of the Assembly, 39th Dist.; Vivian Vaught, Wildlife Chair, Sierra Club; Terry Friedman, Member of the Assembly, 43rd. Dist.; Pete Dangermond, Former Dir., Calif. Dept. of Parks and Recreation.

Arguments Against: The measure takes money from important current programs, such as health care and endangered species protection, and from the Prop. 99 Tobacco Tax Health Fund. Moreover, this measure is more concerned with habitat protection than with public access to park lands.

Endorsers: Robert Beverly, Senator, 29th Dist.; Jonathan Oldham, Pres., San Joaquin Valley Chapter of the Wildlife Society; Richard Golightly, Professional

Wildlife Ecologist and Professor; Dr. Ralph J. Gutierrez, Wildlife Ecologist and Professor.

PROPOSITION 118: Legislature. Reapportionment. Ethics.
Type: Initiative Constitutional Amendment and Statute
Outcome: Rejected
Summary: Amends constitutional provisions for redistricting; redistricting plans to require two-thirds vote of each house and approval of the voters in a referendum. Reschedules years of elections for state Senate. Creates Joint Legislative Ethics Committee and directs legislature to establish ethical standards; regulates honoraria, lobbying, gifts.
Arguments For: The California legislature is a corrupt institution, and legislators receive thousands of dollars from interested parties. This measure will clean up these problems. It will make the redistricting process open and public, and stop manipulation of the process by self-serving politicians.
Endorsers: Bruce Herschensohn, T.V./Radio Commentator; Gerald C. Lubenow, Dir. of Publications, Inst. of Governmental Studies, UC-Berkeley; Gary J. Flynn, Independent Businessman; Gaddi Vasquez, Supervisor, Orange County; Albert Aramburu, Supervisor, Marin County.
Arguments Against: The ethics provisions of this measure have too many loopholes, and will not end the protection of incumbents. The key element in this proposition is reapportionment, and it gives incumbents more power in redrawing districts than they currently have.
Endorsers: John Phillips, Chair, Common Cause; Ed Foglia, Pres. Calif. Teachers Assn.; Jerry Pierson, Secy.-Treas, Calif. Council of Police and Sheriffs; Dan Terry, Pres. Calif. Professional Firefighters; Larry Malmberg, Pres., Peace Officers Research Assn. of Calif.; Daniel Lowenstein, former Chairman, Fair Political Practices Comm.

PROPOSITION 119: Reapportionment by Commission.
Type: Initiative Constitutional Amendment and Statute
Outcome: Rejected
Summary: Twelve-member Independent Citizens Redistricting Commission, appointed by retired appellate justices, will adjust boundaries of Senatorial, Assembly, Congressional, and Board of Equalization districts, by ruling on proposals submitted by any interested citizen.
Arguments For: This approach avoids the conflict of interest inherent in legislators doing their own redistricting, and will end gerrymandering. It is a nonpartisan and public approach to the problem, and will be less expensive than the current procedure.

Endorsers: Carole Wagner Vallianos, Pres., League of Women Voters of Calif.; Stephen Horn, former Vice Chairman, U.S. Comm. on Civil Rights; Tom Huening, Pres., San Mateo County Board of Supervisors; Dan Stanford, former Chairman, Fair Political Practices Comm.

Arguments Against: This measure would create a worthless and expensive new bureaucracy. This idea has twice been rejected by the voters. Proposed plans will be drawn up by special interests, and Commission members will be accountable to the special interests who nominate them. The plan protects the major political parties, but not the people.

Endorsers: Daniel H. Lowenstein, former Chair, Fair Political Practices Comm.; Howard L. Owens, Pres., Congress of Calif. Seniors, Inc.; Bruce W. Sumner, Judge (ret.), former Chair, Constitution Revision Comm.; Tom Noble, Pres., Calif. Assn. of Highway Patrolmen; Ed Foglia, Pres., Calif. Teachers Assn.; Dr. Regene L. Mitchell, Pres., Consumer Fed. of Calif.

Election of November 6, 1990

PROPOSITION 128: Natural Environment, Public Health, Bonds. ["Big Green"]
Type: Initiative Statute/Bond Act
Outcome: Rejected
Summary: Adopts stricter standards for chemicals used in foods, and for pesticides. Establishes new air pollution standards, and regulation of forestry, including $300 million in bonds for state acquisition of "old growth" redwoods. Regulates oil and gas development in state waters, tightens water quality standards. Establishes elected Environmental Advocate.

Arguments For: This measure is necessary to protect the health of Californians and the state's environment. It is needed because special interests have impeded legislative solutions to these problems. The economy will not be seriously hurt by this measure, and costs will be more than compensated for by reduced health costs.

Endorsers: Dr. Jay Hair, Pres., National Wildlife Fed.; Lucy Blake, Exec. Dir., Calif. League of Conservation Voters; Dr. Herb Needleman, M.D., Member, Amer. Academy of Pediatrics, Comm. on Environmental Hazards; Michael Paparian, State Dir., Sierra Club of Calif.

Arguments Against: We already have adequate environmental protections, and this measure will be an economic catastrophe, particularly for California farmers, who will be prohibited from using proven pesticides. New taxes will be required, or current services will have to be cut, to pay for these programs.

Endorsers: Barbara Keating-Edh, Pres., Consumer Alert; Al Stehly, Family Farmer; Larry McCarthy, Pres., Calif. Taxpayers' Assn.; Wallace I. Sampson, M.D., Stanford Univ. School of Medicine; Dr. Judith S. Stern, Prof., Dept. of

Nutrition, Univ. of Calif., Davis; Stephan S. Sternberg, M.D., Sloan-Kettering Inst. for Cancer Research.

PROPOSITION 129: Drug Enforcement, Prevention, Treatment, Prisons. Bonds.
Type: Initiative Constitutional Amendment and Statute/Bond Act
Outcome: Rejected
Summary: Creates California Anti-Drug Superfund, with up to $1.9 billion appropriation for next eight years, for drug enforcement, treatment, and prevention programs. Authorizes $740 million in bonds for new prison construction. Modifies criminal code, including provisions so that changes enacted by Proposition 115 (June 5, 1990) are not construed to alter privacy rights relative to abortion.
Arguments For: This measure will provide real tools in the battle against drugs, and will clarify language in the criminal code that might impinge on a woman's right to abortion. It will also meet the state's great need for additional prison and jail space. There are no "hidden taxes" in this provision.
Endorsers: John Van de Kamp, Atty. Gen. of Calif.; Glen Craig, Sheriff of Sacramento County; Johan Klehs, Chairman, Comm. on Revenue and Taxation, Calif. State Assembly; Frank Jordan, San Francisco Police Chief; Susan Kennedy, Exec. Dir., Calif. Abortion Rights Action League.
Arguments Against: The measure is too broad and complicated, and would dedicate tax revenues to specific government programs. The bond measure will greatly increase government spending outside the constitutional spending limit. State and county governments would have to raise large sums of additional money to implement the anti-drug programs.
Endorsers: Larry McCarthy, Pres., Calif. Taxpayers' Assn.; Quentin L. Kopp, State Senator, 8th Dist.; Richard Gann, Pres. Paul Gann's Citizens Comm.; Daryl Gates, Chief of Police, Los Angeles.

PROPOSITION 130: Forest Acquisition. Timber Harvesting Practices.
Type: Initiative Statute/ Bond Act.
Outcome: Rejected
Summary: Authorizes $742 million in bonds for state purchase of old-growth redwood forests and retraining of people who may lose jobs in the timber industry. Imposes new restrictions on logging and on sale of state-owned timber. Revises qualifications for appointment to the state Board of Forestry.
Arguments For: Our ancient redwood forests are being destroyed, and no law exists to stop clearcutting of these forests. The measure includes reforestation provisions that insure that there will be an ample supply of wood in the future, and also will keep the state Board of Forestry free of industry domination.

Endorsers: Dr. Rupert Cutler, Pres., Defenders of Wildlife; Michael L. Fischer, Exec. Dir., Sierra Club; David Pesonen, former Dir., Calif. Dept. of Forestry; Robert Van Meter, Pres., L. A. Audubon Soc.; Jennifer Jennings, Forest Project Dir., Planning and Conservation League; Jeff DuBonis, Exec. Dir., Assn. of Forest Service Employees for Environmental Ethics.

Arguments Against: This proposal is too radical. It will reduce timber harvesting by 70% and put more than 100,000 Californians out of work. Thousands of lawsuits will result, costing taxpayers untold sums of money. It will politicize the process of timber industry regulation and increase consumer prices for new homes and other wood and paper products.

Endorsers: Gerald L. Partain, former Dir., Calif. Dept. of Forestry and Fire Protection; Phillip G. Lowell, Exec. Dir., Redwood Region Conservation Council; Scott Wall, Pres., Calif. Licensed Foresters Assn.; Sue Granger-Dickson, Wildlife Biologist.

PROPOSITION 131: Limits on Terms of Office. Ethics. Campaign Financing.
Type: Initiative Constitutional Amendment and Statute.
Outcome: Rejected
Summary: Limits statewide officials to eight successive years in office, and state legislators and members of the Board of Equalization to twelve successive years. Changes existing campaign finance laws and enlarges conflict of interest provisions. Permits some public financing of candidacies for public office. Repeals parts of Propositions 68 and 73 (June, 1988).

Arguments For: The measure will combat corruption, self-serving, and the influence of special interests in Calif. politics. The public financing will be voluntary, and therefore not involve additional taxes.

Endorsers: Ralph Nader; John Phillips, Chair, Calif. Common Cause; John Van De Kamp, Atty. General of Calif.; Tom McEnery, Mayor, San Jose; Joan Claybrook, Pres., Public Citizen; David Brower, Founder, Friends of the Earth

Arguments Against: The measure deals with too many issues, and is too complex. It includes a scheme whereby our tax dollars will be used by politicians for their campaigns, $12 million in the first year alone. Such money can go to extremist groups as well as mainstream politicians. And it will repeal the valuable reforms we made in 1988, in Proposition 73.

Endorsers: Dan Stanford, former Chair, Fair Political Practices Comm.; Howard Owens, Pres., Congress of Calif. Seniors; Tom Noble, Pres., Calif. Assn. of Highway Patrolmen; W. Bruce Lee, II, Exec. Dir., Calif. Business League; Wendell Phillips, Pres., Calif. Council of Police and Sheriffs.

PROPOSITION 132: Marine Resources
Type: Initiative Constitutional Amendment

Outcome: Approved

Summary: Establishes marine protection zone within three miles of the coast of Southern California, regulating fishing practices in that area.

Arguments For: The measure will stop the indiscriminate slaughter of marine animals, especially by gill and trammel nets.

Endorsers: Doris Allen, Member, Calif. Assembly, Chairwoman, Comm. to Ban Gill Nets; Stanley M. Minasian, Pres., Marine Mammal Fund; Ann Moss, Pres., The Dolphin Connection; Quentin Kopp, State Senator, 8th Dist.; Dr. John S. Stephens, Jr., James Irvine Prof. of Environmental Biology, Occidental College; Sam La Budde, Earth Island Inst. Research Biologist

Arguments Against: This measure is really designed to save the best fishing off Southern California for wealthy sportfishermen. The vast majority of Californians, who do not ocean fish, will be denied access to fresh local seafood. Thousands of fishermen and fish processing workers will lose their jobs.

Endorsers: Robert E. Ross, Exec. Dir., Calif. Fisheries and Seafood Inst.; Frank Spanger, Jr., Seafood Restaurant Owner; Mrs. Theresa Hoinsky, Pres., Fishermen's Union of American, AFL-CIO; Burr Henneman, former Exec. Dir., Point Reyes Bird Observatory; Alison McCeney, Fisherwoman; Craig Ghio, Vice Pres., Anthony's Seafood Grotto.

PROPOSITION 133: Drug Enforcement and Prevention. Taxes. Prison Terms.

Type: Initiative Statute

Outcome: Rejected

Summary: Increases the state sales tax by one-half percent from July 1, 1991 to July 1, 1995, to create a Safe Streets Fund, the moneys to be used for drug education, enforcement, and treatment, and for prisons and jails.

Arguments For: This measure will make sure that repeat offenders serve their full terms. It will support proven anti-drug programs, and after-school activities that will keep young people away from drugs. It also provides funds to hire thousands of new police officers. The additional tax moneys can only be used for these purposes, and the tax increase will automatically end after four years.

Endorsers: Daryl Gates, Police Chief, Los Angeles; Bill Honig, Supt. of Public Instruction; Leo McCarthy, Lt. Gov.; Chief Don Burnett, Pres., Calif. Police Chiefs Assn.; Dr. Joan E. Hodgman, Dir. of Newborn Care, L. A. County (USC) Medical Center.

Arguments Against: This is just another tax increase for another special interest; it will cost Californians over $7.6 billion. Tax revenues should not be earmarked for specific programs or policies. This is not the right way to support local law enforcement.

Endorsers: Bill Leonard, State Senator, 25th Dist.; Richard Gann, Pres., Paul Gann's Citizens Comm.; Marian Bergeson, State Senator, 37th Dist.

PROPOSITION 134: Alcohol Surtax.
Type: Initiative Constitutional Amendment and Statute
Outcome: Rejected
Summary: Increases surtax on beer, wine and distilled spirits, with all proceeds going to a new Alcohol Surtax Fund. The Fund will spend the money on alcohol and drug abuse prevention and treatment, emergency medical treatment, mental health programs, other health and social services, and on enforcement programs. Also specifies that funding levels for certain other program areas not be decreased. Exempts itself from new taxing regulations which will exist if Proposition 136 is passed.
Arguments For: The tax increase proposed amounts to a "nickel-a-drink," and uses the proceeds to fight alcohol-related programs. Only the liquor industry opposes this, for reasons of its own profits. The measure is widely supported by health, religious, and law enforcement groups. Voters should also vote no on Propositions 126 [a legislative constitutional amendment] and 136, which are sponsored by the liquor industry.
Endorsers: Dr. Donald M. Bowman, Exec. Dir., Calif. Council on Alcohol Problems; Michael P. Trainor, M.D., Pres., Amer. College of Emergency Physicians, State Chapter of Calif.; Thomas A. Noble, Pres., Calif. Assn. of Highway Patrolmen; Harry Snyder, West Coast Dir., Consumers Union; Ric Loya, Exec. Dir., Calif Assn. of School Health Educators; Jacqueline Masso, Santa Clara County Chapter of Mothers Against Drunk Driving (MADD).
Arguments Against: This is not just an alcohol tax. It proposes spending more than the alcohol tax will raise, meaning that funding will come from the taxes of all Californians. It also threatens important current services, and denies any funding to the public schools.
Endorsers: Frank M. Jordan, Police Chief, City and County of San Francisco; Larry McCarthy, Pres., Calif. Taxpayers Assn.; Herbert E. Salinger, former Exec. Dir., Calif. School Boards Assn.; Marc Kern, Ph.D., Addiction Alternatives Research & Treatment Center; Robert B. Hamilton, Pres., Calif. State Fireman's Assn.; Dana W. Reed, former Dir., Calif. Dept. of Traffic Safety.

PROPOSITION 135: Pesticide Regulation.
Type: Initiative Statute
Outcome: Rejected
Summary: Makes changes in the monitoring and regulation of pesticides for food safety, the disposal of pesticides, funding for pest management, and the transportation of hazardous materials. Appropriates money for pesticide-related research. Creates position of state Environmental Advocate, to be filled by the Secretary of Environmental Affairs. Provides that if this measure and

Proposition 128 both pass, only the one receiving the most votes will be implemented in several areas.

Arguments For: Establishes scientific health-protecting measures to control pesticides, protect consumers and farm workers, and protect our food, land, wildlife, air, and water. The opponents of this measure, led by Tom Hayden, want radical, unscientific approaches to the pesticide problem.

Endorsers: Bob L. Vice, Pres., Calif. Farm Bureau Fed.; Dr. Julian R. Youmans, M.D., Ph.D., Prof. of Neurosurgery, Univ. of Calif., Davis; Haruko N. Yasuda, R.D., Registered Dietician; David Moore, Pres., Western Growers Assn.; Don Beaver, Pres., Calif. Growers Assn.

Arguments Against: This is a fraudulent measure, supported by the chemical and pesticide industries, in an effort to defeat Proposition 128. Most of it simply repeats what is already law in California. It includes no meaningful improvements, and will also shift the cost of pesticide testing from the pesticide industry to the taxpayer.

Endorsers: Lucy Blake, Exec. Dir., Calif. League of Conservation Voters; Dan Sullivan, Chair, Sierra Club of Calif.; Al Courchesne, Family Farmer; Al Meyerhoff, Senior Attorney, Natural Resources Defense Council.

PROPOSITION 136: State, Local Taxation.
Type: Initiative Constitutional Amendment
Outcome: Rejected
Summary: Changes the requirements for adopting new or increased state and local taxes. Special (as opposed to general) taxes on personal property must be based on the value of the property, and are restricted to one percent of the value of the property. All new or increased state taxes must be approved by a vote of two-thirds of the legislature. State special taxes enacted through the initiative process must be approved by two-thirds of the voters (state general taxes will continue to require a majority vote). Local government general tax increases must be approved by a majority of the voters. Defines "general" and "special" taxes. Invalidates taxing provisions of other Propositions (including 129, 133, 134) in this election.

Arguments For: This measure guarantees the public's right to vote on prospective tax increases, protects against "special taxes," and stops politicians and special interest groups from pushing through pet tax increases without voter approval.

Endorsers: Joel Fox, Pres., Howard Jarvis' Taxpayers Assn.; Richard Gann, Pres., Paul Gann's Citizens Comm.

Arguments Against: This measure really limits the right to vote and increases the power of special interests. This measure is an effort by the liquor industry to avoid taxation. It violates the principle of majority rule.

Endorsers: Bill Honig, State Supt. of Public Instruction; Ed Davis, State Senator, former Police Chief of Los Angeles; Dan Terry, Pres., Calif. Professional Firefighters; Police Chief Ron Lowenberg, Pres., Police Chiefs Dept. of the League of Calif. Cities; Dorothy Leonard, Pres., Calif. State Parent-Teacher Assn.; Carole Wagner Vallianos, Pres., League of Women Voters of Calif.

PROPOSITION 137: Initiative and Referendum Process.

Type: Initiative Constitutional Amendment
Outcome: Rejected
Summary: Requires that voters approve any changes in state law relative to statewide or local initiative or referendum petition and voting processes
Arguments For: This measure will prevent the politicians from changing the rules for initiatives and referendums, such as increasing the number of signatures required to qualify a measure for the ballot.
Endorsers: Joel Fox, Pres., Howard Jarvis' Taxpayers Assn.; Richard Gann, Paul Gann's Citizens Comm.; Quentin L. Kopp, State Senator, 8th Dist.
Arguments Against: This is an effort by special interests to block reform of the initiative process. It will halt such reforms as disclosure of who is paying for an initiative campaign and regulation of campaign practices.
Endorsers: Daniel H. Lowenstein, former Chair, Fair Political Practices Comm.; Ed Foglia, Pres., Calif. Teachers Assn.; Howard L. Owens, Pres., Congress of Calif. Seniors; Judge Bruce W. Sumner (Ret.), former Chair, Constitution Revision Comm.; Tom Noble, Pres., Calif Assn. of Highway Patrolmen.

PROPOSITION 138: Forestry Programs. Timber Harvesting Practices.

Type: Initiative Statute/Bond Act
Outcome: Rejected
Summary: Revises current restrictions on logging operations, requires the state to conduct studies on "greenhouse gases," places new restrictions on state acquisition of private lands. Authorizes sale of $300 million in bonds to pay for program for forest improvements. Contains provisions to resolve conflicts with parts of Propositions 128 and 130.
Arguments For: We have to protect California's old growth forests, and this proposition is a more reasonable way to do this than that included in Proposition 130. It is also more comprehensive, including wildlife protection and the planting of trees in urban areas. The measure will ban clearcutting, implement massive tree planting to reduce global warming, and strictly regulate forest management.

Endorsers: Gerald L. Partain, former Dir., Calif. Dept. of Forestry and Fire Protection; Phillip G. Lowell, Exec. Dir., Redwood Region Conservation Council; Scott Wall, Pres., Calif. Licensed Foresters Assn; Sue Granger-Dickson, Wildlife Biologist.

Arguments Against: This measure comes from the big timber companies, and is opposed by more than 100 environmental groups.   It does not ban clearcutting, and would subsidize timberland owners with public funds. It will cause massive job losses and a future lack of timber.

Endorsers: George Frampton, Pres., Wilderness Society; Maurice Getty, Pres., Calif. State Park Rangers Assn.; Philip S. Berry, former Vice Chair, Calif. Bd. of Forestry; Gail Lucas, Chair, State Forest Practices Task Force, Sierra Club; Jay D. Hair, Pres., National Wildlife Fed.; John H. Adams, Exec. Dir., Natural Resources Defense Council.

PROPOSITION 139: Prison Inmate Labor. Tax Credit.
Type: Initiative Constitutional Amendment and Statute
Outcome: Approved
Summary: Permits state and local inmates to work for private businesses, governed by contract. Establishes joint venture programs between the Dept. of Corrections and public and private agencies, with an advisory board to direct the program. Regulates wages inmates will receive, and deductions state may make from inmate income; restricts use of inmate labor to replace strikers.

Arguments For: California currently spends $2 billion per year on incarceration. This measure will result in inmates paying for part of their upkeep, and also being able to make restitution to their victims. At the same time, the prisoners will develop skills and work habits that will help them avoid returning to crime when released.

Endorsers: George Deukmejian, Governor; Don Novey, Pres., Calif. Correctional Peace Officers Assn.; Doris Tate, Pres, Coalition of Victims Equal Rights; Pete Wilson, U. S. Senator; Dan Lungren, Attorney.

Arguments Against: The program will lose money, since its expenses will greatly exceed the money returned to the state. It would endanger the public and exacerbate the problem of unemployment among law-abiding citizens. It would discriminate against employers of free labor.

Endorsers: John F. Henning, Exec. Sec.-Treas., Calif. Labor Fed.; Albin J. Gruhn, Pres., Calif. Labor Fed., AFL-CIO; Charles P. Gillingham, Sheriff of Santa Clara County; Michael Hennessey, Sheriff of San Francisco; Melvin H. Jones, Pres., Assn. for Los Angeles Deputy Sheriffs.

PROPOSITION 140: Limits on Terms of Office, Legislator's Retirement, Legislative Operating Costs.

Type: Initiative Constitutional Amendment
Outcome: Approved
Summary: Limits specified state office holders and state senators to two terms, members of the Assembly to three terms. Prohibits legislators from earning any future state retirement benefits, and requires them to join the federal Social Security system. Limits total expenditures of the state legislature for salaries and operating expenses.
Arguments in favor: This will reform our political system by removing an elite of career politicians. The political process will be opened up to new people, and diminish the influence of special interests. It will save millions of dollars by limiting the amount the legislature can spend.
Endorsers: Peter F. Schabarum, Chairman, Los Angeles Country Bd. of Supervisors; Lewis K. Uhler, Pres., National Tax-Limitation Comm.; J. G. Ford, Jr., Pres., Marin United Taxpayers Assn.; W. Bruce Lee, II, Exec. Dir., Calif. Business League; Lee A. Phelps, Chairman, Alliance of Calif. Taxpayers; Art Pagdan, M.D., National 1st. V.P., Filipino-American Political Assn.
Arguments Against: The measure takes away our constitutional right to choose our representatives. It controls more than consecutive terms—legislators will be banned for life from serving again. The retirement provisions will hurt poor and middle class citizens who might run for office.
Endorsers: Dr. Regene L. Mitchell, Pres., Consumer Fed. of Calif.; Lucy Blake, Exec. Dir., Calif. League of Conservation Voters; Dan Terry, Pres., Calif. Professional Firefighters; Ed Foglia, Pres., Calif. Teachers Assn.; Linda M. Tangren, State Chair, Calif. National Women's Political Caucus.

Part III: Selected Bibliography

The pages that follow list references culled from the California Direct Democracy Project research inventory, which now numbers above 750 items. Included are published books, articles, and government documents, plus unpublished master's theses, doctoral dissertations, and scholarly papers. Individuals and groups interested in inquiring further into the subject of the initiative and referendum can use this bibliography as a starting place for such inquiries. The Project continues to expand its research inventory, keeping the list of published materials up to date, and seeking more references to unpublished materials.

BOOKS

Alexander, Herbert E. *Political Reform in California, How Has It Worked??
    An Evaluation of Proposition 9, the Political Reform Act of 1974,
    Following Its Operation in Two Elections.* Los Angeles: Citizens'
    Research Foundation, Center for Study of the American Experience,
    1980.
Anderson, Dewey. *California State Government.* Stanford, CA: Stanford
    Univ. Press, 1942.
Beard, Charles A., and Birl E. Schultz. *Documents On the State-Wide
    Initiative, Referendum, and Recall.* NY: McMillan Co., 1912. Reprinted
    By Da Capo Press, Ny, 1970.
Benedict, Robert, Hugh Bone, Willard Laveal, and Ross Rice. *The Voters
    and Attitudes toward Nuclear Power: A Comparative Study of "Nuclear
    Moratorium" Initiatives.* 1979. (Mimeo.?)
Bicker, William E. *The Vote On Proposition 2: A Post-election Study.*
    Berkeley: University of California, Berkeley, 1972.

Bird, Frederick L. and Francis M. Ryan. *The Recall of Public officers: A Study of the Operation of the Recall in California.* NY: Macmillan, 1930.

Bone, Hugh A. *The Initiative and the Referendum.* NY: National Municipal League, State Constitutional Studies Project, 1975.

Boyle, James. *The Initiative and Referendum.* 2nd Edition. Columbus, Ohio: A. H. Smythe, 1912.

Brandsma, Richard W. *Direct Democracy and Water Policy: A Preliminary Examination of a Special District Election.* Davis: Institute of Governmental Affairs, University of California, 1966.

Brody, Richard A. *North, South, East, and West, It's Prop. 13 We Love....: the Jarvis-Gann Initiative in the Counties of California.* Stanford CA: Stanford University, 1978.

Butler, David, and Austin Ranney. *Referenda.* 1978.

Butler, David, and Austin Ranney. *Referendums: A Comparative Study of Practice and Theory.* Washington, D.C.: American Enterprise Institute, 1978.

Butler, David, and Austin Ranney, eds. *Referendums: A Comparative Study of Practice and Theory.* Washington: American Enterprise Institute, AEI Studies # 216, n.d.

Byrd, Frederick L. and Francis M. Ryan. *The Recall of Public officials: A Study of the Operation of the Recall in California.* NY: Macmillan, 1930.

California Taxpayers' Assn. *Analysis of Measures On the November 5, 1974 Ballot.* Sacramento: California Taxpayers' Assn., 1974.

California State Chamber of Commerce. *We the People: Voter's Guide to the 1974 State and Federal Elections.* San Francisco Sacramento: Calif. State Chamber of Commerce (prepared in Cooperation With American Outlook), 1974.

California Commission on Campaign Financing. *To Govern Ourselves: Ballot Initiatives in California.* Los Angeles: forthcoming, 1991.

California Taxpayer's Assn. *Analysis of Measures on the November 7, 1972 Ballot.* Sacramento: California Taxpayer's Assn., 1972.

California Fair Political Practices Commission. *Historical Overview of Receipts and Expenditures by Ballot Measure Committees: A Summary of Receipts and Expenditures in Connection with California State Ballot Measures, 1976 Through 1986.* Sacramento: The Commission, 1988.

California State Chamber of Commerce, Research Dept. *Initiative Legislation in California: History of the Use of the Initiative and Summary of Various Proposals for Amendment of the Initiative Process.* San Francisco: California State Chamber of Commerce, 1950.

California State Chamber of Commerce, Economic Development and Research Dept. *Initiative Legislation of California: History of the Use of the Initiative and Summary of Various Proposals for Amendment of the Initiative Process.* San Francisco: California State Chamber of Commerce, Revised, 1961.

Cronin, Thomas E. *Direct Democracy: The Politics of Initiative, Referendum, and Recall.* Cambridge, MA: Harvard Univ. Press, 1989

Crouch, Winston W. *The Initiative and Referendum in California.* Los Angeles: John Randolph Haynes and Dora Haynes Foundation, 1950.

Dean, Terry, and Ronald Heckart. *Proposition 13, 1978 California Primary.* [Bibliography] Berkeley, CA: Institute of Governmental Studies, Univ. of California, Berkeley, 1979.

Delmatier, Royce D., Clarence F. Mcintosh, and Earl G. Waters. *The Rumble of California Politics, 1848-1970.* NY: John Wiley and Sons, 1970.

Dubois, Philip, and Floyd Feeney. *Improving the Initiative Process: Options for Change.* Davis, CA, University of California, Davis, forthcoming 1991.

Durkee, Michael P., M. Thomas Jacobson, Thomas C. Wood, and Michael H. Zischke. *Land-use Initiatives and Referenda in California.* Point Arena, CA: Solano Press Books, 1990.

Everson, David H. *Initiatives and Voter Turnout: A Comparative State Analysis.* Springfield: Illinois Legislative Studies Center, Sangamon State Univ., 1980.

Fauber, Richard E. *The Reformer Without A Cause: Hiram Johnson, 1919-1929.* 1960.

Feldman, Esther. *How to Design, Implement and Run A Campaign for A Statewide or Local Land Conservation Initiative.* Sacramento: Planning and Conservation League Foundation, 1988.

Gregg, James E. *California Newspaper Editorial Endorsements: Influence on Ballot Measures.* Davis: University of California, Institute of Governmental Affairs, 1970.

Gregg, James E. *Newspaper Endorsements and Local Elections in California.* Davis: University of California, Institute of Governmental Affairs, 1966.

Groth, Alexander J., and Howard G. Schultz. *Voter Attitudes on the 1976 California Nuclear Initiative.* Institute of Governmental Affairs Environmental Quality Series, No. 25. Davis: Univ. of Calif., 1976.

Guthrie, James W., *et al. School Finance Project: Proposition Thirteen and the Pursuit of Equality and Efficiency for California's Schools.* Berkeley: Univ. of Calif. School of Education, Field Service Center, 1978.

Harris, Joseph P. *California Politics.* 4th Edition. San Francisco: Chandler Publishing Co., 1967.

Heckart, Ronald J., and Terry J. Dean, comps., *Proposition 13 in the 1978 California Primary: A Post-election Bibliography.* Berkeley: Univ. of Calif. Institute of Governmental Studies, 1981.

Hichborn, Franklin. *Story of the Session of the California Legislature of 1921.* San Francisco: Press of James H. Barry, 1922.

Hichborn, Franklin. *The Social Evil in California As A Political Problem.* San Francisco: James H. Barry Co., 1914(?).

Hichborn, Franklin. *Story of the Session of the California Legislature of 1915.* San Francisco: Press of James H. Barry, 1916.

Hichborn, Franklin. *Story of the Session of the California Legislature of 1909.* San Francisco: James H. Barry Co., 1909.

Hichborn, Franklin. *Political Activities of the Power Trust in California.* Public Ownership League of America, 1932.

Hichborn, Franklin. *Story of the Session of the California Legislature of 1911.* San Francisco: James H. Barry Co., 1911.

Hichborn, Franklin. *The Strange Story of California State Irrigation Association.* San Francisco: Issued By the California State Water and Power League, 1926.

Hichborn, Franklin. *Story of the Session of the California Legislature of 1913.* San Francisco: Press of James H. Barry, 1913.

The Initiative: A Brief Bibliography with Emphasis on California. Berkeley, CA: Institute of Governmental Studies, University of California, Berkeley, 1978.

Institute for the Study of Labor and Economic Crisis. *Grassroots Politics in the 1980's: A Case Study.* San Francisco: Synthesis Publications, 1982.

Jarvis, Howard. *I'm Mad As Hell: the Exclusive Story of the Tax Revolt and Its Leader.* NY: Times Books, 1979.

Key, V.O. Jr., and Winston W. Crouch. *The Initiative and Referendum in California.* Berkeley: Univ. of Calif. Press, 1939.

League of Women Voters of California. *Initiative and Referendum in California: A Legacy Lost?* Sacramento: League of Women Voters of California, 1984.

League to Protect the Initiative. *The Initiative and Referendum in Danger! Enemies of Popular Government Renew Effort to Crush Democracy in California.* Los Angeles: n.p., 1922.

Lee, Eugene C. and Larry L. Berg. *The Challenge of California.* 2nd Edition. Boston: Little, Brown, 1976.

Lee, Eugene C. *The Politics of Nonpartisanship.* Berkeley: Univ. of Calif Press, 1960.

Lee, Eugene C. *750 Propositions: The Initiative in Perspective.* California Data Brief, 2:2, Berkeley: Institute of Governmental Studies, University of California, 1978.

Leister, Jack, *et al. California Politics and Government, 1970-1983: A Selected Bibliography.* Berkeley: Institute of Government Studies, University of California, Berkeley, 1984.

Leuthold, David A. *California Politics and Problems, 1900-1936: A Selective Bibliography.* Berkeley, Institute of Government Studies, University of California, 1965. (With supplements, 1964-1968.)

Leuthold, Janet. *Patterns in the Adoption and Use of the Initiative in American States.* Columbia, MO: Missouri Academy of Sciences at the University of Missouri, 1978.

Magleby, David R. *Direct Legislation: Voting On Ballot Propositions in the United States.* Baltimore: John Hopkins, 1984.

McGulkigon, Patrick B. *The Politics of Direct Democracy in the U.S.: Case Studies in Popular Decision Making.* Washington D.C.: Free Congress Research and Education Foundation, 1985.

Mastro, Tandy M., *et al. Taking the Initiative: Corporate Control of the Referendum Process through Media Spending and What to Do About It.* Washington, DC: Media Access Project, 1980.

Mowry, George E. *The California Progressives.* NY: New York Times Book Co., 1951.

Niskanen, William, *et al. Tax and Expenditure Limitation by Constitutional Amendment: Four Perspectives on the California Initiative.* N.p., (1973?).

Oberholtzer, E.P. *The Referendum in America.* New Edition. Ny: Scribner's, 1912.

Olin, Spencer. *California's Prodigal Sons: Hiram Johnson and the Progressives, 1911-1917.* Berkeley: Univ. of Calif. Press, 1968.

Opdahl, Carl. *The Initiative and Referendum: Theories and Uses.* N.p., 1935.

Parris, Kenneth M. *Municipal Government Revenue Sources in Post Proposition 13 California."* Santa Barbara: Univ. of Calif., Santa Barbara Urban Economics Program, 1979.

People's Lobby. *Proposition 9, the Political Reform Act. A Fact for California, a Proposal for America.* Los Angeles: People's Lobby Press, 1974.

Phelps, Edith May, comp. *Selected Articles on the Initiative and Referendum.* 3rd ed. White Plains, NY: H. W. Wilson Co., 1914.

Proposition 13 Impact on Minorities; Proceedings of a Workshop, 2 March 1979. Davis: Univ. of Calif Institute of Governmental Affairs, 1979.

Ranney, Austin, ed. *The Referendum Device.* AEI Symposia. Washington, DC: American Enterprise Institute for Public Policy Research, 1981.

Sabatier, P. A. *Can Regulation Work?: the Implementation of the 1972 California Coastal Initiative.* Plenum Press, 1983. Environmental Policy and Planning Series.

Schmidt, David D., ed. *Ballot Initiatives: History, Research and Analysis of Recent Initiative and Referendum Campaigns.* Washington, DC: Initiative News Service, 1983.

Schmidt, David D. *Citizen Lawmakers: The Ballot Initiative Revolution.* Philadelphia:Temple Univ. Press, 1989.

Schmidt, David D., ed. *Initiative Procedures: A Fifty-State Survey.* Washington, DC: Initiative News Service, 1983.

Schwadron, Terry, Ed., *California and the American Tax Revolt: Proposition 13 Five Years Later.* Berkeley: Univ. of Calif. Press, 1984.

Scott, Stanley. *Governing California's Coast.* Berkeley: Institute of Governmental Studies, Univ. of Calif., 1975.

Sonenblum, Sidney, ed. *The California Tax Limitation.* Los Angeles: UCLA Institute of Government and Public Affairs, (1973?).

Stewart, Alva W. *The Initiative, Referendum, and Recall: Theory and Application.* Monticello, IL: Vance Bibliographies, 1983.

Stolz, Anne B., ed. *The Impact of the Bakke Decision and Proposition 13 on Equity for Women in California Higher Education: Proceedings of A Conference Held May 18-19, 1979 at the University of California, Berkeley.* Berkeley, 1979.

Tallian, Laura. *Direct Democracy: An Historical Analysis of the Initiative, Referendum, and Recall Process.* Los Angeles: People's Lobby Press, 1977.

Young, Nancy. *The Initiative Promise in California.* Los Angeles: Univ. of So. Calif. Law Center Library, 1982.

Zeitlin, Josephine Ver Brugge. *Initiative and Referendum: A Bibliography.* Los Angeles: J.R. Haynes and Dora Haynes Foundation, 1940.

Zeitlin, Josephine Ver Brugge. *Recall: A Bibliography.* Los Angeles: John Randolph and Dora Haynes Foundation, 1941.

Zisk, Betty H. *Money, Media, and the Grass Roots: State Ballot Issues and the Electoral Process.* Newbury Park, CA: Sage Library of Social Research, 1987.

ARTICLES

"A Digest on How the California Public Views a Variety of Matters Relating to the Initiative Process." *California Opinion Index* 1 (Feb. 1983).

"Analysis of June 1978 Ballot Propositions." *Cal-Tax News*, 19:8 (15 April 1978).

"Analysis of November 1978 Ballot Propositions." *Cal-Tax News*, 19:17 (1-14 Sept 1978).

"Analysis of Propositions on Ballot Nov. 8, 1960." *Tax Digest*, 38:8 (Aug. 1960), 38:9 (Sept. 1960).

Anderson, Totton J. "Bibliography on California Politics." *Western Political Q.* (Supplement), 11:4 (Dec. 1958).

Anderson, Totten J. and Eugene C. Lee. "The 1962 Election in California." *Western Political Q.* 16 (June, 1963).

Anderson, Walt. "Decision-making in the Dark: the Proposition 13 Campaigns." *Cry California* (Fall 1978).

Anderson, Jack. "Tax Revolt: the Opening of U.S.-Wide Movement." *Desert News*, 13 June 1978.

"Assembly Kills Move to Amend Law on Initiative." Sacramento *Bee*, 6 June 1939.

"Attacks on Referendum and Initiative Offer Nothing New." Sacramento *Bee*, 26 Dec 1939.

Bailey, Gil. "The Coastal Plan: Battle for the Shoreline." *Cry California* 11,3 (1976).

Baker, Gordon E. "American Conceptions of Direct Vis-a-vis Representative Governance." *Claremont Journal of Public Affairs* 4 (Spring 1977).

Baker, Gordon E. "The Impulse for Direct Democracy." *National Civic Review* 66 (1977).

Balderston, Frederick, I., Michael Heyman, and Wallace F. Smith. "Proposition 13, Property Transfers, and the Real Estate Markets." Berkeley: Univ. of Calif. Institute of Governmental Studies, 1979.

Ballew, Steven E. "The Constitutionality of Budgeting By Statewide Statutory Initiative in California." *Southern California Law Review* 51 (July 1978).

"Ballot Propositions: 1972 General Election." *Calif. Journal*, 1972.

"Ballot Propositions, 1972 General Election." *Calif. Journal*, 3:9 (Oct. 1972).

"Ballot Proposals for June 1970." *The Commonwealth*, 64:18 (4 May 1970).

"Ballot Proposals for November 1966." *The Commonwealth*, 42:40, Part 2 (Oct. 3, 1966).

"Ballot Proposals for November 1968." *The Commonwealth*, 62:40, Part 2 (30 Sept. 1968), 62:43, Part 2 (21 Oct. 1968).

Baratz, J.C. and J.H. Moskowitz. "Proposition 13: How and Why It Happened." *Phi Delta Kappan* 60:9-11 (Sept. 1978.)

Barnett, James D. "Judicial Review of Exceptions From the Referendum." *California Law Review* 10 (July 1922).

Benenson, Robert. "Initiatives and Referendums." *Editorial Research Reports* (22 Oct. 1982).

Berks, J.S., and Others., "Two Roads to School Finance Reform." *Society* 13: 67-72 (Jan. 1976).

"Bill Seeks to Remove Secrecy From Initiative." Sacramento *Bee*, 22 Jan 1937.

Bird, Brian. "Voluntary Suicide May Make California Ballot." *Christianity Today* 32:6 (8 Apr. 1988).

Bliven, B., "Power Politics in California." *New Republic* 114:503 (15 Apr. 1946).

"'Blue Sky,' Non-sale of Game, 'Red Light' and Water Commission Petitions." San Francisco *Call*, 7 Aug 1913.

Brestoff, Nick. "The California Initiative Process: A Suggestion for Reform." *Southern California Law Review* 48 (1975).

Blume, Norman. "Open House Referenda." *Public Opinion Quarterly* 35 (Winter 1971-2).

Bone, Hugh A., and Robert C. Benedict. "Perspectives on Direct Legislation: Washington State's Experience, 1914-1973." *Western Political Quarterly* 28 (1975).

Boyarsky, Nancy. "Proposition 9: The Local-government Loophole." *Calif. Journal* 5:9 (Sept. 1974).

Brestoff, Nick. "The California Initiative Process: A Suggestion for Reform." *Southern California Law Review* 48 (1975).

California Chamber of Commerce. "Initiative Scoreboard: An Historical Perspective." *Calif. Chamber of Commerce Alert*, 5:13 (30 Mar 1979).

California Journal Ballot Proposition Analysis." *Calif. Journal*, 7:6 (May, 1976 and Oct. 1976).

"California's Low-Income Housing Referendum: Equal Protection and the Problem of Economic Discrimination." *Columbia Journal of Law and Social Problems* 8 (1972).

"California's 1974 Political Reform Act: The Implementation and Impact of Proposition 9: Proceedings of A Workshop, May 30, 1975." Davis, Ca: institute of Governmental Affairs, Univ. of Calif., Davis, Sept., 1975.

Carter, Harlon. "Proposition 15 Campaign in Full Swing (California Gun Control Initiative)." *American Rifleman* 130 (Oct. 1982).

Casstevens, Thomas W., "Reflections on the Initiative Process in California State Politics." *Public Affairs Report* 6 (Feb. 1965).

"Change On Initiative Measures is Proposed" Sacramento *Bee*, 1 June 1939.

Cleveland, Willis W., and Charles L. Usher. "The Ecology of Referenda Outcomes in Georgia." *State and Local Government Review* 14 (1982).

Clubb, Jerome M. "National Patterns of Referenda Voting: the 1968 Election." In, Harlan Hahn, ed., *People and Politics in Urban Society.* Beverly Hills, CA: Sage, 1972.

Commonwealth Club of California, "Direct Legislation." *The Commonwealth*, VII:9, Part II (3 Mar. 1931).

Cottrell, Edwin A. "Twenty-five Years of Direct Legislation in California." *Public Opinion Q.* (Jan 1939).

Criuchett, Lawrence Paul. "Assemblyman Byron Rumford: Symbol of An Era." *Calif. History* 66:1 (1987).

Crouch, Winston W. "Initiative and Referendum in Cities. Bibliography." *Amer. Pol. Sci. Rev.* (June 1943).

Crouch, Winston W. "John Randolph Haynes and His Work for Direct Democracy." *Natl. Municipal Review* XXVII:9 (Sept. 1938).

Crouch, Winston W. "The Constitutional Initiative in Operation." *Amer. Pol. Sci. Rev.* (Aug. 1939).

"Danger Is Seen in Bills to Limit Voters' Initiative." Sacramento *Bee*, 6 Jan 1939.

Diamond, Roger J., Peter R.DiDonato, Patrick J. Marley, and Patricia V. Tubert. "California's Political Reform Act: Greater Access to the Initiative Process." *Southwestern University Law Review* 7 (Fall,1975).

Dodd, W. F. "Some Considerations upon the State-wide Initiative and Referendum." *Annals of the American Academy of Political and Social Science* 43 (Sept., 1912).

"Drive for Change in Initiative Law Begins." Sacramento *Bee*, 13 Dec 1939.

Dubois, William. "Proposition 9 Must Be Defeated." *California Farm Bureau Monthly*, 53:4 (Apr. 1972).

"Duck Sale [referendum] Bill Petition Forgeries." San Francisco *Call*, 8 Aug. 1913.

Dzublenski, Joe. "The Continuing Campaign to Inhibit the Initiative." *California Journal* 7 (Aug. 1976).

Ehrman, Sidney M. "Proposals for Revising the Initiative." *California: Magazine of the Pacific* (Dec. 1939).

Everson, David H. "The Effects of Initiatives On Voter Turnout: A Comparative State Analysis." *Western Political Q.* 34 (Sept. 1981).

Feldman, Esther. "Prop. 70: How Californians Won $776 Million to Protect Wildlife, the Coast and Park Lands." *Whole Earth Review* 62 (Spring 1989).

Field, Mervin D., "The Public Pulse: Prop 13--One Year Later." *Taxing and Spending* (July 1979).

Fiorina, Morris P. "The Decline of Collective Responsibility in American Politics." *Daedalus* 109 (Summer, 1980).

Fitzgerald, Maureen S. "Computer Democracy: An Analysis of California's New Love Affair with he Initiative Process." *California Journal* 11 (June 1980).

Fitzgerald, Maureen S. "Initiative Fever: Many Try, But Few Reach the Ballot." *California Journal* 10 (Dec. 1979).

"Forces Line Up to Do Battle Over Euthanasia." *Christianity Today* 31:17 (20 Nov. 1987).

"Four Who Also Shaped Events" (Jarvis-13). *Time*, 113:41 Jan. 1, 1979.

Gable, Richard W. "The Sebastiani Initiative: A California Wine Gone Sour." *Natl. Civic Review* 73:1 (1984).

Gerston, Larry N. "Political Reform, California Style." [Prop. 9, 1974]. *San Jose Studies* 2:2 (1976).

Glenn, Peter G. "State Law Limitations on the Use of Initiatives and Referenda in Connection with Zoning Amendments." *Southern California Law Review* 12 (1979).

Graham, Herbert. "The Direct Initiative Process: Have Unconstitutional Methods of Presenting the Issues Prejudices its Future?" *UCLA Law Review* 27 (1979).

Greenberg, Donald S. "The Scope of the Initiative and Referendum in California." *Calif. Law Rev.* 54 (Oct. 1966).

Groth, Alexander J., and Howard G. Schutz. "Voter Attitudes on the 1976 California Nuclear Initiative." Davis: Univ. of Calif. Institute of Governmental Affairs, 1977.

Gunn, Priscilla F. "Initiatives and Referendums: Direct Democracy and Minority Interests." *Urban Law Annual* 22 (1981).

Hahn, Harlan, and Timothy Almy. "Ethnic Politics and Racial Issues: Voting in Los Angeles." *Western Political Q.* 24 (Dec. 1971).

Hahn, Harlan, and Stephen C. Morton. "Initiative and Referendum—Do they Encourage or Impair Better State Government." *Florida State University Law Review* 5 (1977).

Hamilton, Howard D. "Direct Legislation: Some Implications of Open Housing Referenda." *Amer. Pol. Sci. Rev.* 64 (Mar. 1970).

Hamilton, Howard D. "Voting Behavior in Open Housing Referenda." *Social Science Q.* 51 (Dec. 1970).

Haynes, John R. "The Adoption of the Initiative, Referendum and Recall by the State of California." *West Coast Magazine* 11 (Jan. 1912).

Hendrick, B. J., "Johnson of California." *World's Work* 33: 289-94 (Jan. 1917).

Hennings, Robert E. "California Democratic Politics in the Period of Republican Ascendancy." *Pacific Hist. Review* XXXI (Aug 1962).

Hichborn, Franklin. "California Politics, 1891-1939." Unpublished Typescript, 1949. (Located at UCLA Research Library.)

Hichborn, Franklin. "Sources of Opposition to Direct Legislation in California." *The Commonwealth*, VII:9, (3 Mar. 1931).

"High Initiative Costs Reported." Sacramento *Bee*, 3 Nov 1932.

Holcombe, Randall G., and Paul C. Taylor. "Tax Referenda and the Voluntary Exchange Model of Taxation: A Suggested Implementation." *Public Finance Quarterly* 8 (1980).

Holdren, John P. "The Nuclear Controversy and the Limitations of Decision-Making by Experts." *Bulletin of the Atomic Scientists* 32"2 (1976).

"Information, Credibility and the California Voter: Transcript of Proceedings of Conference Held On 11 Apr. 1980." Sponsored By the Continuing Education Project, Dept. of Humanities and Social Sciences, UCLA Extension, Los Angeles.

"Initiative and Referendum—Power of the Legislature to Affect the Initiative and Referendum Processes by Prohibiting Payment of Compensation to Circulators of Petitions." *Kansas Law Review* 7 (1975).

"Initiative Makes A Big Comeback as Groups Seek to Bypass Legislature." *Calif. Journal*, 3:7 (Aug. 1972).

"Initiative Law Changes Urged to Halt Abuses." Sacramento *Bee*, 18 Dec. 1933.

Institute of Public Affairs, UC Berkeley. "Public Affairs Report." *Institute of Governmental Studies, Public Affairs Report* 6:1 (Feb 1965).

"Is Direct Legislation Unconstitutional?" *Cal Outlook*, 10:6 (15 Apr 1911).

Jaffe, Alvin N. "The Constitutionality of Supermajority Voting Requirements: Gordon v. Lance." *University of Illinois Law Forum* 22 (1971).

"Johnson Urges Care in Revamp of Referendum." Sacramento *Bee*, 22 Dec 1939.

Jordan, David James. "Constitutional Constraints on Initiative and Referendum." *Vanderbilt Law Review* 32 (1979).

"Judicial Review of Initiative Constitutional Amendments." *University of California, Davis Law Review* 14 (1980).

"June 1974 State Ballot Propositions." *The Commonwealth*, 68:19, Pt. 2 (13 May 1974).

"June 1972 State Ballot Propositions." *The Commonwealth*, 66:18, Part 2 (1 May 1972).

Kizer, Kenneth W., Thomas E. Warriner, and Steven A. Book. "Sound Science in the Implementation of Public Policy; A Case Report on California's Proposition 65." (The Safe Drinking Water and Toxic Enforcement Act of 1986). *J. of the American Medical Assn.* 260:7 (19 Aug. 1988).

Krieger, Nancy, and Joyce C. Lashof. "Aids, Policy Analysis and the Electorate: The Role of Schools of Public Health." (Prop 64, La Rouche "prevent Aids Now" Initiative). *Amer. J. of Public Health* 78:4 (Apr. 1988).

Lake, Laura M. "The Environmental Mandate: Activists and the Electorate." *Political Science Q.* 98 (1983).

Lapalombara, J.G. and C.B. Hagin. "Direct Legislation: An Appraisal and A Suggestion." *Amer.Pol. Sci. R.* 45 (June 1951).

"League Attacks Bill Which Would Throttle Initiative Law" Sacramento *Bee*, 20 Mar 1935.

Lee, Eugene C. "The Initiative and Referendum: How California Has Fared." *National Civic Review* 68:2 (1979).

Levy, Mickey. "Voting On California's Tax and Expenditures Limitations Initiative." *National Tax Journal* 28:4 (Dec. 1975).

Lipset, Seymour Martin and Earl Raab. "The Message of Proposition 13." *Commentary* (Sept. 1978).

Lowell, Frederick K., and Teresa A. Craigie. "California's Reapportionment Struggle: A Classic Clash Between Law and Politics." *J. of Law and Politics* 2:2 (1985).

Lowenstein, Daniel H. "California Initiative and the Single Subject Rule." *UCLA Law Review* 30 (1983).

Lowenstein, Daniel H. "Campaign Spending and Ballot Propositions: Recent Experience, Public Choice Theory and the First Amendment." *UCLA Law Review* 29 (1982).

Lutrin, Carl E., and Allen K. Settle. "The Public and Ecology: The Role of Initiatives in California's Environmental Politics." *Western Political Q.* 28:2 (June 1975).

Ma, Louise. "The New Disclosure Law...Charting the Complex Flow of Campaign Contributions." *Calif Journal* 5:9 (Sept. 1974).

McFarland, John. "Progressives and the Initiative: Protestant Reformers Who Thought Politics Was Sin." *California Journal* 15 (1984).

Magleby, David B. "Legislatures and the Initiative: The Politics of Direct Democracy." *J. of State Government* 59:1 (Spring, 1986).

Magleby, David B. "Taking the Initiative: Direct Legislation and Direct Democracy in the 1980's." *ABC Political Science* 21:2 and 21:3 (1988, 1989).

Magleby, David B. "Is Direct Democracy A Failed Democracy? Another Look at Initiative Referenda and Why they Are Popular." *Center Magazine* 18 (Jul.-Aug. 1985).

Mason, P. "Methods of Improving Legislative Procedures." *Ann Am Acad* 195 (Jan. 1938).

Mayer, A., and M. Wheeler. "Referendum Fever." *Atlantic* 244 (Sept. 1979).

McHenry, Dean E. "The Pattern of California Politics." *Western Political Q.* 1 (Mar. 1948).

Mueller, John E. "Choosing Among 133 Candidates." *Public Opinion Q.* 34 (Fall 1970).

Mueller, John E. "The Politics of Fluoridation in Seven California Cities." *Western Political Q.* 19 (Mar. 1966).

Mueller, John E. "Voting On the Propositions: Ballot Pattern and Historical Trends in California." *American Political Science Review* 63 (Dec. 1969).

"Neither of the Major Political Parties Had Used the Initiative." Pubs. of the Univ. of Calif. at Los Angeles in Social Science, 6:4, 1939.

Nelson, Michael. "Power to the People: The Crusade for Direct Democracy: Use of the Initiative." *Saturday Review* 6 (24 Nov 1979).

"1968 Election Special." *Calif. Digest*, 1:3 (Oct. 1968).

"November 1973 State Ballot Proposition: Tax and Expenditure Limitations." *The Commonwealth*, 67:42 (15 Oct. 1973).

"November Ballot Will include Eight Constitutional Changes; Bond Issue." *Cal-Tax*, 9:9 (Sept. 1968).

"November, 1972 State Ballot Propositions." *The Commonwealth*, 66:42, Pt. 2 (16 Oct. 1972).

Ogburn, W. F. "Initiative and Referendum Tested in Hard Times." *Survey* 37:206 (25 Nov 1916).

"Olson is Urged to Seek Curb on Initiative Abuse." Sacramento *Bee*, 10 Nov 1939.

"Olson Wants Law to Halt Misuse of Referendum." Sacramento *Bee*, 3 Mar 1939, 20:4

Owens, John R., and Edward C. Olson. "Campaign Spending and the Electoral Process in California, 1966-1974." *Western Pol. Q.*, 30:4 (Dec. 1977).

Owens, John R., and Larry L. Wade. "Campaign Spending on the California Ballot Propositions, 1924-84." *Western Political Q.* 39:4 (1986).

Peirce, Neal R. "Legislation by Popular Initiative: A Tolerable Compromise that Might Work." *Western City* 55:7 (1979).

Pezoldt, C.W. "Getting the Yes Vote on Bond Referendum." *Parks and Recreation* 10 (Fall 1975).

Phillips, Herbert L. [Series of articles on Nov. 1952 Propositions.] Sacramento *Bee*, 31 July-25 Aug., 1952.

Pillsbury, A. J. "The Initiative, Its Achievements and Abuses." *Commonwealth* 25 (11 Nov. 1931).

Poe, Elizabeth. "Politics and Proposition 15: The Strange Urban-Rural Alliance in California." *Frontier: The Voice of the New West* 12:1 (Nov. 1960).

"Preelection Judicial Review: Taking the Initiative in Voter Protection." *California Law Review* 71 (1983).

Price, Charles M. "The Initiative: A Comparative State Analysis and Reassessment of a Western Phenomenon." *Western Political Q.* 28:2 (June 1975).

Price, Charles M. "The Mercenaries Who Gather Signatures for Ballot Measures." *California Journal* 12 (1981).

Price, Charles M. "Seizing the Initiative: California's New Politics." *Citizen Participation* 15 (1984).

"Proposition 14 Win Spurs New Attacks on Initiative." *The California Statesman*, 1:13 (Dec., 1964).

"Proposition 8 (Tax Reform): 'No' Vote Urged by California Real Estate Association." *California Real Estate Magazine*, 50:7 (May,1970).

"Proposition 9: Can California Afford to Gamble Again?" *Western City*, April 1980.

"Propositions Vote Cost is Set at $1,657,509." Sacramento *Bee*, 8 Dec. 1936.

Quinn, T. Anthony. "Ballot Initiatives: A Politician's Unique Guideposts." *California Journal* 15 (1984).

Quinn, T. Anthony. ""The Specter of 'Black Wednesday': How the Establishment Destroys Unwanted Initiatives Like Jarvis." *California Journal* 9 (1978).

Radabaugh, John Sheldon. "Tendencies of California Direct Legislation." *Southwestern Social Science Q.* 42:1 (June 1961).

Radin, Max. "Popular Legislation in California." *Minnesota Law R.* (Aug. 1939).

Radin, Max. "Popular Legislation in California, 1936-1946." *Calif. Law Rev.*, 35:2 (June 1947).

Ray, Steven W. The California Initiative Process: The Demise of the Single Subject Rule." *Pacific Law Journal* 14 (1983).

"'Red Light' Abatement Bill Petition." San Francisco *Call*, 16 Apr 1913.

Richman, Steven M. "Political Expression by Artificial Persons in Referendum Campaigns." *annual Survey of American Law* (1979).

Roberts, Bob. "What Happened to Proposition 11?" *Pacific Oil World* (July-Aug. 1980).

Roger, Michael. "Progressivism of the California Electorate." *J. of American History* LV (Sept. 1968).

Romer, Thomas, and Howard Rosenthat. "Bureaucrats Versus Voters: On the Political Economy of Resource Allocation by Direct Democracy." *Q. Journal of Economics* 93 (1979).

Scott, Stanley, and Harriet Nathan. "Public Referenda: A Critical Reappraisal." Berkeley: Univ. of Calif. Institute of Governmental Studies, 1970 (Reprint No. 35, from *Urban Affairs Quarterly.*)

"Senate Defeats Plan to Change Initiative Law." Sacramento *Bee*, 17 Mar. 1939.

"Seventh Plan to Curb Abuse of Initiative is Filed for Titling." Sacramento *Bee*, 14 Dec. 1939.

Schmidt, David D. "Referenda & Initiatives: Hot New Campaign Areas." *Campaigns and Elections, The Journal of Political Action* 3:4 (1983).

Schmidt, David D. "Winning an Initiative Big: How they Whipped 'Whoops' in Washington State." *Campaigns and Elections, The Journal of Political Action* 4:3 (1983).

Scott, Stanley, and Harriet Nathan. "Public Referenda, A Critical Reappraisal." *Urban Affairs Q.* 5 (1970).

Sirico, Louis J., Jr. "The Constitutionality of the Initiative and Referendum." *Iowa Law Review* 65 (1980).

Sitton, Tom. "California's Practical Idealist: John Randolph Haynes." *California History* LXVII:1 (Mar. 1988).

Slonim, Marc, and James H. Lowe. "Judicial Review of Laws Enacted by Popular Vote." *Washington Law Review* 55 (1979).

"State and Local Limitations on Ballot Measure Contributions." *Michigan Law Review* 79 (1981).

"State-Wide Referenda Since 1919." *Congressional Digest* 9 (Mar. 1930.).

"The Constitutionality of Municipal Advocacy in Statewide Referendum Campaigns." *Harvard Law Review* 93 (1980).

"The Initiative and Referendum in the United States." *Pacific Municipal Review,* 18 (April, 1908).

"The Indirect Initiative." *National Civic Review* 68 (1979).

"The Reagan Tax Initiative. Is It Necessary to Halt Spiraling State Spending? Or Will It Put California Government in a Straight Jacket?" *Calif. Journal,* 4:9 (Sept. 1973).

Thompson, Julie. "The Incredibly Complex Ballot Facing Democrats in June '76." *Calif. Journal,* 6:3 (Mar. 1975).

Viehe, Fred W. "The First Recall: Los Angeles Urban Reform Or Machine Politics?" *So. Calif. Quarterly,* LXX:1 (Spring, 1988)

Waters, Laughlin E. "The California Housing Initiative." *Los Angeles Bar Bulletin* 39:9 (July 1964).

Wenner, Lettie Mcspadden, and Manfred W. Wenner. "Nuclear Policy and Public Participation." *Am. Behavioral Scientist* 22:2 (1978).

Whitt, J. Allen. "Californians, Cars, and Technological Death." (Prop. 18, 1970) *Society* 10:5 (1973).

Wolffinger, Raymond E., and Fred I. Greenstein. "The Repeal of Fair Housing in California: An Analysis of Referendum Voting." *Am. Pol. Sci. R.* 62:3 (1968).

Woods, William K. "Creative Local Initiative 1982-83: Citizens Take the Lead in All-American Cities." *National Civic Rev.* 73:5 (1984).

Zagoria, S. "Resolving Impasses By Public Referendum." *Missouri Labor R.* 96 (May 1973).

PAPERS

Allswang, John M. "The Origins of Direct Democracy in California: On the Development of an Issue and Its Relationship to Progressivism."

Presented to Conference in Honor of Samuel P. Hays, Pittsburgh, PA, 4-5 May 1991.

Baker, Gordon E. "Judicial Review of Statewide Initiatives in California: Proposition 13 in Recent Historical Prospective." Presented to the Annual Meetings of the American Political Science Association, New York City, August 31-September 3, 1978.

Berg, Larry. "The Initiative Process and Public Policy-Making in the States: 1904-1976." Presented at the Annual Meetings of the American Political Science Association, New York City, August 31-September 3, 1978.

Debow, Ken. "Tilting at the Windmill of Special interest Lobbying Power: the Case of California Under Proposition 9." Presented at the Meetings of the Western Political Science Association, Portland, Oregon. March 22-24, 1979.

Everson, David H. "Initiatives and Voter Turnout: the Case of 1978." Presented at the Meetings of the Southwestern Political Science Association, Houston, Texas April 2-5, 1980.

Hamilton, Howard D. "Political Ethos: The Evidence in Referenda Survey Data." Presented at the Meetings of the American Political Science Association, New Orleans, 4-9 Sept. 1973.

Radosevich, Ted C. "Electoral Analysis of the Clean Water Bond Law of 1974: Patterns of Support in a Continuing Environmental Issue." Institute of Governmental Studies, Working Paper No. 15. University of California, Berkeley, August, 1975.

Magleby, David B., *et al.* "The Initiative in the 1980s: Popular Support, Issue Agendas, and Legislative Reform of the Process." Presented at Meetings of the American Political Science Association, Denver, 2-6 Sept. 1982.

Magleby, David B. "Legal Provisions for Direct Legislation and the Growth of an Initiative Industry." Presented to Meetings of the American Political Science Association, 28-31 Aug. 1980.

Magleby, David B. "Plebiscitary Democracy: The Initiative and Referendum in American Politics." Prepared for Center for the Study of Democratic Institutions, Santa Barbara, CA., 16 Dec. 1983.

Neiman, Max, and M. Gottdiener. "The Secondary Effects of Initiative Politics: The Mobilized Petition Signer." Presented to Meetings of the American Political Science Association, Chicago, 1-4 Sept. 1983.

Newquest, Marilyn Fuller. "The Political Reform Act of 1974: A Case Study of California's Initiative Process." Presented to Meetings of the Western Political Science Association, Denver, 26-28 Mar. 1981.

Shockley, John S. "Direct Democracy, Campaign Finance, and the Courts: The Difficulty of Reform." Presented to meetings of the American Political Science Association, New York, 3-6 Sept. 1981.

Soule, John W., and Strand Paul J. "Public attitudes toward Homosexuality: the Proposition 6 Case in California." Presented at the Meetings of the Western Political Science Association, Portland, Oregon, 22-24, March, 1979.

Zisk, Betty H. "Winning State Referenda: Money vs. Peoplepower." Presented to Meetings of the American Political Science Association, Chicago, 1-4 Sept. 1983.

THESES/DISSERTATIONS

Adams, James Ring. "The Tax Revolt Tradition in American Politics and Law." Ph.D. Dissertation, Cornell University, 1983.

Bates, Jack. "The Southern Pacific Railroad in California Politics." M.A. Thesis, College of the Pacific, 1942.

Best, Wallace Hill. "Initiative and Referendum Politics in California, 1912-1952." Ph.D. Dissertation, University of Southern California, 1958.

Bidwell, Roy Norbert. "Alternative Funding of Community Services in California Community Colleges." Ed.D Dissertation, University of Southern California, 1987.

Blue, Margret Roemer. "Economic Initiative Voter Behavior: Some Data in the Search of Theory." Ph.D. Dissertation, Claremont Graduate School, 1984.

Borges, William George. "The Politics of Proposition 13: California, Public Education, and Moreno Valley United School District." Ph.D. Dissertation, University of California, Riverside, 1980.

Braitman, Jacqueline R. "Katherine Phelps Edson: A Progressive Feminist in California's Era of Reform." Ph.D. Dissertation, University of California, Los Angeles, 1988.

Bratton, J. Wesley. "The Extent and Nature of Educational Legislation Obtained Through the Initiative and Referendum in the United States With Special Application to the State of California." Ph.D. Dissertation, University of Southern California, 1951.

Clodius, Albert H. "The Quest for Good Government in Los Angeles, 1890-1910. Ph.D. Dissertation, Claremont Graduate School, 1953.

Cohn, Carl A. "The Jarvis II Initiative Campaign: A Case Study of An Educational Interest Group Coalition." Ph.D. Dissertation, University of California, Los Angeles, 1981.

Cohn, Carl Anthony. "The Jarvis II Initiative Campaign: A Case Study of An Educational Interest Group Coalition." Ed.D Dissertation, University of California, Los Angeles, 1981.

Everett, Miles C. "Chester Harvey Rowell: Pragmatic Humanist and California Progressive." Ph.D. Dissertation, University of California, Berkeley, 1966.

Jaques, Janice. "The Political Reform Movement in Los Angeles, 1900--1909." M.A. Thesis, Claremont Graduate School, 1948.

Lee, Eun Jae. "Cutback Management in the City of Alhambra (California)." Ph.D. Dissertation, Claremont Graduate School 1986.

Magleby, David Blyth. "Direct Legislation: Voting On Ballot Propositions in the United States." Ph.D. Dissertation, University of California, Berkeley, 1980.

McCoy, Candace Sue. "Plea Bargaining and Proposition 8 Politics: the Impact of the 'Victims' Bill of Rights' in California. Ph.D. Dissertation, University of California. Berkeley, 1987.

McDonald, Glenn D. Financial Assistance and Control of Public Educational Institutions By the Initiative and Referendum in the States of Washington, Oregon, and California. Ph.D. Dissertation, the University of Texas at Austin, 1955.

Mederros, Francine M. "Edward A. Dickson: A Study in Progressivism." Ph.D. Dissertation, University of California, Los Angeles, 1968.

Minar, David William. "Voting Behavior on Recent Labor Measures in California." M. A. Thesis, University of California, Berkeley, 1951

Mueller, John E. "Reason and Caprice: Ballot Pattern in California." Ph.D. Dissertation, University of California, Los Angeles, 1965.

Newquest, Marilyn Jean Fuller. "The Political Reform Act of 1974: A Case Study in California's Initiative Process." M.A. Thesis, California State University, Long Beach, 1977.

Peterson, Eric F. "Prelude to Progressivism in California: Election Reform, 1870-1909." Ph.D. Dissertation, University of California, Los Angeles, 1969.

Pitchell, Robert J. "Twentieth Century California Voting Behavior." Ph.D. Dissertation, University of California, Los Angeles, 1955.

Posner, Russell M. "State Politics and the Bank of America, 1920-1934" Ph.D. Dissertation, University of California 1956.

Rose, Alice, "The Rise of California Insurgency: Origins of the League of Lincoln-Roosevelt Republican Clubs, 1900-1907." Ph.D. Dissertation, Stanford University, 1942.

Rosenbaum, Walter A. "Legislative Participation in California Direct Legislation, 1940-1960." Ph.D. Dissertation, Princeton University, 1964.

Schade, John Jean. "The Effects of Proposition 13 on Special District Financing in Orange County." Ph.D. Dissertation, Claremont Graduate School, 1981.

Shenk, Edward Jackson. "Description of the Effects of Proposition 13 On the Mission of the California Community College System. Ed.D. Dissertation, University of Oregon, 1981.

Smith, Kenneth L. Beating the Big Boys: Common Cause and the California Campaign for Political Reform." D.P.A. Dissertation, University of Southern California, 1978.

Uhimchuk, George A. "Constitutional Tax Limits at the State Level: An Overview and Selected Case Studies." Ph.D. Dissertation, Virginia Polytechnic institute and State University, 1980.

Wilkening, David Lester. "Political History of California State Legislative Reapportionment, 1849-1977." M.A. thesis, Calif. State University, Sacramento, n.d.

DOCUMENTS

California Constitution Revision Commission. *Minutes of the Article XXIII Committee.* (1968?)

California Fair Political Practices Commission. *Campaign Contribution and Spending Report.* Sacramento: the Commission, 1978.

California Fair Political Practices Commission. *Campaign Costs: How Much Have they increased and Why? A Study of State Elections, 1958-78.* Sacramento: the Commission, 1980.

California Legislative Analyst. *An Analysis of Proposition No.1, the Governor's State Expenditure Limitation Proposal, on the November 1973 Ballot.* Sacramento: 1973.

California Legislature, Assembly, Committee on Elections and Reapportionment. *Initiative Process.* Transcript of Public Hearing, Los Angeles, 10 Oct. 1972. Sacramento: 1972.

California Legislature, Assembly, Committee on Revenue and Taxation. *Proposition 13 Assessment Issues: A Briefing Book for Oversight Hearings.* Sacramento: Assembly Publications Office, 1980.

California Legislature, Assembly, Committee on Elections and Reapportionment. *Public Hearing on the Initiative Process.* Los Angeles, Oct. 10, 1972 Sacramento: the Committee, 1972.

California Legislature, Assembly, Committee on Finance and Insurance. *Oversight Hearing on Proposition 103.* Sacramento: Joint Publications Office, 1989.

California Legislature, Assembly, Interim Committee on Constitutional Amendments. *Article XXIV, the State Civil Service System, the Initiative.* Meeting of Full Committee, Montebello, 13 Jan 1966. Pico Rivera: the Committee, 1966.

California Legislature, Assembly, Interim Committee on Constitutional Amendments. *The Initiative.* Transcript of Proceedings, 17 Nov. 1965. San Francisco: the Committee, 1965.

California Legislature, Assembly, Interim Committee on Constitutional Amendments. *Final Report: The Initiative and the Effective Dates of Statutes.* Sacramento: Assembly Interim Committee Reports, V. 27, No. 5. 1967.

California Legislature, Assembly, Interim Committee on Constitutional Amendments. *The Initiative and Effective Dates of Statutes.* Meeting of Full Committee, Los Angeles, 13-14 Dec. 1965. N.p., 1965.

California Legislature, Assembly, Interim Committee on Constitutional Amendments. *Background Study on the Initiative.* (2 Vols.) Sacramento: 1965.

California Legislature, Assembly, Interim Committee on Constitutional Amendments. *The Initiative and the Effective Dates of Statutes: Final Report.* Sacramento: the Committee, 1967.

California Legislature, Assembly, Interim Committee on Constitutional Amendments. *Review of Work of California Constitution Revision Commission.* (Transcript of Proceedings, 2-3 Dec. 1965.) Sacramento, 1965.

California Legislature, Senate, Committee on Insurance, Claims, and Corporations. *Hearing on Proposition 103.* Sacramento: Joint Publications Office (1989?).

California Legislature, Senate, Committee on Revenue and Taxation. *Post-Proposition 13 Restrictions and Exemptions.* Hearing, Los Angeles, Oct. 24, 1980. Sacramento: the Committee, 1980.

California Legislature, Senate, Committee on Elections. *Joint Hearing on Propositions 68 and 73.* Sacramento: Joint Publications, 1988.

California Legislature, Senate, Committee on Elections. *A Guide to Proposition 73.* Sacramento: Joint Publications, 1988.

California Legislature, Senate, Committee on General Research, Subcommittee on Revenue and Taxation. *Proposition 9 Relating to Property Taxation.* Transcript of Joint Hearing. Los Angeles, 15-16 Oct. 1968 Sacramento:1968.

California Legislature, Senate, Committee on Toxics and Public Safety Management. *Proposition 65 Implementation: Joint Hearing.* Sacramento: Joint Publications, 1987.

California Legislature, Senate, Committee on Revenue and Taxation. *Interim Hearing on Proposition 13: Equity Alternatives.* County Hall of Administration, Los Angeles, Ca, Oct. 23, 1980 Sacramento: the Committee, 1980.

California Legislature, Senate, Committee on Revenue and Taxation. *Interim Hearing on Proposition 13: Taxation of Unsecured Property for the*

1978-79 Fiscal Year. Sacramento: Senate Committee on Revenue and Taxation, 1980.

California Legislature, Senate, Committee on Revenue and Taxation. *Proposition 13: State and Local Fiscal Outlook.* Joint Interim Hearing, Los Angeles, Nov. 14, 1978. Sacramento: the Committee, 1979.

California Legislature, Senate, Office of Research. *June 1990 Ballot: Analysis of Propositions.* Sacramento: the Office, 1990.

California Legislature, Senate Office of Research. *November 1988 Ballot: Analysis of Propositions.* Sacramento: the Office, 1988.

California Legislature. *Proposition 102: Reporting Exposure to the Aids Virus Initiative: Legislative Hearing.* Sacramento: Joint Publications, 1988.

California Legislature. *Proposition 62: Analysis of Issues and Provisions.* Sacramento: Joint Publications, (1986?).

California Legislature. *Uncodified Initiative Measures and Statues, Annotated: including Uncodified Acts of A General and Permanent Nature, Set Out in Full Or By Title, With Legislative Histories, Through the Regular Session of 1972.* Annotated and Indexed by the Publisher's Editorial Staff. San Francisco: Bancroft-whitney, 1973.

California Secretary of State. *Amendments to the Constitution: Proposed Statues With Arguments Respecting the Same, 1883-.* Microform, Sunnyvale, CA: Library Microfilms, 1979-.

California State Legislature, Assembly, Committee on Elections and Reapportionment. *Public Hearing on the Initiative Process.* October 10, 1972. Sacramento: 1972.

California State Legislature, Assembly, Interim Committee on Constitutional Amendments. *Background Study on the Initiative.* Sacramento: the Committee, 1965.

Connecticut, General Assembly, Office of Legislative Research. *Government Openness/Accessibility in Connecticut in Comparison with States Which have Initiative and Referendum Process.* Hartford, CT: the Office, 1978.

Duffy, Gordon. *Analysis of the Potential Impact of Proposition 9.* California Legislature, Assembly, Minority Ways and Means Committee, 1980.

Duke, Kathryn. *Proposition 64, the Aids Initiative in California.* Sacramento: Senate Office of Research, 1986.

Dwight, Allen., comp. *A Study of Ballot Measures, 1884-1980.* Compiled by the Office of the Secretary of State. Sacramento: The Office of the Secretary of State, (1981?).

Eu, March Fong. *A History of the California Initiative Process.* Sacramento: State of California, Office of the Secretary of State. 1989.

Governor's Office of Planning and Research. *The Growth Revolt: After-shock of Proposition 13?* Sacramento: the Office, (1980).

Graham, Virginia, comp. *A Compilation of Statewide Initiative Proposals Appearing on the Ballot through 1978.* Washington D.C.; Congressional Research Service, Library of Congress, 1978.

Hardie v. Eu. 18 C.3rd 371; 134 Cal. Rptr. 201, 556 P 2d. 301. (Re: limits on expenditures for petition circulation.)

Heimke, Martin. *Jarvis IV, Key Provisions and Issues.* Sacramento: Senate Office of Research, 1984.

Hensler, Deborah R., and Carl Hensler. *Evaluating Nuclear Power: Voter Choice on the California Nuclear Initiative.* Santa Monica: Rand Corporation, 1979.

Hodson, Timothy A. *Proposition 39, Reapportionment Commission Initiative: A Special Report....* Sacramento: Joint Publications, 1984.

Hodson, Timothy A. *Proposition 61: An Analysis of the Text and Context of the Gann Salary Limitation Initiative.* Sacramento: Joint Publications, 1986.

Illinois, Legislative Council. *Lawmaking by Initiative.* Springfield, IL: the Council, 1982.

Initiative Resource Center. *Initiative and Referendum: The Power of the People.* Washington D.C.: Initiative Resource Center, 1986.

League of California Cities. *Proposition 9: The State income Tax Reduction Initiative, Special Bulletin.* Sacramento, California: League of California Cities, 1980.

Low, Kathleen, comp. *Initiative and Referendum.* Sacramento: California State Library, State Information and Reference Center, 1989.

Morris, Gabrielle. "Paul Gann, Oral History Interview. Unpublished Typescript, 1987. (Bancroft Library, University of California, Berkeley.)

New York, State Legislature, Senate, Task Force on Critical Problems. *The Popular Interest versus the Public Interest ... a Report on the Popular Initiative.* 1979.

Pillsbury, A.J., "A Study of Direct Legislation in All of Its forms As Exemplified in the Government of the State of California in State Affairs only From the Adoption of the Constitution of 1849 to the Presidential Election of 1928." Carbon of Typescript, "for the Consideration of the Direct Legislation Section of the Commonwealth Club of California" (3 Parts: 1, 1849-1879; 2, 1879-1911; 3, 1911-1921). No Date, ca. 500 pages. (In Hichborn Papers, UCLA.)

Snyder, David L., comp. *Records of the Elections Division, California Secretary of State. California State Archives Inventory No. 3.* Sacramento: California State Archives, Office of the Secretary of State, 1972.

U. S. Congressional Budget Office. *Proposition 13: Its Impact on the Nation's Economy, Federal Revenues, and Federal Expenditures.* (Background Paper) Washington: 1978.

Index